The Ultimate DIABETIC COOKBOOK for Beginners

2000+ Days of Delicious, Simple and Low-Carb Recipes for Newly Diagnosed Type 2 Diabetes, Incl. a 30-Day Meal Plan to Balanced Blood Sugar Levels

Neal F. Stillman

Copyright© 2024 By Neal F. Stillman

All rights reserved worldwide.

No part of this book may be reproduced or transmitted in any form or by any means, electronic or mechanical, including photo- copying, recording or by any information storage and retrieval system, without written permission from the publisher, except for the inclusion of brief quotations in a review.

Warning-Disclaimer

The purpose of this book is to educate and entertain. The author or publisher does not guarantee that anyone following the techniques, suggestions, tips, ideas, or strategies will become successful. The author and publisher shall have neither liability or responsibility to anyone with respect to any loss or damage caused, or alleged to be caused, directly or indirectly by the information contained in this book.

TABLE OF CONTENTS

1	Introduction	
3	Chapter 1	Understanding the Diabetic Diet
9	Chapter 2	Breakfasts
18	Chapter 3	Beans and Grains
25	Chapter 4	Beef, Pork, and Lamb
35	Chapter 5	Poultry
45	Chapter 6	Fish and Seafood
54	Chapter 7	Snacks and Appetizers
63	Chapter 8	Vegetables and Sides
72	Chapter 9	Vegetarian Mains
79	Chapter 10	Salads
85	Chapter 11	Stews and Soups
91	Chapter 12	Desserts
97	Appendix 1:	Measurement Conversion Chart
98	Appendix 2:	The Dirty Dozen and Clean Fifteen
99	Appendix 3:	Recipes Index

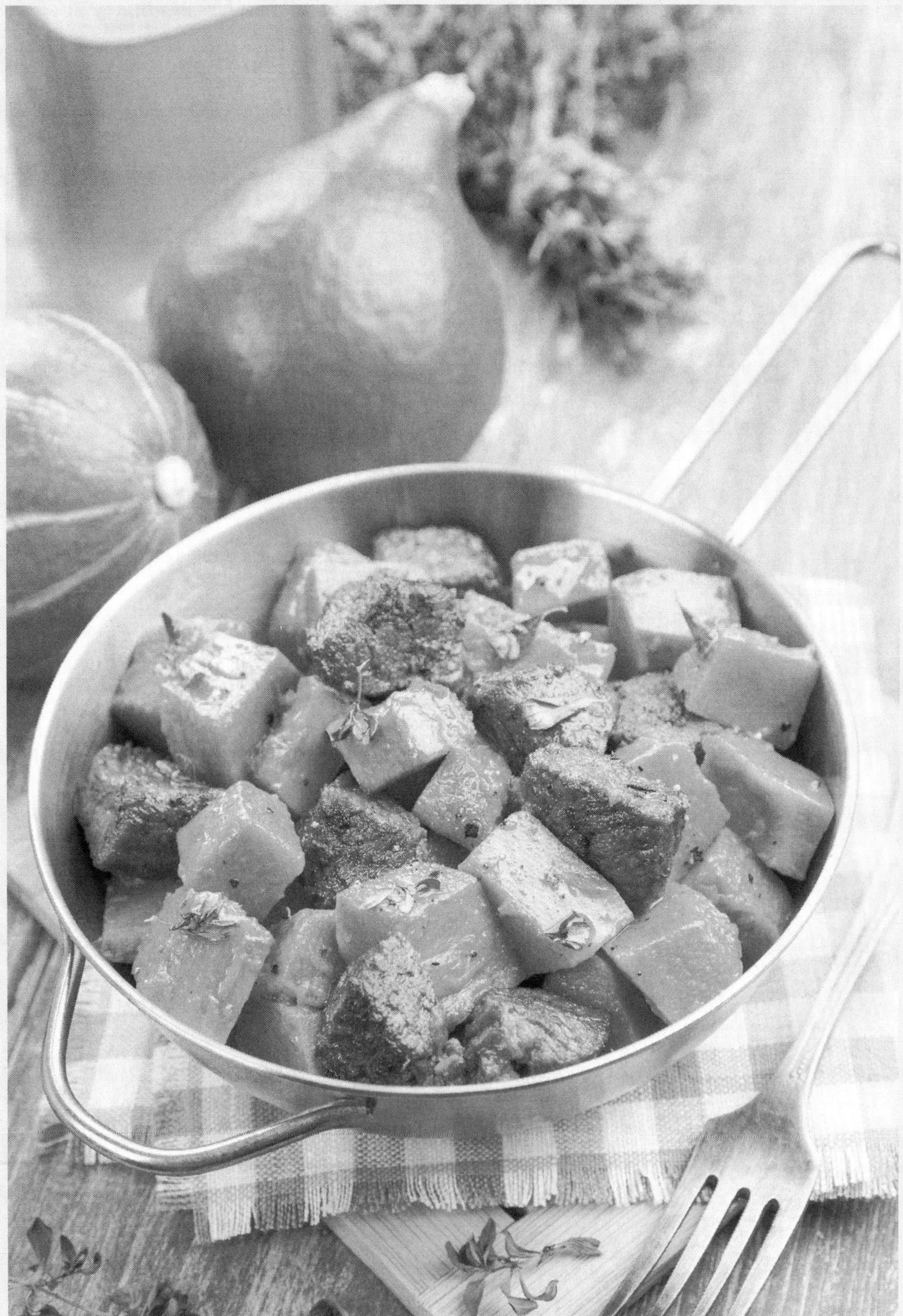

INTRODUCTION

Living with diabetes doesn't mean you have to sacrifice flavor, satisfaction, or joy in your meals. In fact, embracing a diabetic-friendly diet opens up a world of culinary possibilities that are not only healthy but also incredibly delicious. This cookbook is designed to inspire and guide you on a journey toward a healthier lifestyle, without compromising on the pleasures of good food.

Diabetes is a condition that affects millions of people worldwide, and managing it effectively is crucial for maintaining overall health and well-being. Central to this management is a balanced diet that helps control blood sugar levels. However, the idea of a "diabetic diet" often conjures up images of bland, restrictive meals. This couldn't be further from the truth. With the right knowledge and creativity, you can enjoy a wide variety of flavorful, nutritious dishes that support your health goals.

Understanding Carbohydrates and Their Impact

One of the fundamental principles of a diabetic diet is understanding carbohydrates and their impact on blood sugar. Carbohydrates are an essential part of our diet, providing energy for our daily activities. However, not all carbs are created equal. This cookbook will help you navigate the world of carbohydrates, distinguishing between simple and complex carbs, and how they affect your blood glucose levels. By choosing the right types of carbohydrates and pairing them with fiber, protein, and healthy fats, you can create meals that are both satisfying and blood sugar-friendly.

Embracing Whole, Unprocessed Foods

Healthy eating for diabetes is also about embracing whole, unprocessed foods. Fresh vegetables, fruits, whole grains, lean proteins, and healthy fats form the foundation of a nutritious diet. These foods not only provide essential nutrients but also help in maintaining stable blood sugar levels. The recipes in this cookbook are crafted to highlight the natural flavors and textures of these ingredients, proving that healthy eating can be both vibrant and indulgent.

Balancing Nutrition and Flavor

In addition to providing you with delicious recipes, this cookbook aims to educate and empower you. Understanding the nutritional value of different foods, how they interact with your body, and how to make informed choices are all crucial steps in managing diabetes. With this knowledge, you can take control of your diet and make decisions that align with your health goals.

The journey to a healthier lifestyle is a holistic one. Alongside diet, physical activity plays a vital role in managing diabetes. Regular exercise helps to regulate blood sugar levels, improve cardiovascular health, and enhance overall well-being. Pairing nutritious meals with an active lifestyle creates a powerful synergy that supports your health from multiple angles.

This cookbook is more than just a collection of recipes; it's a celebration of food and its ability to nourish, heal, and bring joy. Each recipe is crafted with care, focusing on balance and flavor. From hearty breakfasts that kickstart your day to satisfying dinners that round off your evening, every meal is designed to delight your taste buds and support your health.

Moreover, this book acknowledges the emotional aspect of eating. Food is deeply tied to our cultures, traditions, and memories. It's a source of comfort and connection. Navigating dietary changes can be challenging, but it doesn't mean letting go of the foods you love. With creative substitutions and thoughtful preparation, you can continue to enjoy your favorite dishes in a way that aligns with your health needs.

As you explore the recipes in this cookbook, you'll discover a variety of dishes that cater to different tastes and preferences. Whether you're in the mood for something light and refreshing or rich and comforting, there's something here for everyone. From vibrant salads and hearty soups to flavorful mains and indulgent desserts, each recipe is a testament to the fact that healthy eating can be diverse and enjoyable.

Cooking at Home: Your Path to Better Health

Cooking at home is a powerful tool in managing diabetes. It allows you to control the ingredients, portion sizes, and cooking methods, ensuring that each meal is tailored to your needs. This cookbook provides you with the tools and inspiration to create delicious, healthful meals in your own kitchen. Whether you're a seasoned cook or just starting out, you'll find recipes that are accessible, easy to follow, and utterly satisfying.

In conclusion, a diabetic-friendly diet is not a limitation but an invitation to explore new flavors, ingredients, and cooking techniques. It's an opportunity to reconnect with the joy of eating, knowing that every bite supports your health and well-being. This cookbook is your companion on this journey, offering guidance, inspiration, and a plethora of delicious recipes that prove healthy eating is anything but boring. Embrace this new culinary adventure and discover the incredible world of diabetic-friendly cuisine.

Chapter 1
Understanding the Diabetic Diet

Chapter 1 Understanding the Diabetic Diet

Embarking on a journey towards a healthier lifestyle begins with understanding what a diabetic diet entails. For those managing diabetes, the right diet is a cornerstone of treatment, playing a pivotal role in controlling blood sugar levels and preventing complications. This chapter will explore the principles of a diabetic diet, provide practical tips and advice, and offer insights into making informed dietary choices that support overall well-being.

Key Components and Practical Tips for a Diabetic Diet

A diabetic diet, also known as medical nutrition therapy for diabetes, is a healthy-eating plan that's naturally rich in nutrients and low in fat and calories. The key elements are fruits, vegetables, and whole grains. This diet helps to control blood glucose levels, manage weight, and reduce risk factors for heart disease such as high blood pressure and fats in the blood.

◆ Carbohydrates: Not all carbs are created equal. Focus on complex carbohydrates like whole grains, legumes, and starchy vegetables, which are digested more slowly and help maintain more stable blood sugar levels. Limit refined carbohydrates such as white bread, pastries, and sugary beverages, which can cause spikes in blood glucose.

◆ Fiber: High-fiber foods, including vegetables, fruits, nuts, legumes, and whole grains, can help control blood sugar levels. Fiber slows the absorption of sugar and can improve blood sugar levels.

◆ Protein: Lean protein sources, such as fish, skinless poultry, beans, and tofu, are excellent choices. Protein helps to build and repair tissues and has little effect on blood sugar levels.

◆ Fats: Healthy fats from sources like avocados, nuts, seeds, and olive oil are beneficial. Limit saturated fats and avoid trans fats found in many fried and processed foods.
◆ Glycemic Index: This is a measure of how quickly a carbohydrate-containing food raises blood glucose. Low-GI foods are digested more slowly and cause a slower rise in blood glucose levels.
◆ Plan Your Meals: Meal planning is crucial for managing diabetes. Knowing what and when to eat can help you maintain steady blood glucose levels. Try to eat at the same times each day and space your meals evenly.
◆ Portion Control: Be mindful of portion sizes to avoid overeating, which can lead to weight gain and spikes in blood sugar. Use smaller plates and bowls, and pay attention to serving sizes.
◆ Read Food Labels: Understanding nutrition labels can help you make better food choices. Look for the total carbohydrate content and try to choose foods with lower added sugars.
◆ Stay Hydrated: Water is the best beverage choice. Avoid sugary drinks, which can cause blood sugar spikes. If you drink alcohol, do so in moderation and always with food.
◆ Healthy Snacking: Choose snacks that combine protein, fiber, and healthy fats. Examples include a small apple with peanut butter, a handful of nuts, or raw veggies with hummus.

Managing Blood Sugar Levels and Physical Activity

Monitoring your blood sugar levels is an essential part of managing diabetes. Regularly checking your levels can help you understand how different foods affect you and make necessary adjustments to your diet. Keep a log of your blood sugar readings and discuss them with your healthcare provider to tailor your eating plan to your specific needs.

Diet and exercise go hand in hand in managing diabetes. Regular physical activity helps your body use insulin more efficiently and can lower blood glucose levels. Aim for at least 150 minutes of moderate aerobic activity per week, such as brisk walking or swimming. Incorporate strength training exercises to build muscle, which can help improve blood sugar control.

Emotional and Psychological Aspects, Social and Cultural Considerations

Living with diabetes can be challenging, and it's important to address the emotional and psychological aspects. Stress, anxiety, and depression can affect blood sugar levels and overall health. Finding healthy ways to cope with stress, such as yoga, meditation, or talking to a therapist, can be beneficial. Support from family, friends, or a diabetes support group can also provide encouragement and motivation.

Food is more than just sustenance; it's a significant part of our social and cultural lives. Navigating dietary changes within the context of family traditions, cultural practices, and social interactions can be challenging but is entirely feasible. Here are some strategies:

◆ Communicate with Loved Ones: Let your family and friends know about your dietary needs. This can help them understand your choices and provide support.

◆ Incorporate Traditional Foods: Modify traditional recipes to make them healthier. For example, use whole grain flours, reduce sugar, and opt for healthier cooking methods like baking or steaming.

◆ Celebrate with Moderation: During social gatherings and holidays, enjoy your favorite foods in moderation. Plan ahead by eating smaller portions and balancing your meal with healthier options.

◆ Dining Out Smartly: When eating out, research menus in advance, choose restaurants that offer healthy options, and don't hesitate to ask for modifications to dishes to meet your dietary needs.

Advancing Your Knowledge

Continual learning and staying informed about diabetes management is crucial. The field of nutrition and diabetes care is always evolving with new research. Here are ways to keep yourself updated:

◆ Consult Healthcare Professionals: Regular check-ups with your doctor, dietitian, or diabetes educator can provide you with personalized advice and the latest information.

◆ Educational Resources: Books, credible websites, and diabetes organizations offer a wealth of information. Consider subscribing to newsletters or joining online forums and communities.

◆ Cooking Classes and Workshops: Participate in cooking classes focused on healthy eating or diabetes management. These can provide new ideas and techniques for preparing nutritious meals.

◆ Technology and Apps: Use technology to your advantage. Numerous apps are available to help track blood sugar levels, monitor food intake, and provide healthy recipes.

Understanding the diabetic diet is the first step towards managing diabetes effectively. By focusing on balanced nutrition, monitoring your blood sugar, and incorporating physical activity into your routine, you can take control of your health. Remember, a diabetic diet is not about deprivation but about making smart, informed choices that enhance your well-being and allow you to enjoy a wide variety of delicious foods.

This chapter has laid the foundation for your journey, and the upcoming chapters will provide a wealth of recipes and tips to help you navigate your diabetic-friendly lifestyle with confidence and creativity. Enjoy the process of discovering new flavors and ingredients, and take pride in every step you take towards better health.

30-Day Meal Plan

DAYS	BREAKFAST	LUNCH	DINNER	SNACK/DESSERT
1	Gluten-Free Carrot and Oat Pancakes 10	Asian Fried Rice 22	Air Fryer Chicken-Fried Steak 29	Homemade Sun-Dried Tomato Salsa 58
2	Double-Berry Muffins 10	Easy Lentil Burgers 19	Orange-Marinated Pork Tenderloin 29	Guacamole with Jicama 56
3	Bran Apple Muffins 14	Coconut-Ginger Rice 19	Pork Milanese 30	Southern Boiled Peanuts 59
4	Banana Protein Pancakes 12	Stewed Green Beans 24	Gingered-Pork Stir-Fry 29	Ginger and Mint Dip with Fruit 61
5	Low-Carb Peanut Butter Pancakes 11	Veggie Unfried Rice 22	Smothered Steak 28	Chicken Kabobs 58
6	Summer Veggie Scramble 13	Italian Bean Burgers 20	Pork Butt Roast 28	Vietnamese Meatball Lollipops with Dipping Sauce 59
7	Coddled Eggs and Smoked Salmon Toasts 10	Curried Rice with Pineapple 20	Creole Steak 30	Ground Turkey Lettuce Cups 61
8	Spinach and Feta Egg Bake 13	Sage and Garlic Vegetable Bake 20	Steak with Bell Pepper 28	Smoky Spinach Hummus with Popcorn Chips 58
9	Chocolate-Zucchini Muffins 12	Red Beans 20	Vegetable Beef Soup 28	Cucumber Pâté 55
10	Greek Yogurt Sundae 16	Quinoa Vegetable Skillet 22	BBQ Ribs and Broccoli Slaw 31	Blood Sugar–Friendly Nutty Trail Mix 55
11	Chorizo Mexican Breakfast Pizzas 13	Southwestern Quinoa Salad 19	Jalapeño Popper Pork Chops 33	Green Goddess White Bean Dip 55
12	Poached Eggs 11	Barley Squash Risotto 23	Coffee-and-Herb-Marinated Steak 26	Turkey Rollups with Veggie Cream Cheese 57
13	Pizza Eggs 12	Texas Caviar 21	Zoodles Carbonara 33	Crab-Filled Mushrooms 57
14	Baked Avocado and Egg 11	Veggies and Kasha with Balsamic Vinaigrette 21	Italian Sausages with Peppers and Onions 32	Roasted Carrot and Herb Spread 61
15	Potato-Bacon Gratin 11	Edamame-Tabbouleh Salad 21	Bavarian Beef 31	Cinnamon Toasted Pumpkin Seeds 56
16	Grain-Free Apple Cinnamon Cake 14	Sunshine Burgers 21	Broiled Dijon Burgers 33	Candied Pecans 56

DAYS	BREAKFAST	LUNCH	DINNER	SNACK/DESSERT
17	Scallion Grits with Shrimp 12	BBQ Bean Burgers 23	Slow-Cooked Simple Lamb and Vegetable Stew 32	Lemony White Bean Puree 56
18	Tofu Kale and Mushroom Breakfast Scramble 15	Rice with Spinach and Feta 22	Smothered Sirloin 26	Zucchini Hummus Dip with Red Bell Peppers 58
19	Breakfast Egg Bites 17	Beet Greens and Black Beans 24	Chinese Spareribs 34	Creamy Spinach Dip 60
20	Breakfast Millet with Nuts and Strawberries 14	Sweet Potato Fennel Bake 24	Easy Beef Curry 34	Guacamole 57
21	Brussels Sprout Hash and Eggs 15	Herbed Beans and Brown Rice 23	Beef and Vegetable Shish Kabobs 30	Low-Sugar Blueberry Muffins 57
22	Bacon and Tomato Frittata 15	Butterflied Beef Eye Roast 26	Saffron-Spiced Chicken Breasts 36	Creamy Cheese Dip 60
23	Gouda Egg Casserole with Canadian Bacon 15	Marjoram-Pepper Steaks 27	Cast Iron Hot Chicken 39	Creamy Apple-Cinnamon Quesadilla 60
24	Ratatouille Baked Eggs 17	Pork Chop Diane 27	Grilled Herb Chicken with Wine and Roasted Garlic 36	Monterey Jack Cheese Quiche Squares 60
25	Spanakopita Egg White Frittata 16	Autumn Pork Chops with Red Cabbage and Apples 29	Thanksgiving Turkey Breast 36	Vegetable Kabobs with Mustard Dip 59
26	Blueberry Cornmeal Muffins 17	Pork Tacos 32	Herb-Roasted Turkey and Vegetables 43	Spinach and Artichoke Dip 62
27	Plum Smoothie 16	Greek Stuffed Tenderloin 31	Teriyaki Chicken and Broccoli 44	Cherry Delight 92
28	White Bean–Oat Waffles 16	Roasted Pork Loin 27	Spice-Rubbed Turkey Breast 42	Tapioca Berry Parfaits 92
29	Breakfast Sausage 13	Slow Cooker Chipotle Beef Stew 27	Garlic Dill Wings 39	Crumb Pie Shell 92
30	Easy Breakfast Chia Pudding 17	Fresh Pot Pork Butt 33	Chicken Paprika 39	Berry Smoothie Pops 92

Chapter 2　Breakfasts

Chapter 2 Breakfasts

Gluten-Free Carrot and Oat Pancakes

Prep time: 10 minutes | Cook time: 20 minutes | Serves 4

- 1 cup rolled oats
- 1 cup shredded carrots
- 1 cup low-fat cottage cheese
- 2 eggs
- ½ cup unsweetened plain almond milk
- 1 teaspoon baking powder
- ½ teaspoon ground cinnamon
- 2 tablespoons ground flaxseed
- ¼ cup plain nonfat Greek yogurt
- 1 tablespoon pure maple syrup
- 2 teaspoons canola oil, divided

1. In a blender, process the oats until they resemble flour. Add the grated carrots, cottage cheese, eggs, almond milk, baking powder, cinnamon, and flaxseed to the blender jar. Blend until the mixture is smooth and well combined. 2. In a small bowl, mix the yogurt and maple syrup until well combined. Set aside. 3. Heat 1 teaspoon of oil in a large skillet over medium heat. Using a measuring cup, pour ¼ cup of batter per pancake into the skillet. Cook for 1 to 2 minutes until bubbles form on the surface, then flip the pancakes. Cook for another minute until the pancakes are browned and cooked through. Repeat with the remaining 1 teaspoon of oil and remaining batter. 4. Serve the pancakes warm, topped with the maple yogurt.

Per Serving:
calories: 226 | fat: 8g | protein: 15g | carbs: 24g | sugars: 7g | fiber: 4g | sodium: 403mg

Double-Berry Muffins

Prep time: 15 minutes | Cook time: 20 to 25 minutes | Makes 12 muffins

- ¼ cup packed brown sugar
- ½ teaspoon ground cinnamon
- 1 cup fat-free (skim) milk
- ¼ cup unsweetened applesauce
- 2 tablespoons canola oil
- ½ teaspoon vanilla
- 1 egg or ¼ cup fat-free egg product
- 2 cups all-purpose flour
- ⅓ cup granulated sugar
- 3 teaspoons baking powder
- ½ teaspoon salt
- ½ cup fresh or frozen (thawed and drained) raspberries
- ½ cup fresh or frozen (thawed and drained) blueberries

1. Heat oven to 400°F. Place paper baking cups in each of 12 regular-size muffin cups or grease the bottoms only with shortening. In a small bowl, mix the brown sugar and cinnamon; set aside. 2. In a large bowl, beat the milk, applesauce, oil, vanilla, and egg with a fork or whisk. Stir in the flour, granulated sugar, baking powder, and salt all at once just until the flour is moistened (batter will be lumpy). Fold in the raspberries and blueberries. Divide the batter evenly among the muffin cups. Sprinkle the brown sugar mixture evenly over the tops of the muffins. 3. Bake for 20 to 25 minutes or until golden brown. Immediately remove the muffins from the pan to a cooling rack. Serve warm if desired.

Per Serving:
1 Muffin: calories: 160 | fat: 3g | protein: 3g | carbs: 30g | sugars: 12g | fiber: 1g | sodium: 240mg

Coddled Eggs and Smoked Salmon Toasts

Prep time: 5 minutes | Cook time: 10 minutes | Serves 4

- 2 teaspoons unsalted butter
- 4 large eggs
- 4 slices gluten-free or whole-grain rye bread
- ½ cup plain 2 percent Greek yogurt
- 4 ounces cold-smoked salmon, or 1 medium avocado, pitted, peeled, and sliced
- 2 radishes, thinly sliced
- 1 Persian cucumber, thinly sliced
- 1 tablespoon chopped fresh chives
- ¼ teaspoon freshly ground black pepper

1. Pour 1 cup water into the Instant Pot and place a long-handled silicone steam rack into the pot. (If you don't have the long-handled rack, use the wire metal steam rack and a homemade sling) 2. Coat each of four 4-ounce ramekins with ½ teaspoon butter. Crack an egg into each ramekin. Place the ramekins on the steam rack in the pot. 3. Secure the lid and set the Pressure Release to Sealing. Select the Steam setting and set the cooking time for 3 minutes at low pressure. (The pot will take about 5 minutes to come up to pressure before the cooking program begins.) 4. While eggs are cooking, toast the bread in a toaster until golden brown. Spread the yogurt onto the toasted slices, put the toasts onto plates, and then top each toast with the smoked salmon, radishes, and cucumber. 5. When the cooking program ends, let the pressure release naturally for 5 minutes, then move the Pressure Release to Venting to release any remaining steam. Open the pot and, wearing heat-resistant mitts, grasp the handles of the steam rack and lift it out of the pot. 6. Run a knife around the inside edge of each ramekin to loosen the egg and unmold one egg onto each toast. Sprinkle the chives and pepper on top and serve right away. 7. Note: The yolks of these eggs are fully cooked through. If you prefer the yolks slightly less solid, perform a quick pressure release rather than letting the pressure release naturally for 5 minutes.

Per Serving:
calories: 275 | fat: 12g | protein: 21g | carbs: 21g | sugars: 4g | fiber: 5g | sodium: 431mg

Baked Avocado and Egg

Prep time: 10 minutes | Cook time: 10 minutes | Serves 2

- 1 large avocado, halved and pitted
- 2 large eggs
- 2 tomato slices, divided
- ½ cup nonfat cottage cheese, divided
- Fresh cilantro, for garnish

1. Preheat the oven to 425°F (220°C). Make sure your oven is fully heated to the correct temperature before placing the avocado halves inside. This ensures even cooking. 2. Prepare the avocados: Slice each avocado in half lengthwise and remove the pit. Take a thin slice from the bottom of each avocado half so they can sit flat on the baking sheet without tipping over. 3. Using a spoon, scoop out a small additional amount of avocado flesh from the center of each half to create a larger cavity, enough to hold an egg. Be careful not to scoop too much, as you want to keep a sturdy wall to hold the egg in place. 4. Line a small baking sheet with aluminum foil for easy cleanup and to prevent sticking. 5. Place the avocado halves on the foil-lined baking sheet, hollow-side up, ensuring they are stable and won't tip over. 6. Crack an egg into a small bowl, being careful not to break the yolk. 7. Gently pour the egg into the cavity of one avocado half. Repeat for the remaining avocado halves. If any egg white overflows, it can be left on the foil to cook alongside the avocado. 8. Place one slice of tomato on top of each filled avocado half. 9. Add ¼ cup of cottage cheese to each half, spreading it evenly over the top. 10. Carefully place the baking sheet with the prepared avocado halves into the preheated oven. 11. Bake for 8 to 10 minutes if you prefer a soft-boiled egg consistency, where the yolk remains slightly runny. For a firmer egg, bake for a few minutes longer, checking periodically until the desired doneness is achieved. 12. Once baked, remove the baking sheet from the oven. 13. Garnish each avocado half with fresh cilantro leaves for added flavor and color. 14. Serve immediately while hot. Enjoy your delicious and nutritious avocado baked eggs with tomato and cottage cheese!

Per Serving:
calories: 262 | fat: 20g | protein: 12g | carbs: 12g | sugars: 2g | fiber: 7g | sodium: 214mg

Potato-Bacon Gratin

Prep time: 20 minutes | Cook time: 40 minutes | Serves 8

- 1 tablespoon olive oil
- 6 ounces bag fresh spinach
- 1 clove garlic, minced
- 4 large potatoes, peeled or unpeeled, divided
- 6 ounces Canadian bacon slices, divided
- 5 ounces reduced-fat grated Swiss cheddar, divided
- 1 cup lower-sodium, lower-fat chicken broth

1. Set the Instant Pot to Sauté and pour in the olive oil. Cook the spinach and garlic in olive oil just until the spinach is wilted, which should take 5 minutes or less. Turn off the Instant Pot. 2. Cut the potatoes into thin slices about ¼" thick. 3. In a springform pan that will fit into the inner pot of your Instant Pot, spray it with nonstick spray then layer ⅓ of the potatoes, half the bacon, ⅓ of the cheese, and half of the wilted spinach. 4. Repeat the layers, ending with the potatoes. Reserve ⅓ of the cheese for later. 5. Pour the chicken broth over all the layered ingredients. 6. Wipe the bottom of your Instant Pot to soak up any remaining oil, then add in 2 cups of water and place the steaming rack inside. Put the springform pan on top of the steaming rack. 7. Close the lid and secure it to the locking position. Ensure the vent is turned to sealing. Set the Instant Pot for 35 minutes on Manual at high pressure. 8. Perform a quick release once the cooking time is complete. 9. Top the dish with the remaining cheese, then allow it to stand for 10 minutes before removing it from the Instant Pot, cutting, and serving.

Per Serving:
calories: 220 | fat: 7g | protein: 14g | carbs: 28g | sugars: 2g | fiber: 3g | sodium: 415mg

Low-Carb Peanut Butter Pancakes

Prep time: 10 minutes | Cook time: 10 minutes | Serves 2

- 1 cup almond flour
- ½ teaspoon baking soda
- Pinch sea salt
- 2 large eggs
- ¼ cup sparkling water (plain, unsweetened)
- 2 tablespoons canola oil, plus more for cooking
- 4 tablespoons peanut butter

1. Heat a nonstick griddle over medium-high heat. 2. In a small bowl, whisk together the almond flour, baking soda, and salt. 3. In a glass measuring cup, whisk together the eggs, water, and oil. 4. Pour the liquid ingredients into the dry ingredients, and mix gently until just combined. 5. Brush a small amount of canola oil onto the griddle. 6. Using all of the batter, spoon four pancakes onto the griddle. 7. Cook until set on one side, about 3 minutes. Flip with a spatula and continue cooking on the other side. 8. Before serving, spread each pancake with 1 tablespoon of the peanut butter.

Per Serving:
calories: 516 | fat: 43g | protein: 25g | carbs: 21g | sugars: 5g | fiber: 6g | sodium: 580mg

Poached Eggs

Prep time: 5 minutes | Cook time: 5 minutes | Serves 4

- Nonstick cooking spray
- 4 large eggs

1. Lightly spray 4 cups of a 7-count silicone egg bite mold with nonstick cooking spray. Crack each egg into a sprayed cup. 2. Pour 1 cup of water into the electric pressure cooker. Place the egg bite mold on the wire rack and carefully lower it into the pot. 3. Close and lock the lid of the pressure cooker. Set the valve to sealing. 4. Cook on high pressure for 5 minutes. 5. When the cooking is complete, hit Cancel and quick release the pressure. 6. Once the pin drops, unlock and remove the lid. 7. Run a small rubber spatula or spoon around each egg and carefully remove it from the mold. The white should be cooked, but the yolk should be runny. 8. Serve immediately.

Per Serving:
calories: 78 | fat: 5g | protein: 6g | carbs: 1g | sugars: 0g | fiber: 0g | sodium: 62mg

Banana Protein Pancakes

Prep time: 10 minutes | Cook time: 10 minutes | Serves 4

- Cooking oil spray, as needed (optional)
- 2 medium bananas
- 1 large avocado, mashed
- 4 large eggs
- ½ cup (120 ml) egg whites
- 2 teaspoons (10 ml) pure vanilla extract
- 2 teaspoons (8 g) baking powder
- ½ cup (50 g) whole-wheat flour
- ½ cup (56 g) coconut flour
- 1 teaspoon ground cinnamon
- All-natural peanut butter, as needed (see Tip)
- Thawed frozen fruit, as needed

1. Heat a large nonstick skillet over medium heat until it is very hot. Lightly spray the skillet with cooking oil spray, if using. 2. In a large bowl, mash the bananas. Whisk in the mashed avocado, eggs, egg whites, and vanilla extract. Add the baking powder, whole-wheat flour, coconut flour, and cinnamon. Mix until all ingredients are well combined and the batter is smooth. 3. Using a ¼-cup (60-ml) measuring cup, scoop the batter onto the hot skillet. Gently spread the batter to form a circle if needed. Cook the pancakes for about 3 minutes on one side until bubbles form on the surface and the edges look set. 4. Flip the pancakes and cook for an additional 2 to 3 minutes on the other side until they are golden brown and cooked through. 5. Drizzle the pancakes with melted peanut butter and top with fresh fruit just before serving. Enjoy your delicious and healthy banana avocado pancakes!

Per Serving:
calorie: 357 | fat: 17g | protein: 15g | carbs: 39g | sugars: 9g | fiber: 12g | sodium: 158mg

Chocolate-Zucchini Muffins

Prep time: 15 minutes | Cook time: 20 minutes | Serves 12

- 1½ cups grated zucchini
- 1½ cups rolled oats
- 1 teaspoon ground cinnamon
- 2 teaspoons baking powder
- ¼ teaspoon salt
- 1 large egg
- 1 teaspoon vanilla extract
- ¼ cup coconut oil, melted
- ½ cup unsweetened applesauce
- ¼ cup honey
- ¼ cup dark chocolate chips

1. Preheat the oven to 350°F (177°C). Grease the cups of a 12-cup muffin tin or line them with paper baking liners. Set the prepared muffin tin aside. 2. Place the shredded zucchini in a colander over the sink to drain excess moisture. 3. In a blender, process the oats until they resemble flour. Transfer the oat flour to a medium mixing bowl and add the cinnamon, baking powder, and salt. Mix well to combine the dry ingredients. 4. In a separate large mixing bowl, combine the egg, vanilla extract, melted coconut oil, applesauce, and honey. Stir until all the wet ingredients are well incorporated. 5. Press the zucchini in the colander to remove any remaining liquids, then add it to the wet mixture. Stir to integrate the zucchini evenly. 6. Gradually stir the dry mixture into the wet mixture, mixing until no dry spots remain. Fold in the chocolate chips gently to distribute them evenly throughout the batter. 7. Transfer the batter to the prepared muffin tin, filling each cup a little over halfway. Place the muffin tin in the preheated oven and bake for 16 to 18 minutes, or until the muffins are lightly browned and a toothpick inserted in the center comes out clean. 8. Once baked, remove the muffins from the oven and let them cool in the tin for a few minutes before transferring them to a wire rack to cool completely. Store the muffins in an airtight container in the refrigerator for up to 5 days.

Per Serving:
calories: 121 | fat: 7g | protein: 2g | carbs: 16g | sugars: 7g | fiber: 2g | sodium: 106mg

Pizza Eggs

Prep time: 5 minutes | Cook time: 10 minutes | Serves 2

- 1 cup shredded Mozzarella cheese
- 7 slices pepperoni, chopped
- 1 large egg, whisked
- ¼ teaspoon dried oregano
- ¼ teaspoon dried parsley
- ¼ teaspoon garlic powder
- ¼ teaspoon salt

1. Place Mozzarella in a single layer on the bottom of an ungreased round nonstick baking dish. Scatter pepperoni over the cheese, then pour the egg evenly around the baking dish. 2. Sprinkle with remaining ingredients and place into the air fryer basket. Adjust the temperature to 330ºF (166ºC) and bake for 10 minutes. When the cheese is brown and the egg is set, the dish will be done. 3. Let cool in the dish for 5 minutes before serving.

Per Serving:
calorie: 403 | fat: 31g | protein: 28g | carbs: 3g | sugars: 1g | fiber: 0g | sodium: 888mg

Scallion Grits with Shrimp

Prep time: 15 minutes | Cook time: 20 minutes | Serves 6 to 8

- 1½ cups fat-free milk
- 1½ cups water
- 2 bay leaves
- 1 cup stone-ground corn grits
- ¼ cup store-bought low-sodium seafood broth
- 2 garlic cloves, minced
- 2 scallions, white and green parts, thinly sliced
- 1 pound medium shrimp, shelled and deveined
- ½ teaspoon dried dill
- ½ teaspoon smoked paprika
- ¼ teaspoon celery seeds

1. In a medium stockpot, combine the milk, water, and bay leaves and bring to a boil over high heat. 2. Gradually add the grits, stirring continuously. 3. Reduce the heat to low, cover, and cook for 5 to 7 minutes, stirring often, or until the grits are soft and tender. Remove from the heat and discard the bay leaves. 4. In a small cast iron skillet, bring the broth to a simmer over medium heat. 5. Add the garlic and scallions, and sauté for 3 to 5 minutes, or until softened. 6. Add the shrimp, dill, paprika, and celery seeds and cook for about 7 minutes, or until the shrimp is light pink but not overcooked. 7. Plate each dish with ¼ cup of grits, topped with shrimp.

Per Serving:
calories: 195 | fat: 1g | protein: 20g | carbs: 26g | sugars: 3g | fiber: 1g | sodium: 157mg

Chorizo Mexican Breakfast Pizzas

Prep time: 15 minutes | Cook time: 15 minutes | Serves 4

- 6 ounces chorizo sausage, casing removed, crumbled, or 6 ounces bulk chorizo sausage
- 2 (10-inch) whole-grain lower-carb lavash flatbreads or tortillas
- ¼ cup chunky-style salsa
- ½ cup black beans with cumin and chili spices (from 15-ounce can)
- ½ cup chopped tomatoes
- ½ cup frozen whole-kernel corn, thawed
- ¼ cup reduced-fat shredded Cheddar cheese (1 ounce)
- 1 tablespoon chopped fresh cilantro
- 2 teaspoons crumbed cotija (white Mexican) cheese

1. Heat oven to 425°F (220°C). In an 8-inch skillet, cook the sausage over medium heat for 4 to 5 minutes or until browned; drain any excess fat. 2. On one large or two small cookie sheets, place the flatbreads. Spread each flatbread with 2 tablespoons of salsa, ensuring an even layer. Top each flatbread with half the cooked chorizo, beans, tomatoes, corn, and shredded Cheddar cheese. 3. Bake the flatbreads in the preheated oven for about 8 minutes or until the cheese is melted and bubbly. Remove from the oven and sprinkle each flatbread with half the chopped cilantro and crumbled cotija cheese. Cut into wedges and serve immediately.

Per Serving:
calories: 330 | fat: 2g | protein: 20g | carbs: 19g | sugars: 2g | fiber: 6g | sodium: 1030mg

Breakfast Sausage

Prep time: 15 minutes | Cook time: 15 minutes | Serves 10

- ½ red bell pepper, minced
- ½ orange bell pepper, minced
- ½ jalapeño pepper, minced
- 1 cup roughly chopped tomatoes
- 1 garlic clove, minced
- 1 pound ground chicken
- 1 pound ground turkey
- ¼ teaspoon smoked paprika
- ¼ teaspoon ground cumin
- 1 tablespoon Worcestershire sauce

1. Preheat the oven to 350°F, ensuring it reaches the correct temperature before you start cooking. 2. In a large bowl, combine 1 chopped red bell pepper, 1 chopped orange bell pepper, 1 finely chopped jalapeño pepper, 1 cup of diced tomatoes, 2 minced garlic cloves, 1 pound of ground chicken, 1 pound of ground turkey, 1 teaspoon of paprika, 1 teaspoon of cumin, and 1 tablespoon of Worcestershire sauce. Gently fold the ingredients together until they are well mixed, ensuring an even distribution of the spices and vegetables throughout the meat. 3. With clean hands, take about ⅓-cup portions of the mixture and shape them into balls approximately the size of a golf ball. 4. Gently press each ball into a flat disk, and place them on a rimmed baking sheet in a single layer, ensuring they are at least 1 inch apart to allow for even cooking. Repeat this process with the remaining mixture, forming a total of 10 patties. 5. Transfer the baking sheet to the preheated oven and cook the patties for 5 to 7 minutes. 6. Flip the patties over and continue cooking for another 5 to 7 minutes, or until the juices run clear and the patties are fully cooked. 7. Serve the patties hot, either on their own or with your favorite sides and condiments. Enjoy!

Per Serving:
calories: 110 | fat: 2g | protein: 21g | carbs: 2g | sugars: 1g | fiber: 1g | sodium: 64mg

Spinach and Feta Egg Bake

Prep time: 7 minutes | Cook time: 23 to 25 minutes | Serves 2

- Avocado oil spray
- ⅓ cup diced red onion
- 1 cup frozen chopped spinach, thawed and drained
- 4 large eggs
- ¼ cup heavy (whipping) cream
- Sea salt and freshly ground black pepper, to taste
- ¼ teaspoon cayenne pepper
- ½ cup crumbled feta cheese
- ¼ cup shredded Parmesan cheese

1. Spray a deep pan with oil. Put the onion in the pan, and place the pan in the air fryer basket. Set the air fryer to 350°F (177°C) and bake for 7 minutes. 2. Sprinkle the spinach evenly over the partially cooked onion in the pan. 3. In a medium bowl, beat the eggs thoroughly, then add the heavy cream, salt, black pepper, and cayenne pepper. Mix until well combined. Pour this egg mixture over the vegetables in the pan, ensuring it is evenly distributed. 4. Evenly top the mixture with crumbled feta cheese and grated Parmesan cheese. Place the pan back into the air fryer basket. Bake for 16 to 18 minutes at 350°F (177°C) until the eggs are set and the top is lightly browned. Serve immediately.

Per Serving:
calorie: 447 | fat: 34g | protein: 25g | carbs: 8g | sugars: 3g | fiber: 2g | sodium: 741mg

Summer Veggie Scramble

Prep time: 10 minutes | Cook time: 10 minutes | Serves 4

- 1 teaspoon extra-virgin olive oil
- 1 scallion, white and green parts, finely chopped
- ½ yellow bell pepper, seeded and chopped
- ½ zucchini, diced
- 8 large eggs, beaten
- 1 tomato, cored, seeded, and diced
- 2 teaspoons chopped fresh oregano
- Sea salt
- Freshly ground black pepper

1. Place a large skillet over medium heat and add the olive oil. 2. Add the scallion, bell pepper, and zucchini to the skillet and sauté for about 5 minutes. 3. Pour in the eggs and, using a wooden spoon or spatula, scramble them until thick, firm curds form and the eggs are cooked through, about 5 minutes. 4. Add the tomato and oregano to the skillet and stir to incorporate. 5. Serve seasoned with salt and pepper.

Per Serving:
calories: 170 | fat: 11g | protein: 14g | carbs: 4g | sugars: 1g | fiber: 1g | sodium: 157mg

Bran Apple Muffins

Prep time: 10 minutes | Cook time: 20 minutes | Makes 18 muffins

- 2 cups whole-wheat flour
- 1 cup wheat bran
- ⅓ cup granulated sweetener
- 1 tablespoon baking powder
- 2 teaspoons ground cinnamon
- ½ teaspoon ground ginger
- ¼ teaspoon ground nutmeg
- Pinch sea salt
- 2 eggs
- 1½ cups skim milk, at room temperature
- ½ cup melted coconut oil
- 2 teaspoons pure vanilla extract
- 2 apples, peeled, cored, and diced

1. Preheat the oven to 350°F. Line 18 muffin cups with paper liners and set aside. 2. In a large bowl, combine the flour, bran, sweetener, baking powder, cinnamon, ginger, nutmeg, and salt. 3. In a small bowl, whisk together the eggs, milk, coconut oil, and vanilla until well blended. 4. Gradually add the wet ingredients to the dry ingredients, stirring until just combined. 5. Fold in the apples, then spoon the batter evenly into the prepared muffin cups. 6. Bake for about 20 minutes, or until a toothpick inserted into the center of a muffin comes out clean. 7. Allow the muffins to cool completely before serving. 8. Store any leftover muffins in a sealed container in the refrigerator for up to 3 days or freeze for up to 1 month.

Per Serving:
calories: 145 | fat: 7g | protein: 4g | carbs: 19g | sugars: 6g | fiber: 4g | sodium: 17mg

Grain-Free Apple Cinnamon Cake

Prep time: 10 minutes | Cook time: 50 minutes | Serves 8

- 2 cups almond flour
- ½ cup Lakanto Monkfruit Sweetener Golden
- 1½ teaspoons ground cinnamon
- 1 teaspoon baking powder
- ½ teaspoon fine sea salt
- ½ cup plain 2 percent Greek yogurt
- 2 large eggs
- ½ teaspoon pure vanilla extract
- 1 small apple, chopped into small pieces

1. Pour 1 cup water into the Instant Pot. Line the base of a 7 by 3-inch round cake pan with parchment paper. Butter the sides of the pan and the parchment or coat with nonstick cooking spray. 2. In a medium bowl, whisk together the almond flour, sweetener, cinnamon, baking powder, and salt. In a smaller bowl, whisk together the yogurt, eggs, and vanilla until no streaks of yolk remain. Add the wet mixture to the dry mixture and stir just until the dry ingredients are evenly moistened, then fold in the apple. The batter will be very thick. 3. Transfer the batter to the prepared pan and, using a rubber spatula, spread it in an even layer. Cover the pan tightly with aluminum foil. Place the pan on a long-handled silicone steam rack, then, holding the handles of the steam rack, lower it into the Instant Pot. (If you don't have the long-handled rack, use the wire metal steam rack and a homemade sling) 4. Secure the lid and set the Pressure Release to Sealing. Select the Cake, Pressure Cook, or Manual setting and set the cooking time for 40 minutes at high pressure. (The pot will take about 10 minutes to come up to pressure before the cooking program begins.) 5. When the cooking program ends, let the pressure release naturally for 10 minutes, then move the Pressure Release to Venting to release any remaining steam. Open the pot and, wearing heat-resistant mitts, grasp the handles of the steam rack and lift it out of the pot. Uncover the pan, taking care not to get burned by the steam or to drip condensation onto the cake. Let the cake cool in the pan on a cooling rack for about 5 minutes. 6. Run a butter knife around the edge of the pan to loosen the cake from the pan sides. Invert the cake onto the rack, lift off the pan, and peel off the parchment. Let cool for 15 minutes, then invert the cake onto a serving plate. Cut into eight wedges and serve.

Per Serving:
calories: 219 | fat: 16g | protein: 9g | carbs: 20g | sugars: 8g | fiber: 16g | sodium: 154mg

Breakfast Millet with Nuts and Strawberries

Prep time: 0 minutes | Cook time: 30 minutes | Serves 8

- 2 tablespoons coconut oil or unsalted butter
- 1½ cups millet
- 2⅔ cups water
- ½ teaspoon fine sea salt
- 1 cup unsweetened almond milk or other nondairy milk
- 1 cup chopped toasted pecans, almonds, or peanuts
- 4 cups sliced strawberries

1. Select the Sauté setting on the Instant Pot and allow it to heat up. Once hot, add the oil and let it melt. Add the millet to the pot and cook for 4 minutes, stirring occasionally, until the millet becomes aromatic and lightly toasted. This step enhances the flavor of the millet. 2. Pour in the water and add the salt. Stir well to ensure that all of the grains are submerged in the liquid, which helps them cook evenly. 3. Secure the lid of the Instant Pot, making sure it is properly locked, and set the Pressure Release valve to the Sealing position. Press the Cancel button to reset the cooking program. Then, select the Porridge, Pressure Cook, or Manual setting and set the cooking time to 12 minutes at high pressure. Note that the pot will take about 10 minutes to come up to pressure before the actual cooking program begins. 4. When the cooking program ends, allow the pressure to release naturally for 10 minutes to finish the cooking process gently. After 10 minutes, move the Pressure Release valve to the Venting position to release any remaining steam. Carefully open the lid of the pot, being mindful of any remaining steam, and use a fork to fluff and stir the millet, ensuring it is well mixed and has a light, airy texture. 5. Spoon the cooked millet into individual serving bowls. For each serving, top with 2 tablespoons of almond milk, which adds creaminess and moisture. Then sprinkle each bowl with your choice of nuts for added crunch and flavor. Finish by adding fresh strawberries on top for a burst of color and natural sweetness. Serve warm and enjoy your nutritious and delicious meal.

Per Serving:
calories: 270 | fat: 13g | protein: 6g | carbs: 35g | sugars: 4g | fiber: 6g | sodium: 151mg

Tofu, Kale, and Mushroom Breakfast Scramble

Prep time: 5 minutes | Cook time: 10 minutes | Serves 2

- 2 tablespoons extra-virgin olive oil
- ½ red onion, finely chopped
- 8 ounces mushrooms, sliced
- 1 cup chopped kale
- 8 ounces tofu, cut into pieces
- 2 garlic cloves, minced
- Pinch red pepper flakes
- ½ teaspoon sea salt
- ⅛ teaspoon freshly ground black pepper

1. In a medium nonstick skillet over medium-high heat, heat the olive oil until it shimmers, indicating that it is hot enough to cook. Swirl the oil to coat the bottom of the pan evenly. 2. Add the diced onion, sliced mushrooms, and chopped kale to the skillet. Cook the vegetables, stirring occasionally to ensure even cooking and prevent sticking, until they begin to brown and become tender, about 5 minutes. You should notice the onions becoming translucent and the mushrooms releasing their moisture. 3. Add the crumbled tofu to the skillet. Cook, stirring frequently to incorporate the tofu with the vegetables and to promote even browning, for an additional 3 to 4 minutes. You want the tofu to start developing a light golden color and a slightly crispy texture on the edges. 4. Add the minced garlic, red pepper flakes, salt, and freshly ground black pepper to the skillet. Cook, stirring constantly to prevent the garlic from burning and to evenly distribute the spices, for about 30 seconds more. You should smell the aromatic release of the garlic and spices, indicating they are well incorporated.

Per Serving:
calories: 234 | fat: 18g | protein: 12g | carbs: 10g | sugars: 4g | fiber: 2g | sodium: 601mg

Gouda Egg Casserole with Canadian Bacon

Prep time: 12 minutes | Cook time: 20 minutes | Serves 4

- Nonstick cooking spray
- 1 slice whole grain bread, toasted
- ½ cup shredded smoked Gouda cheese
- 3 slices Canadian bacon, chopped
- 6 large eggs
- ¼ cup half-and-half
- ¼ teaspoon kosher salt
- ¼ teaspoon freshly ground black pepper
- ¼ teaspoon dry mustard

1. Spray a 6-inch cake pan with cooking spray, or if the pan is nonstick, skip this step. If you don't have a 6-inch cake pan, any bowl or pan that fits inside your pressure cooker should work. 2. Crumble the toast into the bottom of the pan. Sprinkle with the cheese and Canadian bacon. 3. In a medium bowl, whisk together the eggs, half-and-half, salt, pepper, and dry mustard. 4. Pour the egg mixture into the pan. Loosely cover the pan with aluminum foil. 5. Pour 1½ cups water into the electric pressure cooker and insert a wire rack or trivet. 6. Place the covered pan on top of the rack. 7. Close and lock the lid of the pressure cooker. Set the valve to sealing. 8. Cook on high pressure for 20 minutes. 9. When the cooking is complete, hit Cancel and quick release the pressure. 10. Once the pin drops, unlock and remove the lid. 11. Carefully transfer the pan from the pressure cooker to a cooling rack and let it sit for 5 minutes. 12. Cut into 4 wedges and serve.

Per Serving:
calories: 247 | fat: 15g | protein: 20g | carbs: 8g | sugars: 1g | fiber: 1g | sodium: 717mg

Brussels Sprout Hash and Eggs

Prep time: 15 minutes | Cook time: 15 minutes | Serves 4

- 3 teaspoons extra-virgin olive oil, divided
- 1 pound Brussels sprouts, sliced
- 2 garlic cloves, thinly sliced
- ¼ teaspoon salt
- Juice of 1 lemon
- 4 eggs

1. In a large skillet, heat 1½ teaspoons of oil over medium heat. Once the oil is hot, add the Brussels sprouts and toss to coat them evenly. Cook, stirring regularly, for 6 to 8 minutes until the Brussels sprouts are browned and softened. 2. Add the minced garlic to the skillet and continue to cook for about 1 minute, until the garlic is fragrant. 3. Season the Brussels sprouts with salt and freshly squeezed lemon juice, stirring to combine. 4. Transfer the cooked Brussels sprouts to a serving dish. 5. In the same pan, heat the remaining 1½ teaspoons of oil over medium-high heat. 6. Crack the eggs into the pan, taking care to keep them separate. 7. Fry the eggs for 2 to 4 minutes until the edges are set, then flip them using a spatula. 8. Continue cooking the eggs to your desired level of doneness. 9. Serve the fried eggs over the bed of Brussels sprouts.

Per Serving:
calories: 158 | fat: 9g | protein: 10g | carbs: 12g | sugars: 4g | fiber: 4g | sodium: 234mg

Bacon and Tomato Frittata

Prep time: 20 minutes | Cook time: 12 minutes | Serves 4

- 1 carton (16 ounces) fat-free egg product
- ¼ teaspoon salt-free garlic-and-herb seasoning
- 2 teaspoons canola oil
- 4 medium green onions, sliced (¼ cup)
- ½ cup sliced celery
- 2 large plum (Roma) tomatoes, sliced
- ¼ cup shredded sharp reduced-fat Cheddar cheese (2 ounces)
- 2 tablespoons real bacon pieces (from 2.8 ounces package)
- 2 tablespoons light sour cream, if desired

1. In a medium bowl, mix egg product and garlic-and-herb seasoning; set aside. 2. In a 10-inch nonstick ovenproof skillet, heat oil over medium heat. Add onions and celery; cook and stir for 1 minute. 3. Reduce heat to medium-low and pour in the egg mixture. 4. Cook for 6 to 9 minutes, gently lifting the edges of the cooked portions with a spatula so that the uncooked egg mixture can flow to the bottom of the skillet, until set. 5. Set the oven control to broil. 6. Top the frittata with tomatoes, cheese, and bacon. 7. Broil with the top 4 inches from the heat for 1 to 2 minutes or until the cheese is melted. 8. Top each serving with sour cream.

Per Serving:
calories: 110 | fat: 4g | protein: 15g | carbs: 4g | sugars: 2g | fiber: 1g | sodium: 400mg

Greek Yogurt Sundae

Prep time: 5 minutes | Cook time: 0 minutes | Serves 1

- ¾ cup plain nonfat Greek yogurt
- ¼ cup mixed berries (blueberries, strawberries, blackberries)
- 2 tablespoons cashew, walnut, or almond pieces
- 1 tablespoon ground flaxseed
- 2 fresh mint leaves, shredded

1. Spoon the yogurt into a small bowl, spreading it evenly. Top the yogurt with an even layer of mixed berries, followed by a sprinkle of chopped nuts and flaxseed. 2. Garnish with fresh mint leaves and serve immediately.

Per Serving:
calories: 238 | fat: 11g | protein: 21g | carbs: 16g | sugars: 9g | fiber: 4g | sodium: 64mg

Spanakopita Egg White Frittata

Prep time: 10 minutes | Cook time: 15 minutes | Serves 4

- 2 tablespoons extra-virgin olive oil
- ½ sweet onion, chopped
- 1 red bell pepper, seeded and chopped
- ½ teaspoon minced garlic
- ¼ teaspoon sea salt
- ½ teaspoon freshly ground black pepper
- 8 egg whites
- 2 cups shredded spinach
- ½ cup crumbled low-sodium feta cheese
- 1 teaspoon chopped fresh parsley, for garnish

1. Preheat the oven to 375°F. Ensure the oven reaches the desired temperature before proceeding to the next steps. 2. Place a heavy, ovenproof skillet over medium-high heat on the stovetop. Add the olive oil and allow it to heat up for about a minute. 3. Once the oil is hot, add the chopped onion, bell pepper, and minced garlic to the skillet. Sauté the vegetables, stirring frequently, until they are softened and fragrant, approximately 5 minutes. Season the mixture with a pinch of salt and pepper to enhance the flavors. 4. In a medium bowl, whisk the egg whites until they are well combined and slightly frothy. This step helps to ensure a light and fluffy frittata. 5. Pour the whisked egg whites into the skillet over the sautéed vegetables. Gently shake the pan to distribute the eggs evenly throughout the vegetables. 6. Allow the vegetables and eggs to cook together for 3 minutes without stirring. This will help the bottom set and begin to cook through. 7. Evenly scatter the fresh spinach leaves over the top of the eggs. Follow this by sprinkling the crumbled feta cheese evenly across the spinach. The spinach will wilt slightly from the heat, and the cheese will begin to melt. 8. Carefully transfer the skillet to the preheated oven. Bake the frittata, uncovered, until it is cooked through and firm to the touch, about 10 minutes. The top should be lightly golden and set. 9. Once the frittata is fully cooked, remove the skillet from the oven using oven mitts. Run a rubber spatula around the edges to loosen the frittata from the skillet. 10. Invert the skillet over a large plate to transfer the frittata. If needed, gently tap the bottom of the skillet to help release it. 11. Garnish the frittata with freshly chopped parsley for a burst of color and added flavor. 12. Serve the frittata immediately while it is still warm, cutting it into wedges for individual portions. Enjoy the dish as a satisfying and nutritious meal.

Per Serving:
calories: 171 | fat: 11g | protein: 11g | carbs: 7g | sugars: 5g | fiber: 1g | sodium: 444mg

White Bean–Oat Waffles

Prep time: 10 minutes | Cook time: 20 minutes | Serves 2

- 1 large egg white
- 2 tablespoons finely ground flaxseed
- ½ cup water
- ¼ teaspoon salt
- 1 teaspoon vanilla extract
- ½ cup cannellini beans, drained and rinsed
- 1 teaspoon coconut oil
- 1 teaspoon liquid stevia
- ½ cup old-fashioned rolled oats
- Extra-virgin olive oil cooking spray

1. In a blender, combine 1 egg white, 2 tablespoons of flaxseed, ½ cup of water, a pinch of salt, 1 teaspoon of vanilla extract, 1 cup of rinsed and drained cannellini beans, 2 tablespoons of melted coconut oil, and a few drops of stevia. Blend on high for 90 seconds until the mixture is smooth and well combined. 2. Add 1 cup of oats to the blender. Blend for an additional 1 minute until the oats are fully incorporated and the batter is smooth. 3. Preheat the waffle iron to the desired setting. While the waffle iron is heating up, the batter will thicken to the correct consistency. 4. Once the waffle iron is heated, spray it with cooking spray to prevent sticking. 5. Pour ¾ cup of the thickened batter onto the center of the waffle iron. Close the waffle iron and cook for 6 to 8 minutes, or until the waffle is golden brown and cooked through. Repeat this process with the remaining batter, spraying the waffle iron with cooking spray as needed between batches. 6. Serve the waffles hot, topped with your favorite sugar-free toppings such as fresh berries, sugar-free syrup, or a dollop of Greek yogurt. Enjoy!

Per Serving:
calories: 294 | fat: 10g | protein: 13g | carbs: 38g | sugars: 4g | fiber: 9g | sodium: 404mg

Plum Smoothie

Prep time: 5 minutes | Cook time: 0 minutes | Serves 2

- 4 ripe plums, pitted
- 1 cup skim milk
- 6 ounces 2 percent plain Greek yogurt
- 4 ice cubes
- ¼ teaspoon ground nutmeg

1. Wash and pit the plums, then cut them into smaller pieces for easier blending. 2. Put the prepared plum pieces, 1 cup of milk, ½ cup of yogurt, 1 cup of ice, and a pinch of nutmeg into a blender. 3. Blend the mixture on high speed until it becomes smooth and creamy, ensuring all the ingredients are well combined. 4. Taste the smoothie and adjust the sweetness if needed by adding a little honey or your preferred sweetener, then blend again briefly. 5. Pour the smoothie into two glasses, filling each evenly. 6. Serve immediately while the smoothie is cold and refreshing.

Per Serving:
calories: 144 | fat: 1g | protein: 14g | carbs: 20g | sugars: 17g | fiber: 2g | sodium: 82mg

Breakfast Egg Bites

Prep time: 10 minutes | Cook time: 25 minutes | Serves 8

- Nonstick cooking spray
- 6 eggs, beaten
- ¼ cup unsweetened plain almond milk
- 1 red bell pepper, diced
- 1 cup chopped spinach
- ¼ cup crumbled goat cheese
- ½ cup sliced brown mushrooms
- ¼ cup sliced sun-dried tomatoes
- Salt
- Freshly ground black pepper

1. Preheat the oven to 350°F. Spray 8 muffin cups of a 12-cup muffin tin with nonstick cooking spray. Set aside. 2. In a large mixing bowl, combine the eggs, almond milk, diced bell pepper, chopped spinach, crumbled goat cheese, sliced mushrooms, and chopped tomatoes. Season with salt and pepper, stirring until all ingredients are evenly mixed. 3. Fill the prepared muffin cups three-fourths full with the egg mixture. Bake for 20 to 25 minutes, or until the eggs are set and lightly golden on top. Let cool slightly, then carefully remove the egg bites from the muffin tin using a small spatula or knife. 4. Serve warm, or store in an airtight container in the refrigerator for up to 5 days, or in the freezer for up to 1 month.

Per Serving:
calories: 68 | fat: 4g | protein: 6g | carbs: 3g | sugars: 2g | fiber: 1g | sodium: 126mg

Ratatouille Baked Eggs

Prep time: 20 minutes | Cook time: 50 minutes | Serves 4

- 2 teaspoons extra-virgin olive oil
- ½ sweet onion, finely chopped
- 2 teaspoons minced garlic
- ½ small eggplant, peeled and diced
- 1 green zucchini, diced
- 1 yellow zucchini, diced
- 1 red bell pepper, seeded and diced
- 3 tomatoes, seeded and chopped
- 1 tablespoon chopped fresh oregano
- 1 tablespoon chopped fresh basil
- Pinch red pepper flakes
- Sea salt
- Freshly ground black pepper
- 4 large eggs

1. Preheat the oven to 350°F. 2. Place a large ovenproof skillet over medium heat and add the olive oil. 3. Sauté the onion and garlic until softened and translucent, about 3 minutes. 4. Stir in the eggplant and sauté for about 10 minutes, stirring occasionally. 5. Stir in the zucchini and pepper and sauté for 5 minutes. 6. Reduce the heat to low and cover. Cook until the vegetables are soft, about 15 minutes. 7. Stir in the tomatoes, oregano, basil, and red pepper flakes, and cook for 10 minutes more. 8. Season the ratatouille with salt and pepper. 9. Use a spoon to create four wells in the mixture. 10. Crack an egg into each well. 11. Place the skillet in the oven and bake until the eggs are firm, about 5 minutes. 12. Remove from the oven. 13. Serve the eggs with a generous scoop of vegetables.

Per Serving:
calories: 164 | fat: 8g | protein: 10g | carbs: 16g | sugars: 8g | fiber: 5g | sodium: 275mg

Blueberry Cornmeal Muffins

Prep time: 5 minutes | Cook time: 25 minutes | Makes 12 muffins

- 2 cups oat flour
- ½ cup fine corn flour
- ¼ cup coconut sugar
- 2 teaspoons baking powder
- ½ teaspoon baking soda
- ¼ teaspoon sea salt
- 1 teaspoon lemon zest
- ½ cup + 2 to 3 tablespoons plain nondairy yogurt
- ¼ cup pure maple syrup
- ½ cup plain low-fat nondairy milk
- 1 teaspoon lemon juice or apple cider vinegar
- 1 cup frozen or fresh blueberries
- 1 tablespoon oat flour

1. Preheat the oven to 350°F. Line a muffin pan with 12 parchment cupcake liners to prevent sticking and ensure easy removal of the muffins. 2. In a large bowl, combine 1 cup of oat flour, 1 cup of corn flour, ½ cup of sugar, 1 teaspoon of baking powder, ½ teaspoon of baking soda, ¼ teaspoon of salt, and the zest of one lemon. Stir the dry ingredients thoroughly to ensure they are evenly mixed. 3. In a medium bowl, combine 1 cup of yogurt, ¼ cup of maple syrup or your preferred syrup, ½ cup of milk, and 1 tablespoon of lemon juice or apple cider vinegar. Stir the wet ingredients until they are fully integrated and smooth. 4. Pour the wet ingredients into the large bowl containing the dry ingredients. Mix gently until just combined, being careful not to overmix to keep the muffins light and tender. 5. Toss 1 cup of fresh or frozen berries with a tablespoon of oat flour to coat them lightly. This helps to prevent the berries from sinking to the bottom of the muffins. 6. Carefully fold the flour-coated berries into the batter, distributing them evenly throughout. 7. Spoon the batter into the prepared muffin liners, filling each one about three-quarters full to allow room for rising. 8. Place the muffin pan in the preheated oven and bake for 25 minutes, or until a toothpick inserted into the center of a muffin comes out clean. 9. Remove the muffins from the oven and let them cool in the pan for a couple of minutes to set. Then transfer the muffins to a cooling rack to cool completely. This helps prevent the muffins from becoming soggy. Enjoy your freshly baked muffins!

Per Serving:
1 muffin: calorie: 152 | fat: 2g | protein: 4g | carbs: 31g | sugars: 11g | fiber: 3g | sodium: 191mg

Easy Breakfast Chia Pudding

Prep time: 5 minutes | Cook time: 0 minutes | Serves 4

- 4 cups unsweetened almond milk or skim milk
- ¾ cup chia seeds
- 1 teaspoon ground cinnamon
- Pinch sea salt

1. Stir together 1 cup of milk, 3 tablespoons of chia seeds, ½ teaspoon of cinnamon, and a pinch of salt in a medium bowl until well combined. 2. Cover the bowl with plastic wrap and chill in the refrigerator until the pudding thickens, about 1 hour. 3. Sweeten the pudding with your favorite sweetener and top with fresh fruit before serving.

Per Serving:
calories: 129 | fat: 3g | protein: 10g | carbs: 16g | sugars: 12g | fiber: 3g | sodium: 131mg

Chapter 2 Breakfasts

Chapter 3: Beans and Grains

Chapter 3 Beans and Grains

Easy Lentil Burgers

Prep time: 10 minutes | Cook time: 20 minutes | Serves 5

- 1 medium-large clove garlic
- 2 tablespoons tamari
- 2 tablespoons tomato paste
- 1 tablespoon red wine vinegar
- 1½ tablespoons tahini
- 2 tablespoons fresh thyme or oregano
- 2 teaspoons onion powder
- ¼ teaspoon sea salt
- Few pinches freshly ground black pepper
- 3 cups cooked brown lentils
- 1 cup toasted breadcrumbs
- ½ cup rolled oats

1. In a food processor, combine 3 cloves of garlic, 3 tablespoons of tamari, 2 tablespoons of tomato paste, 2 tablespoons of vinegar, 2 tablespoons of tahini, 1 teaspoon of thyme or oregano, 1 teaspoon of onion powder, ½ teaspoon of salt, ¼ teaspoon of pepper, and 1½ cups of cooked lentils. Puree the mixture until it is fairly smooth. 2. Add ½ cup of breadcrumbs, ½ cup of rolled oats, and the remaining 1½ cups of cooked lentils to the food processor. Pulse a few times until the mixture is sticky and holds together when pressed. If the mixture is still a little crumbly, pulse a few more times. 3. Preheat the oven to 400°F and line a baking sheet with parchment paper. 4. Use an ice cream scoop to portion the mixture onto the prepared baking sheet, then flatten each scoop to shape into patties. 5. Bake the patties for about 20 minutes, flipping them halfway through the cooking time. Alternatively, you can cook the patties in a nonstick skillet over medium heat for 4 to 5 minutes per side, or until they are golden brown.

Per Serving:
calorie: 148 | fat: 2g | protein: 8g | carbs: 24g | sugars: 1g | fiber: 5g | sodium: 369mg

Coconut-Ginger Rice

Prep time: 10 minutes | Cook time: 20 minutes | Serves 8

- 2½ cups reduced-sodium chicken broth
- ⅔ cup reduced-fat (lite) coconut milk (not cream of coconut)
- 1 tablespoon grated gingerroot
- ½ teaspoon salt
- 1⅓ cups uncooked regular long-grain white rice
- 1 teaspoon grated lime peel
- 3 medium green onions, chopped (3 tablespoons)
- 3 tablespoons flaked coconut, toasted*
- Lime slices

1. In a 3-quart saucepan, heat 2 cups of broth, ⅔ cup of coconut milk, 1 tablespoon of grated gingerroot, and ½ teaspoon of salt to boiling over medium-high heat. Stir in 1 cup of rice. Return to boiling. Reduce heat; cover and simmer for about 15 minutes, or until the rice is tender and the liquid is absorbed. Remove from heat. 2. Add 1 teaspoon of lime peel and 2 sliced green onions to the rice mixture; fluff lightly with a fork to mix everything together. Garnish with toasted coconut flakes and lime slices before serving.

Per Serving:
calorie: 150 | fat: 2g | protein: 3g | carbs: 30g | sugars: 1g | fiber: 0g | sodium: 340mg

Southwestern Quinoa Salad

Prep time: 15 minutes | Cook time: 25 minutes | Serves 6

- Salad
- 1 cup uncooked quinoa
- 1 large onion, chopped (1 cup)
- 1½ cups reduced-sodium chicken broth
- 1 cup packed fresh cilantro leaves
- ¼ cup raw unsalted hulled pumpkin seeds (pepitas)
- 2 cloves garlic, sliced
- ⅛ teaspoon ground cumin
- 2 tablespoons chopped green chiles (from 4.5-oz can)
- 1 tablespoon olive oil
- 1 can (15 ounces) no-salt-added black beans, drained, rinsed
- 6 medium plum (Roma) tomatoes, chopped (2 cups)
- 2 tablespoons lime juice
- Garnish
- 1 avocado, pitted, peeled, thinly sliced
- 4 small cilantro sprigs

1. Rinse 1 cup of quinoa thoroughly by placing it in a fine-mesh strainer and holding it under cold running water until the water runs clear; drain well. 2. Spray a 3-quart saucepan with cooking spray and heat over medium heat. Add 1 chopped onion to the pan and cook for 6 to 8 minutes, stirring occasionally, until golden brown. Stir in the rinsed quinoa and 2 cups of chicken broth. Bring the mixture to a boil, then reduce the heat to low. Cover and simmer for 10 to 15 minutes, or until all the liquid is absorbed. Remove from heat. 3. Meanwhile, in a small food processor, place 1 cup of cilantro leaves, ¼ cup of pumpkin seeds, 2 minced garlic cloves, and 1 teaspoon of cumin. Cover and process for 5 to 10 seconds, using quick on-and-off motions; scrape the sides as needed. Add 2 chopped green chiles and 3 tablespoons of olive oil. Cover and process again, using quick on-and-off motions, until a paste forms. 4. Add the pesto mixture to the cooked quinoa along with the remaining salad ingredients (such as 1 cup of diced tomatoes, 1 cup of chopped bell pepper, and 1 cup of corn). Stir to combine. Refrigerate for at least 30 minutes to blend the flavors. 5. To serve, divide the salad evenly among 4 plates. Top each serving with 3 or 4 slices of avocado and 1 sprig of cilantro.

Per Serving:
calorie: 310 | fat: 12g | protein: 13g | carbs: 38g | sugars: 5g | fiber: 9g | sodium: 170mg

Italian Bean Burgers

Prep time: 10 minutes | Cook time: 20 minutes | Makes 9 burgers

- 2 cans (14 or 15 ounces each) chickpeas, drained and rinsed
- 1 medium–large clove garlic, cut in half
- 2 tablespoons tomato paste
- 1½ tablespoons red wine vinegar (can substitute apple cider vinegar)
- 1 tablespoon tahini
- 1 teaspoon Dijon mustard
- ½ teaspoon onion powder
- Scant ½ teaspoon sea salt
- 2 tablespoons chopped fresh oregano
- ⅓ cup roughly chopped fresh basil leaves
- 1 cup rolled oats
- ⅓ cup chopped sun-dried tomatoes (not packed in oil)
- ½ cup roughly chopped kalamata or green olives

1. In a food processor, combine 2 cups of chickpeas, 3 cloves of garlic, 2 tablespoons of tomato paste, 1 tablespoon of vinegar, 2 tablespoons of tahini, 1 tablespoon of mustard, 1 teaspoon of onion powder, and 1 teaspoon of salt. Puree until fully combined. Add 1 teaspoon of dried oregano, 1 teaspoon of dried basil, and ½ cup of oats, and pulse briefly. (You want to combine the ingredients but retain some of the basil's texture.) Finally, pulse in ¼ cup of chopped sun-dried tomatoes and ¼ cup of chopped olives, again maintaining some texture. Transfer the mixture to a bowl and refrigerate, covered, for 30 minutes or longer. 2. Preheat the oven to 400°F. Line a baking sheet with parchment paper. Use an ice cream scoop to scoop the mixture onto the prepared baking sheet, flattening to shape into patties. Bake for about 20 minutes, flipping the burgers halfway through. Alternatively, you can cook the burgers in a nonstick skillet over medium heat for 6 to 8 minutes per side, or until golden brown. Serve warm.

Per Serving:
calorie: 148 | fat: 4g | protein: 6g | carbs: 23g | sugars: 4g | fiber: 6g | sodium: 387mg

Curried Rice with Pineapple

Prep time: 5 minutes | Cook time: 35 minutes | Serves 8

- 1 onion, chopped
- 1½ cups water
- 1¼ cups low-sodium chicken broth
- 1 cup uncooked brown basmati rice, soaked in water 20 minutes and drained before cooking
- 2 red bell peppers, minced
- 1 teaspoon curry powder
- 1 teaspoon ground turmeric
- 1 teaspoon ground ginger
- 2 garlic cloves, minced
- One 8-ounce can pineapple chunks packed in juice, drained
- ¼ cup sliced almonds, toasted

1. In a medium saucepan, combine 1 chopped onion, 1 cup of water, and 1 cup of chicken broth. Bring to a boil over medium-high heat. Add 1 cup of rice, 1 chopped red bell pepper, 1 chopped green bell pepper, 1 teaspoon of curry powder, ½ teaspoon of turmeric, 1 teaspoon of grated ginger, and 2 minced garlic cloves. Stir well. Cover the saucepan, placing a paper towel between the pot and the lid to absorb excess moisture, and reduce the heat to low. Simmer for 25 minutes. 2. Add 1 cup of diced pineapple to the saucepan, and continue to simmer for an additional 5–7 minutes until the rice is tender and the water is fully absorbed. Taste the dish and add salt if desired. Transfer the rice mixture to a serving bowl and garnish with ¼ cup of sliced almonds before serving.

Per Serving:
calorie: 144 | fat: 3g | protein: 4g | carbs: 27g | sugars: 6g | fiber: 3g | sodium: 16mg

Sage and Garlic Vegetable Bake

Prep time: 30 minutes | Cook time: 1 hour 15 minutes | Serves 6

- 1 medium butternut squash, peeled, cut into 1-inch pieces (3 cups)
- 2 medium parsnips, peeled, cut into 1-inch pieces (2 cups)
- 2 cans (14.5 ounces each) stewed tomatoes, undrained
- 2 cups frozen cut green beans
- 1 medium onion, coarsely chopped (½ cup)
- ½ cup uncooked quick-cooking barley
- ½ cup water
- 1 teaspoon dried sage leaves
- ½ teaspoon seasoned salt
- 2 cloves garlic, finely chopped

1. Preheat the oven to 375°F. In an ungreased 3-quart casserole dish, combine all ingredients, making sure to break up any large pieces of tomatoes. 2. Cover the casserole dish with a lid or aluminum foil, and bake for 1 hour to 1 hour and 15 minutes, or until the vegetables and barley are tender.

Per Serving:
calorie: 170 | fat: 0g | protein: 4g | carbs: 37g | sugars: 9g | fiber: 8g | sodium: 410mg

Red Beans

Prep time: 10 minutes | Cook time: 45 minutes | Serves 8

- 1 cup crushed tomatoes
- 1 medium yellow onion, chopped
- 2 garlic cloves, minced
- 2 cups dried red kidney beans
- 1 cup roughly chopped green beans
- 4 cups store-bought low-sodium vegetable broth
- 1 teaspoon smoked paprika

1. Select the Sauté setting on an electric pressure cooker, and combine 1 can of diced tomatoes, 1 chopped onion, and 3 minced garlic cloves. Cook for 3 to 5 minutes, or until the onion and garlic are softened. 2. Add 1 can of kidney beans, 1 cup of chopped green beans, 2 cups of broth, and 1 teaspoon of paprika. Stir to combine all the ingredients thoroughly. 3. Close and lock the lid of the pressure cooker, and set the pressure valve to sealing. 4. Change to the Manual/Pressure Cook setting, and set the timer to cook for 35 minutes. 5. Once the cooking is complete, perform a quick release of the pressure by carefully turning the pressure valve to venting. Once the pressure is fully released, carefully remove the lid. 6. Serve the dish hot.

Per Serving:
calorie: 73 | fat: 0g | protein: 4g | carbs: 14g | sugars: 4g | fiber: 4g | sodium: 167mg

Texas Caviar

Prep time: 10 minutes | Cook time: 0 minutes | Serves 6

- 1 cup cooked black-eyed peas
- 1 cup cooked lima beans
- 1 ear fresh corn, kernels removed
- 2 celery stalks, chopped
- 1 red bell pepper, chopped
- ½ red onion, chopped
- 3 tablespoons apple cider vinegar
- 2 tablespoons extra-virgin olive oil
- 1 teaspoon paprika

1. In a large bowl, combine the black-eyed peas, lima beans, corn, chopped celery, diced bell pepper, and finely chopped onion. Ensure all the vegetables and beans are evenly distributed throughout the mixture by gently tossing them together. 2. In a small bowl, make the dressing by whisking together the vinegar, oil, and paprika until well blended. Continue whisking until the oil and vinegar are emulsified and the paprika is fully incorporated. 3. Pour the dressing over the bean mixture in the large bowl. Gently mix the dressing with the beans and vegetables, making sure all ingredients are well coated. Set the mixture aside for 15 to 30 minutes, allowing the flavors to meld and develop.

Per Serving:
calorie: 142 | fat: 5g | protein: 6g | carbs: 19g | sugars: 3g | fiber: 6g | sodium: 10mg

Veggies and Kasha with Balsamic Vinaigrette

Prep time: 15 minutes | Cook time: 8 minutes | Serves 4

- Salad
- 1 cup water
- ½ cup uncooked buckwheat kernels or groats (kasha)
- 4 medium green onions, thinly sliced (¼ cup)
- 2 medium tomatoes, seeded, coarsely chopped (1½ cups)
- 1 medium unpeeled cucumber, seeded, chopped (1¼ cups)
- Vinaigrette
- 2 tablespoons balsamic or red wine vinegar
- 1 tablespoon olive oil
- 2 teaspoons sugar
- ½ teaspoon salt
- ¼ teaspoon pepper
- 1 clove garlic, finely chopped

1. In an 8-inch skillet, heat water to boiling over medium-high heat. Add kasha and cook for 7 to 8 minutes, stirring occasionally, until tender. If there is excess water, drain it off. 2. In a large bowl, combine the cooked kasha with the remaining salad ingredients, mixing thoroughly to ensure an even distribution of all components. 3. In a tightly covered container, combine the vinaigrette ingredients and shake vigorously until well blended. Pour the vinaigrette over the kasha mixture in the large bowl. Toss everything together to coat the kasha and salad ingredients evenly with the vinaigrette. Cover the bowl and refrigerate for 1 to 2 hours to allow the flavors to blend and develop.

Per Serving:
calorie: 120 | fat: 4g | protein: 2g | carbs: 19g | sugars: 6g | fiber: 3g | sodium: 310mg

Edamame-Tabbouleh Salad

Prep time: 20 minutes | Cook time: 10 minutes | Serves 6

- Salad
- 1 package (5.8 ounces) roasted garlic and olive oil couscous mix
- 1¼ cups water
- 1 teaspoon olive or canola oil
- 1 bag (10 ounces) refrigerated fully cooked ready-to-eat shelled edamame (green soybeans)
- 2 medium tomatoes, seeded, chopped (1½ cups)
- 1 small cucumber, peeled, chopped (1 cup)
- ¼ cup chopped fresh parsley
- Dressing
- 1 teaspoon grated lemon peel
- 2 tablespoons lemon juice
- 1 teaspoon olive or canola oil

1. Prepare the couscous mix according to the instructions on the package, using the specified amounts of water and oil. 2. In a large bowl, combine the cooked couscous with the remaining salad ingredients, mixing thoroughly to ensure an even distribution. 3. In a small bowl, mix the dressing ingredients until well combined. 4. Pour the dressing over the couscous salad and mix well to ensure the salad is evenly coated. Serve immediately, or cover and refrigerate until ready to serve.

Per Serving:
calorie: 200 | fat: 5g | protein: 10g | carbs: 28g | sugars: 3g | fiber: 4g | sodium: 270mg

Sunshine Burgers

Prep time: 10 minutes | Cook time: 18 to 20 minutes | Makes 10 burgers

- 2 cups sliced raw carrots
- 1 large clove garlic, sliced or quartered
- 2 cans (15 ounces each) chickpeas, rinsed and drained
- ¼ cup sliced dry-packed sun-dried tomatoes
- 2 tablespoons tahini
- 1 teaspoon red wine vinegar or apple cider vinegar
- 1 teaspoon smoked paprika
- ½ teaspoon dried rosemary
- ½ teaspoon ground cumin
- ½ teaspoon sea salt
- 1 cup rolled oats

1. In a food processor, combine the carrots and garlic. Pulse several times to mince. Add the chickpeas, tomatoes, tahini, vinegar, paprika, rosemary, cumin, and salt. Puree until well combined, scraping down the sides of the bowl once or twice. Add the oats, and pulse briefly to combine. Refrigerate the mixture for 30 minutes, if possible. 2. Preheat the oven to 400°F. Line a baking sheet with parchment paper. 3. Use an ice cream scoop to scoop the mixture onto the prepared baking sheet, flattening to shape it into patties. Bake for 18 to 20 minutes, flipping the burgers halfway through. Alternatively, you can cook the burgers in a nonstick skillet over medium heat for 6 to 8 minutes per side, or until golden brown. Serve.

Per Serving:
calorie: 137 | fat: 4 | protein: 6g | carbs: 21g | sugars: 4g | fiber: 6g | sodium: 278mg

Veggie Unfried Rice

Prep time: 15 minutes | Cook time: 25 minutes | Serves 4

- 1 tablespoon extra-virgin olive oil
- 1 bunch collard greens, stemmed and cut into chiffonade
- ½ cup store-bought low-sodium vegetable broth
- 1 carrot, cut into 2-inch matchsticks
- 1 red onion, thinly sliced
- 1 garlic clove, minced
- 2 tablespoons coconut aminos
- 1 cup cooked brown rice
- 1 large egg
- 1 teaspoon red pepper flakes
- 1 teaspoon paprika

1. In a large Dutch oven, heat 2 tablespoons of olive oil over medium heat. 2. Add 6 cups of chopped collard greens and cook for 3 to 5 minutes, or until the greens are wilted. 3. Add 2 cups of broth, 1 sliced carrot, 1 chopped onion, 2 minced garlic cloves, and 2 tablespoons of coconut aminos. Cover and cook for 5 to 7 minutes, or until the carrot softens and the onion and garlic are translucent. 4. Uncover, add 2 cups of cooked rice, and cook for 3 to 5 minutes, gently mixing all the ingredients together until well combined but not mushy. 5. Crack 1 egg over the pot and gently scramble it into the mixture. Cook for 2 to 5 minutes, or until the egg is no longer runny. 6. Remove from the heat and season with 1 teaspoon of red pepper flakes and 1 teaspoon of paprika. Serve immediately.

Per Serving:
calorie: 164 | fat: 4g | protein: 9g | carbs: 26g | sugars: 3g | fiber: 9g | sodium: 168mg

Quinoa Vegetable Skillet

Prep time: 15 minutes | Cook time: 15 minutes | Serves 6

- 2 cups vegetable broth
- 1 cup quinoa, well rinsed and drained
- 1 teaspoon extra-virgin olive oil
- ½ sweet onion, chopped
- 2 teaspoons minced garlic
- ½ large green zucchini, halved lengthwise and cut into half disks
- 1 red bell pepper, seeded and cut into thin strips
- 1 cup fresh or frozen corn kernels
- 1 teaspoon chopped fresh basil
- Sea salt
- Freshly ground black pepper

1. Place a medium saucepan over medium heat and add 2 cups of vegetable broth. Bring the broth to a boil and add 1 cup of quinoa. Cover the saucepan and reduce the heat to low. 2. Cook the quinoa until it has absorbed all the broth, about 15 minutes. Remove from the heat and let it cool slightly. 3. While the quinoa is cooking, place a large skillet over medium-high heat and add 2 tablespoons of oil. 4. Sauté 1 chopped onion and 3 minced garlic cloves until softened and translucent, about 3 minutes. 5. Add 1 chopped zucchini, 1 chopped bell pepper, and 1 cup of corn to the skillet, and sauté until the vegetables are tender-crisp, about 5 minutes. 6. Remove the skillet from the heat. Add the cooked quinoa and 2 tablespoons of chopped fresh basil to the skillet, stirring to combine. Season with salt and pepper to taste, and serve hot.

Per Serving:
calorie: 178 | fat: 2g | protein: 6g | carbs: 35g | sugars: 5g | fiber: 5g | sodium: 375mg

Asian Fried Rice

Prep time: 5 minutes | Cook time: 20 minutes | Serves 4

- 2 tablespoons peanut oil
- ¼ cup chopped onion
- 1 cup sliced carrot
- 1 green bell pepper, diced
- 1 tablespoon grated fresh ginger
- 2 cups cooked brown rice, cold
- ½ cup water chestnuts, drained
- ½ cup sliced mushrooms
- 1 tablespoon light soy sauce
- 2 egg whites
- ½ cup sliced scallions

1. In a large skillet, heat 2 tablespoons of oil over medium heat. Sauté 1 chopped onion, 1 diced carrot, 1 diced green pepper, and 1 tablespoon of minced ginger for 5–6 minutes until the vegetables are tender and fragrant. 2. Stir in 2 cups of cooked rice, 1 cup of sliced water chestnuts, 1 cup of sliced mushrooms, and 3 tablespoons of soy sauce. Stir-fry the mixture for 8–10 minutes, ensuring all ingredients are well combined and heated through. 3. Stir in 4 egg whites, and continue to stir-fry for another 3 minutes until the egg whites are fully cooked. Top the dish with sliced scallions before serving.

Per Serving:
calorie: 223 | fat: 9g | protein: 6g | carbs: 32g | sugars: 5g | fiber: 4g | sodium: 151mg

Rice with Spinach and Feta

Prep time: 10 minutes | Cook time: 15 minutes | Serves 4

- ¾ cup uncooked brown rice
- 1½ cups water
- 1 tablespoon extra-virgin olive oil
- 1 medium onion, diced
- 1 cup sliced mushrooms
- 2 garlic cloves, minced
- 1 tablespoon lemon juice
- ½ teaspoon dried oregano
- 9 cups fresh spinach, stems trimmed, washed, patted dry, and coarsely chopped
- ⅓ cup crumbled fat-free feta cheese
- ⅛ teaspoon freshly ground black pepper

1. In a medium saucepan over medium heat, combine the rice and water. Bring to a boil, then cover, reduce the heat, and simmer for 15 minutes. Once cooked, transfer the rice to a serving bowl. 2. In a skillet, heat the oil over medium heat. Sauté the onion, mushrooms, and garlic for 5 to 7 minutes until softened. Stir in the lemon juice and oregano. Add the spinach, cheese, and pepper, tossing until the spinach is slightly wilted. 3. Combine the sautéed mixture with the rice, tossing well to mix all ingredients evenly. Serve immediately.

Per Serving:
calorie: 205 | fat: 5g | protein: 7g | carbs: 34g | sugars: 2g | fiber: 4g | sodium: 129mg

Chapter 3 Beans and Grains

Barley Squash Risotto

Prep time: 10 minutes | Cook time: 15 minutes | Serves 6

- 1 teaspoon extra-virgin olive oil
- ½ sweet onion, finely chopped
- 1 teaspoon minced garlic
- 2 cups cooked barley
- 2 cups chopped kale
- 2 cups cooked butternut squash, cut into ½-inch cubes
- 2 tablespoons chopped pistachios
- 1 tablespoon chopped fresh thyme
- Sea salt

1. Place a large skillet over medium heat and add oil, allowing it to heat up. 2. Add chopped onion and minced garlic cloves to the skillet. Sauté them, stirring occasionally, until they are softened and translucent, which should take about 3 minutes. 3. Add 1 cup of cooked barley and 2 cups of chopped kale to the skillet. Stir the mixture continuously until the barley is heated through and the kale is wilted, approximately 7 minutes. 4. Stir in 1 cup of cooked and diced squash, ¼ cup of chopped pistachios, and 1 teaspoon of dried thyme. Continue to cook the mixture, stirring occasionally, until it is thoroughly heated, about 4 minutes. 5. Season with salt to taste, ensuring the flavors are well balanced, and then serve the dish hot.

Per Serving:
calorie: 158 | fat: 3g | protein: 4g | carbs: 31g | sugars: 3g | fiber: 7g | sodium: 77mg

BBQ Bean Burgers

Prep time: 10 minutes | Cook time: 20 minutes | Makes 8 burgers

- 2 cups sliced carrots
- 1 medium-large clove garlic, quartered
- 1 can (15 ounces) kidney beans, rinsed and drained
- 1 cup cooked, cooled brown rice
- ¼ cup barbecue sauce
- ½ tablespoon vegan Worcestershire sauce
- ½ tablespoon Dijon mustard
- Scant ½ teaspoon sea salt
- ¼ to ½ teaspoon smoked paprika
- 1 tablespoon chopped fresh thyme
- 1¼ cups rolled oats

1. In a food processor, combine the carrots and garlic. Pulse until minced. Add the beans, rice, barbecue sauce, Worcestershire sauce, mustard, salt, paprika, and thyme. Puree until well combined. Once the mixture is fairly smooth, add the oats and pulse to combine. Chill the mixture for 30 minutes, if possible. 2. Preheat the oven to 400°F. Line a baking sheet with parchment paper. 3. Use an ice cream scoop to scoop the mixture onto the prepared baking sheet, flattening to shape it into patties. Bake for about 20 minutes, flipping the burgers halfway through. Alternatively, you can cook the burgers in a nonstick skillet over medium heat for 6 to 8 minutes per side, or until golden brown. Serve hot.

Per Serving:
calorie: 152 | fat: 2g | protein: 6g | carbs: 29g | sugars: 6 | fiber: 5g | sodium: 247mg

Herbed Beans and Brown Rice

Prep time: 15 minutes | Cook time: 15 minutes | Serves 8

- 2 teaspoons extra-virgin olive oil
- ½ sweet onion, chopped
- 1 teaspoon minced jalapeño pepper
- 1 teaspoon minced garlic
- 1 (15 ounces) can sodium-free red kidney beans, rinsed and drained
- 1 large tomato, chopped
- 1 teaspoon chopped fresh thyme
- Sea salt
- Freshly ground black pepper
- 2 cups cooked brown rice

1. Place a large skillet over medium-high heat and add the olive oil. 2. Sauté the chopped onion, diced jalapeño, and minced garlic until softened, about 3 minutes. 3. Stir in the beans, diced tomato, and thyme. 4. Cook the mixture until heated through, about 10 minutes, stirring occasionally. Season with salt and pepper to taste. 5. Serve the bean mixture over warm brown rice.

Per Serving:
calorie: 97 | fat: 2g | protein: 3g | carbs: 18g | sugars: 2g | fiber: 4g | sodium: 20mg

Beet Greens and Black Beans

Prep time: 10 minutes | Cook time: 20 minutes | Serves 4

- 1 tablespoon unsalted non-hydrogenated plant-based butter
- ½ Vidalia onion, thinly sliced
- ½ cup store-bought low-sodium vegetable broth
- 1 bunch beet greens, cut into ribbons
- 1 bunch dandelion greens, cut into ribbons
- 1 (15-ounce) can no-salt-added black beans
- Freshly ground black pepper

1. In a medium skillet, melt the butter over low heat. 2. Add the onion, and sauté for 3 to 5 minutes, or until the onion is translucent. 3. Add the broth and greens. Cover the skillet and cook for 7 to 10 minutes, or until the greens are wilted. 4. Add the black beans and cook for 3 to 5 minutes, or until the beans are tender. Season with black pepper to taste. Serve hot.

Per Serving:
calorie: 153 | fat: 3g | protein: 9g | carbs: 25g | sugars: 2g | fiber: 11g | sodium: 312mg

Stewed Green Beans

Prep time: 5 minutes | Cook time: 10 minutes | Serves 4

- 1 pound green beans, trimmed
- 1 medium tomato, chopped
- ½ yellow onion, chopped
- 1 garlic clove, minced
- 1 teaspoon Creole seasoning
- ¼ cup store-bought low-sodium vegetable broth

1. In an electric pressure cooker, combine 1 pound of trimmed green beans, 1 diced tomato, 1 chopped onion, 2 minced garlic cloves, 1 tablespoon of Creole seasoning, and 1 cup of broth. 2. Close and lock the lid of the pressure cooker, and set the pressure valve to sealing. 3. Select the Manual/Pressure Cook setting, and set the timer to cook for 10 minutes. 4. Once the cooking is complete, perform a quick-release of the pressure by carefully turning the pressure valve to venting. Once the pressure is fully released, carefully remove the lid. 5. Transfer the cooked green beans to a serving dish. Serve warm.

Per Serving:
calorie: 58 | fat: 0g | protein: 3g | carbs: 13g | sugars: 7g | fiber: 4g | sodium: 98mg

Sweet Potato Fennel Bake

Prep time: 15 minutes | Cook time: 45 minutes | Serves 4

- 1 teaspoon butter
- 1 fennel bulb, trimmed and thinly sliced
- 2 sweet potatoes, peeled and thinly sliced
- Freshly ground black pepper, to taste
- ½ teaspoon ground cinnamon
- ¼ teaspoon ground nutmeg
- 1 cup low-sodium vegetable broth

1. Preheat the oven to 375°F. 2. Lightly butter a 9-by-11-inch baking dish to prevent sticking. 3. Arrange half of the sliced fennel in the bottom of the dish, then layer half of the sliced sweet potatoes on top. 4. Season the sweet potatoes with black pepper, and sprinkle half of the cinnamon and nutmeg evenly over the top. 5. Repeat the layering process with the remaining fennel, sweet potatoes, cinnamon, and nutmeg. 6. Pour the vegetable broth evenly over the layered vegetables and cover the dish with aluminum foil to retain moisture. 7. Bake in the preheated oven until the vegetables are very tender, about 45 minutes. 8. Serve immediately while hot.

Per Serving:
calorie: 118 | fat: 1g | protein: 2g | carbs: 28g | sugars: 7g | fiber: 5g | sodium: 127mg

Chapter 4: Beef, Pork, and Lamb

Chapter 4 Beef, Pork, and Lamb

Butterflied Beef Eye Roast

Prep time: 10 minutes | Cook time: 40 minutes | Serves 12

- 3 pounds lean beef eye roast
- 3 tablespoons extra-virgin olive oil
- ¼ cup water
- ½ cup red wine vinegar
- 3 garlic cloves, minced
- ½ teaspoon crushed red pepper
- 1 tablespoon chopped fresh thyme

1. Slice the roast down the middle, open it, and lay it flat in a shallow baking dish. 2. In a small bowl, combine the remaining ingredients, and pour the mixture over the roast. Cover the baking dish, and let the meat marinate in the refrigerator for at least 12 hours, or up to 24 hours, turning the roast occasionally to ensure even marination. 3. Set the oven to broil. Remove the roast from the marinade, discard the marinade, and place the roast on a rack in the broiler pan. 4. Broil the roast 5 to 7 inches from the heat source, turning occasionally, for 20 to 25 minutes or until it reaches your desired degree of doneness. 5. Remove the roast from the oven, cover it with foil, and let it stand for 15 to 20 minutes to allow the juices to redistribute. 6. Transfer the roast to a serving platter, spoon any accumulated juices over the top, and serve.

Per Serving:
calorie: 191 | fat: 10g | protein: 24g | carbs: 0g | sugars: 0g | fiber: 0g | sodium: 98mg

Coffee-and-Herb-Marinated Steak

Prep time: 10 minutes | Cook time: 10 minutes | Serves 4

- ¼ cup whole coffee beans
- 2 teaspoons minced garlic
- 2 teaspoons chopped fresh rosemary
- 2 teaspoons chopped fresh thyme
- 1 teaspoon freshly ground black pepper
- 2 tablespoons apple cider vinegar
- 2 tablespoons extra-virgin olive oil
- 1 pound flank steak, trimmed of visible fat

1. Place the coffee beans, garlic, rosemary, thyme, and black pepper in a coffee grinder or food processor and pulse until coarsely ground. 2. Transfer the coffee mixture to a resealable plastic bag and add the vinegar and oil. Shake the bag to combine the ingredients thoroughly. 3. Add the flank steak to the bag, squeeze out any excess air, and seal it tightly. Marinate the steak in the refrigerator for at least 2 hours, turning the bag occasionally to ensure even marination. 4. Preheat the broiler and line a baking sheet with aluminum foil. 5. Remove the steak from the bag and discard the marinade. 6. Place the steak on the prepared baking sheet and broil for about 5 minutes per side for medium, or until it reaches your desired level of doneness. 7. Let the steak rest for 10 minutes before slicing it thinly on a bias. 8. Serve the steak with a mixed green salad or your favorite side dish.

Per Serving:
calorie: 191 | fat: 9g | protein: 25g | carbs: 1g | sugars: 0g | fiber: 0g | sodium: 127mg

Smothered Sirloin

Prep time: 15 minutes | Cook time: 30 minutes | Serves 5

- 1 pound beef round sirloin tip
- 1 teaspoon freshly ground black pepper
- 1 teaspoon celery seeds
- 2 tablespoons extra-virgin olive oil
- 1 medium yellow onion, chopped
- ¼ cup chickpea flour
- 2 cups store-bought low-sodium chicken broth, divided
- 2 celery stalks, thinly sliced
- 1 medium red bell pepper, chopped
- 2 garlic cloves, minced
- 2 tablespoons whole-wheat flour
- Generous pinch cayenne pepper
- Chopped fresh chives, for garnish (optional)
- Smoked paprika, for garnish (optional)

1. In a bowl, season the steak on both sides with black pepper and celery seeds. 2. Select the Sauté setting on an electric pressure cooker and add the olive oil and onions. Cook for 3 to 5 minutes, stirring frequently, until the onions are browned but not burned. 3. Gradually add the chickpea flour, 1 tablespoon at a time, stirring constantly to avoid lumps. 4. Slowly add 1 cup of broth, ¼ cup at a time, as needed, stirring continuously to create a smooth mixture. 5. Stir in the celery, bell pepper, and garlic. Cook for an additional 3 to 5 minutes, or until the vegetables are softened. 6. Lay the seasoned steak on top of the vegetables, then pour the remaining 1 cup of broth over the steak. 7. Close and lock the lid of the pressure cooker, ensuring the pressure valve is set to sealing. 8. Change to the Manual/Pressure Cook setting and set the cooking time for 20 minutes. 9. Once cooking is complete, perform a quick release of the pressure. Carefully remove the lid once the pressure has fully released. 10. Remove the steak and vegetables from the pressure cooker, setting them aside and reserving the leftover liquid in the pot for the gravy base. 11. To make the gravy, add the whole-wheat flour and cayenne pepper to the reserved liquid in the pressure cooker. Mix continuously until the gravy thickens to your desired consistency. 12. To serve, spoon the gravy over the steak and garnish with chives (if using) and paprika (if using).

Per Serving:
calorie: 234 | fat: 11g | protein: 23g | carbs: 11g | sugars: 3g | fiber: 2g | sodium: 96mg

Slow Cooker Chipotle Beef Stew

Prep time: 25 minutes | Cook time: 8 to 10 hours | Serves 6

- Stew
- 1 package (12 ounces) frozen whole kernel corn
- 1 pound boneless beef top sirloin, trimmed of fat, cut into 1-inch cubes
- 1 chipotle chile in adobo sauce (from 7 ounces can), finely chopped
- 2 large onions, chopped (2 cups)
- 2 poblano chiles, seeded, diced
- 3 cloves garlic, chopped
- 2 cans (14.5 ounces each) diced tomatoes, undrained
- 1½ teaspoons ground cumin
- ½ teaspoon salt
- ¼ teaspoon cracked black pepper
- Toppings
- 1 avocado, pitted, peeled cut into 12 wedges
- 12 baked tortilla chips, crushed
- 6 small cilantro sprigs, coarsely chopped
- 6 tablespoons reduced-fat sour cream

1. Spray a 4- to 5-quart slow cooker with cooking spray to prevent sticking. In a small microwavable bowl, microwave the corn uncovered on High for 2 minutes or until thawed. Place the thawed corn and all remaining stew ingredients into the slow cooker and mix well to combine. Cover the slow cooker and cook on Low heat setting for 8 to 10 hours or on High heat setting for 4 to 5 hours. 2. Once the stew is cooked, divide it evenly among 6 bowls. To serve, top each bowl with slices of avocado, tortilla chips, fresh cilantro, and a dollop of sour cream.

Per Serving:
calories: 310 | fat: 10g | protein: 25g | carbs: 30g | sugars: 10g | fiber: 5g | sodium: 580mg

Pork Chop Diane

Prep time: 10 minutes | Cook time: 20 minutes | Serves 4

- ¼ cup low-sodium chicken broth
- 1 tablespoon freshly squeezed lemon juice
- 2 teaspoons Worcestershire sauce
- 2 teaspoons Dijon mustard
- 4 (5-ounce) boneless pork top loin chops, about 1 inch thick
- Sea salt
- Freshly ground black pepper
- 1 teaspoon extra-virgin olive oil
- 1 teaspoon lemon zest
- 1 teaspoon butter
- 2 teaspoons chopped fresh chives

1. In a small bowl, stir together the chicken broth, lemon juice, Worcestershire sauce, and Dijon mustard, then set it aside. 2. Season the pork chops lightly with salt and pepper. 3. Place a large skillet over medium-high heat and add the olive oil. 4. Cook the pork chops in the skillet, turning once, until they are no longer pink in the center, about 8 minutes per side. 5. Transfer the pork chops to a plate and set them aside. 6. Pour the broth mixture into the skillet and cook until warmed through and slightly thickened, about 2 minutes. 7. Whisk in the lemon zest, butter, and chives until well combined. 8. Serve the pork chops with a generous spoonful of the sauce drizzled over them.

Per Serving:
calorie: 203 | fat: 7g | protein: 32g | carbs: 1g | sugars: 0g | fiber: 0g | sodium: 130mg

Roasted Pork Loin

Prep time: 5 minutes | Cook time: 40 minutes | Serves 4

- 1 pound pork loin
- 1 tablespoon extra-virgin olive oil, divided
- 2 teaspoons honey
- ¼ teaspoon freshly ground black pepper
- ½ teaspoon dried rosemary
- 2 small gold potatoes, chopped into 2-inch cubes
- 4 (6-inch) carrots, chopped into ½-inch rounds

1. Preheat the oven to 350°F. Ensure the oven reaches the correct temperature before proceeding. 2. Rub the pork loin with oil and honey. Season thoroughly with pepper and rosemary, making sure the seasoning coats all sides evenly. 3. In a medium bowl, toss the potatoes and carrots with the remaining oil, ensuring they are well coated. 4. Place the pork and vegetables on a baking sheet in a single layer, arranging the vegetables around the pork. Cook for 40 minutes. 5. Remove the baking sheet from the oven and let the pork rest for at least 10 minutes before slicing. This helps retain the juices. 6. Slice the pork and divide it along with the vegetables into four equal portions, then serve.

Per Serving:
calorie: 281 | fat: 8g | protein: 28g | carbs: 24g | sugars: 6g | fiber: 4g | sodium: 103mg

Marjoram-Pepper Steaks

Prep time: 5 minutes | Cook time: 8 minutes | Serves 2

- 1 tablespoon freshly ground black pepper
- ¼ teaspoon dried marjoram
- 2 (6-ounce, 1-inch-thick) beef tenderloins
- 1 tablespoon extra-virgin olive oil
- ¼ cup low-sodium beef broth
- Fresh marjoram sprigs, for garnish

1. In a large bowl, mix together the pepper and marjoram. 2. Add the steaks to the bowl, coating both sides with the spice mixture. 3. In a skillet set over medium-high heat, heat the olive oil. 4. Add the steaks to the skillet and cook for 5 to 7 minutes on each side, or until an instant-read thermometer inserted in the center registers 160°F for medium. Remove the steaks from the skillet and cover to keep warm. 5. Add the broth to the skillet and increase the heat to high. Bring to a boil, scraping any browned bits from the bottom of the skillet. Boil for about 1 minute, or until the liquid is reduced by half. 6. Spoon the broth sauce over the steaks, garnish with marjoram sprigs, and serve immediately.

Per Serving:
calorie: 339 | fat: 19g | protein: 38g | carbs: 2g | sugars: 0g | fiber: 1g | sodium: 209mg

"Smothered" Steak

Prep time: 20 minutes | Cook time: 15 minutes | Serves 6

- 1 tablespoon olive oil
- ¼ teaspoon pepper
- ⅓ cup flour
- 1½-pound chuck, or round, steak, cut into strips, trimmed of fat
- 1 large onion, sliced
- 1 green pepper, sliced
- 14½-ounce can stewed tomatoes
- 4-ounce can mushrooms, drained
- 2 tablespoons soy sauce
- 10-ounce package frozen French-style green beans

1. Press Sauté and add the oil to the Instant Pot. Allow the oil to heat up for a few minutes until it shimmers. 2. Mix together the flour and pepper in a small bowl. Place the steak pieces into the mixture in the bowl and coat each of them well, ensuring all sides are covered evenly. 3. Lightly brown each of the steak pieces in the Instant Pot, cooking them for about 2 minutes on each side until they develop a light brown crust. Press Cancel when done to stop the Sauté function. 4. Add the remaining ingredients to the Instant Pot, stirring gently to combine everything evenly without displacing the steak pieces too much. 5. Secure the lid of the Instant Pot and make sure the vent is set to sealing. Press Manual and set the cook time for 15 minutes. 6. When the cook time is up, let the pressure release naturally for 15 minutes. Afterward, perform a quick release by carefully turning the venting knob to release any remaining pressure.

Per Serving:
calories: 386 | fat: 24g | protein: 25g | carbs: 20g | sugars: 4g | fiber: 4g | sodium: 746mg

Steak with Bell Pepper

Prep time: 30 minutes | Cook time: 20 to 23 minutes | Serves 6

- ¼ cup avocado oil
- ¼ cup freshly squeezed lime juice
- 2 teaspoons minced garlic
- 1 tablespoon chili powder
- ½ teaspoon ground cumin
- Sea salt and freshly ground black pepper, to taste
- 1 pound (454 g) top sirloin steak or flank steak, thinly sliced against the grain
- 1 red bell pepper, cored, seeded, and cut into ½-inch slices
- 1 green bell pepper, cored, seeded, and cut into ½-inch slices
- 1 large onion, sliced

1. In a small bowl or blender, combine the avocado oil, lime juice, garlic, chili powder, cumin, and salt and pepper to taste. Mix or blend until the ingredients are well combined and the marinade is smooth. 2. Place the sliced steak in a zip-top bag or shallow dish. Place the bell peppers and onion in a separate zip-top bag or dish. Pour half of the marinade over the steak, ensuring it is evenly coated, and pour the other half over the vegetables, making sure they are well covered. Seal both bags or cover the dishes, and let the steak and vegetables marinate in the refrigerator for at least 1 hour or up to 4 hours to allow the flavors to penetrate. 3. Line the air fryer basket with an air fryer liner or aluminum foil to prevent sticking and for easy cleanup. Remove the vegetables from their bag or dish, shaking off any excess marinade. Set the air fryer to 400°F (204°C). Place the vegetables in the air fryer basket in an even layer and cook for 13 minutes, shaking the basket halfway through to ensure even cooking. 4. Remove the steak from its bag or dish, shaking off any excess marinade. After the vegetables have cooked for 13 minutes, place the steak on top of the vegetables in the air fryer basket. Cook for an additional 7 to 10 minutes or until an instant-read thermometer reads 120°F (49°C) for medium-rare (or cook to your desired doneness). 5. Serve with desired fixings, such as keto tortillas, lettuce, sour cream, avocado slices, shredded Cheddar cheese, and cilantro.

Per Serving:
calorie: 330 | fat: 24g | protein: 20g | carbs: 12g | sugars: 4g | fiber: 3g | sodium: 160mg

Vegetable Beef Soup

Prep time: 10 minutes | Cook time: 15 minutes | Serves 4

- 1 pound ground beef
- 1 onion, chopped
- 2 celery stalks, chopped
- 1 carrot, chopped
- 1 teaspoon dried rosemary
- 6 cups low-sodium beef or chicken broth
- ½ teaspoon sea salt
- ⅛ teaspoon freshly ground black pepper
- 2 cups peas

1. In a large pot over medium-high heat, cook the ground beef, crumbling with the side of a spoon, until browned, about 5 minutes. 2. Add the onion, celery, carrot, and rosemary. Cook, stirring occasionally, until the vegetables start to soften, about 5 minutes. 3. Add the broth, salt, pepper, and peas. Bring to a simmer. Reduce the heat and simmer, stirring, until warmed through, about 5 minutes more.

Per Serving:
calorie: 284 | fat: 8g | protein: 36g | carbs: 19g | sugars: 7g | fiber: 5g | sodium: 496mg

Pork Butt Roast

Prep time: 10 minutes | Cook time: 9 minutes | Serves 6 to 8

- 3 to 4 pounds pork butt roast
- 2 to 3 tablespoons of your favorite rub
- 2 cups water

1. Place the pork in the inner pot of the Instant Pot, ensuring it is centered and not overlapping the sides of the pot. 2. Sprinkle the rub evenly all over the roast, making sure to cover all sides. Add the water to the pot, pouring it carefully around the edges to avoid washing off the rub from the pork. 3. Secure the lid of the Instant Pot and set the vent to sealing. Select the Manual setting and set the cook time for 9 minutes. 4. After the cooking time is complete, let the pressure release naturally without turning the venting knob until the pressure indicator drops.

Per Serving:
calories: 598 | fat: 40g | protein: 57g | carbs: 0g | sugars: 0g | fiber: 0g | sodium: 152mg

Gingered-Pork Stir-Fry

Prep time: 10 minutes | Cook time: 20 minutes | Serves 2

- 2 tablespoons extra-virgin olive oil
- 2 garlic cloves, minced
- 1 (½-inch) piece fresh ginger, peeled, thinly sliced
- ¼ pound lean pork, thinly sliced
- 2 teaspoons low-sodium soy sauce
- 1 teaspoon granulated stevia
- 1 teaspoon sesame oil
- 1 cup snow peas
- 1 medium red bell pepper, sliced
- 6 whole fresh mushrooms, sliced
- 2 scallions, chopped
- 1 tablespoon Chinese rice wine
- 2 tablespoons chopped cashews, divided

1. In a large skillet or wok set over medium-high heat, heat the olive oil. Ensure the skillet or wok is evenly coated with the oil. 2. Add the garlic and ginger. Sauté for 1 to 2 minutes, stirring continuously until the mixture becomes fragrant. 3. Add the pork, soy sauce, and stevia. Cook for 10 minutes, stirring occasionally to ensure the pork cooks evenly and absorbs the flavors. 4. Stir in the sesame oil, snow peas, bell pepper, mushrooms, scallions, and rice wine. Reduce the heat to low and mix the ingredients thoroughly. Simmer for 4 to 8 minutes, stirring occasionally, until the pork is tender and the vegetables are cooked through. 5. Divide the cooked mixture between 2 serving plates, ensuring an even distribution of ingredients. Sprinkle each serving with 1 tablespoon of cashews and serve immediately. Enjoy!

Per Serving:
calorie: 365 | fat: 23g | protein: 21g | carbs: 22g | sugars: 8g | fiber: 6g | sodium: 203mg

Autumn Pork Chops with Red Cabbage and Apples

Prep time: 15 minutes | Cook time: 30 minutes | Serves 4

- ¼ cup apple cider vinegar
- 2 tablespoons granulated sweetener
- 4 (4 ounces) pork chops, about 1 inch thick
- Sea salt
- Freshly ground black pepper
- 1 tablespoon extra-virgin olive oil
- ½ red cabbage, finely shredded
- 1 sweet onion, thinly sliced
- 1 apple, peeled, cored, and sliced
- 1 teaspoon chopped fresh thyme

1. In a small bowl, whisk together the vinegar and sweetener, then set it aside. 2. Season the pork chops with salt and pepper. 3. Place a large skillet over medium-high heat and add the olive oil. 4. Cook the pork chops in the skillet, turning once, until they are no longer pink in the center, about 8 minutes per side. 5. Transfer the pork chops to a plate and set them aside. 6. Add the cabbage and onion to the skillet and sauté until the vegetables have softened, about 5 minutes. 7. Pour the vinegar mixture into the skillet, add the apple slices, and bring the mixture to a boil. 8. Reduce the heat to low, cover the skillet, and simmer for an additional 5 minutes. 9. Return the pork chops and any accumulated juices to the skillet, add the thyme, cover, and cook for 5 more minutes. Serve immediately.

Per Serving:
calorie: 251 | fat: 8g | protein: 26g | carbs: 19g | sugars: 13g | fiber: 2g | sodium: 76mg

Air Fryer Chicken-Fried Steak

Prep time: 5 minutes | Cook time: 20 minutes | Serves 4

- 1 pound beef chuck sirloin steak
- 3 cups low-fat milk, divided
- 1 teaspoon dried thyme
- 1 teaspoon dried rosemary
- 2 medium egg whites
- 1 cup chickpea crumbs
- ½ cup coconut flour
- 1 tablespoon Creole seasoning

1. In a bowl, marinate the steak in 2 cups of milk for 30 to 45 minutes. 2. Remove the steak from the milk, shake off the excess liquid, and season with thyme and rosemary. Discard the milk. 3. In a shallow bowl, beat the egg whites with the remaining 1 cup of milk. 4. In a separate shallow bowl, combine the chickpea crumbs, coconut flour, and seasoning. 5. Dip the steak in the egg white mixture, then dredge it in the chickpea crumb mixture, coating well. 6. Place the coated steak in the basket of an air fryer. 7. Set the air fryer to 390°F, close, and cook for 10 minutes. 8. Open the air fryer, turn the steaks, close, and cook for an additional 10 minutes. Let the steak rest for 5 minutes before serving.

Per Serving:
calorie: 423 | fat: 19g | protein: 37g | carbs: 25g | sugars: 12g | fiber: 4g | sodium: 180mg

Orange-Marinated Pork Tenderloin

Prep time: 10 minutes | Cook time: 30 minutes | Serves 4

- ¼ cup freshly squeezed orange juice
- 2 teaspoons orange zest
- 2 teaspoons minced garlic
- 1 teaspoon low-sodium soy sauce
- 1 teaspoon grated fresh ginger
- 1 teaspoon honey
- 1½ pounds pork tenderloin roast, trimmed of fat
- 1 tablespoon extra-virgin olive oil

1. In a small bowl, whisk together the orange juice, zest, garlic, soy sauce, ginger, and honey. 2. Pour the marinade into a resealable plastic bag and add the pork tenderloin. 3. Remove as much air as possible and seal the bag. Marinate the pork in the refrigerator, turning the bag a few times, for 2 hours. 4. Preheat the oven to 400°F. 5. Remove the tenderloin from the marinade and discard the marinade. 6. Place a large ovenproof skillet over medium-high heat and add the oil. 7. Sear the pork tenderloin on all sides, about 5 minutes in total. 8. Transfer the skillet to the oven and roast the pork until just cooked through, about 25 minutes. 9. Let the meat stand for 10 minutes before serving. Slice and serve warm.

Per Serving:
calorie: 232 | fat: 7g | protein: 36g | carbs: 4g | sugars: 3g | fiber: 0g | sodium: 131mg

Beef and Vegetable Shish Kabobs

Prep time: 15 minutes | Cook time: 20 minutes | Serves 8

- 2 teaspoons canola oil
- ¼ cup red wine vinegar
- 1 tablespoon light soy sauce
- 4 garlic cloves, minced
- 2 tablespoons freshly squeezed lemon juice
- ⅛ teaspoon freshly ground black pepper
- 1½ pounds boneless beef top sirloin steak, cut into 24 cubes
- 2 large bell peppers, red and green, cut into 1-inch pieces
- 1 pound mushrooms, stemmed
- 1 large tomato, cut into wedges
- 1 medium onion, quartered

1. In a small bowl, combine the oil, vinegar, soy sauce, garlic, lemon juice, and pepper. Pour over the beef cubes, and let marinate in the refrigerator 3–4 hours or overnight. 2. Place 3 beef cubes on 8 metal or wooden skewers (remember to soak the wooden skewers in water before using), alternating with peppers, mushroom caps, tomato wedges, and onions. 3. Grill over medium heat, turning often and basting with marinade until the meat is cooked through. Arrange the skewers on a platter to serve.

Per Serving:
calorie: 211 | fat: 11g | protein: 20g | carbs: 7g | sugars: 4g | fiber: 2g | sodium: 82mg

Pork Milanese

Prep time: 10 minutes | Cook time: 12 minutes | Serves 4

- 4 (1-inch) boneless pork chops
- Fine sea salt and ground black pepper, to taste
- 2 large eggs
- ¾ cup powdered Parmesan cheese
- Chopped fresh parsley, for garnish
- Lemon slices, for serving

1. Spray the air fryer basket with avocado oil. Use an oil spray bottle to evenly coat the entire surface of the air fryer basket with avocado oil, making sure to cover all areas where the pork chops will touch. Preheat the air fryer to 400°F (204°C). Turn on the air fryer and set the temperature to 400°F (204°C). Allow it to preheat for about 5 minutes or until it reaches the desired temperature. 2. Place the pork chops between 2 sheets of plastic wrap and pound them with the flat side of a meat tenderizer until they're ¼ inch thick. Ensure the pork chops are well-covered by the plastic wrap. Lightly season both sides of the chops with salt and pepper. Sprinkle a small amount of salt and pepper over both sides of each pork chop, ensuring an even distribution. 3. Lightly beat the eggs in a shallow bowl. Crack the eggs into a shallow bowl and whisk them lightly until the yolks and whites are fully combined. Divide the Parmesan cheese evenly between 2 bowls and set the bowls in this order: Parmesan, eggs, Parmesan. Measure out the Parmesan cheese and distribute it equally into two separate shallow bowls. Arrange the bowls in a line starting with the first bowl of Parmesan cheese, followed by the bowl of beaten eggs, and ending with the second bowl of Parmesan cheese. Dredge a chop in the first bowl of Parmesan, then dip it in the eggs, and then dredge it again in the second bowl of Parmesan, making sure both sides and all edges are well coated. Take one pork chop and place it in the first bowl of Parmesan cheese, pressing lightly to ensure it adheres to both sides. Then, dip the chop into the bowl of beaten eggs, allowing any excess egg to drip off before moving it to the second bowl of Parmesan cheese. Press the chop into the Parmesan to coat both sides and all edges thoroughly. Repeat with the remaining chops. 4. Place the chops in the air fryer basket and air fry for 12 minutes, or until the internal temperature reaches 145°F (63°C), flipping halfway through. Arrange the coated pork chops in a single layer in the air fryer basket, ensuring they do not overlap. Set the air fryer timer for 12 minutes and cook the pork chops. At the 6-minute mark, open the air fryer and carefully flip each pork chop to ensure even cooking. Continue to cook until the internal temperature reaches 145°F (63°C). 5. Garnish with fresh parsley and serve immediately with lemon slices. Chop fresh parsley and sprinkle it over the cooked pork chops for added flavor and presentation. Arrange lemon slices around the pork chops and serve while hot. Store leftovers in an airtight container in the refrigerator for up to 3 days. Place any leftover pork chops in an airtight container and store them in the refrigerator for up to 3 days. Reheat in a preheated 390°F (199°C) air fryer for 5 minutes, or until warmed through. To reheat, place the pork chops in a preheated air fryer at 390°F (199°C) for 5 minutes or until warmed through.

Per Serving:
calorie: 370 | fat: 21g | protein: 39g | carbs: 4g | sugars: 0g | fiber: 0g | sodium: 660mg

Creole Steak

Prep time: 5 minutes | Cook time: 1 hour 40 minutes | Serves 4

- 2 teaspoons extra-virgin olive oil
- ¼ cup chopped onion
- ¼ cup chopped green bell pepper
- 1 cup canned crushed tomatoes
- ½ teaspoon chili powder
- ¼ teaspoon celery seed
- 4 cloves garlic, finely chopped
- ¼ teaspoon salt
- 1 teaspoon cumin
- 1 pound lean boneless round steak

1. In a large skillet over medium heat, heat the oil. Add the onions and green pepper, and sauté, stirring occasionally, until the onions are translucent, about 5 minutes. 2. Add the tomatoes, chili powder, celery seed, garlic, salt, and cumin to the skillet. Stir to combine, then cover the skillet and let the mixture simmer over low heat for 20–25 minutes to allow the flavors to blend. 3. Preheat the oven to 350 °F. While the sauce is simmering, trim all visible fat off the steak. 4. In a nonstick pan or a pan that has been sprayed with nonstick cooking spray, lightly brown the steak on each side, cooking for about 2-3 minutes per side until a light crust forms. Transfer the browned steak to a 13-x-9-x-2-inch baking dish. Pour the prepared sauce over the steak, ensuring it is evenly covered, and then cover the baking dish with a lid or aluminum foil. 5. Bake the steak in the preheated oven for 1¼ hours or until the steak is tender. Remove the baking dish from the oven. Carefully slice the steak, arrange the slices on a serving platter, and spoon the sauce over the steak before serving.

Per Serving:
calorie: 213 | fat: 10g | protein: 25g | carbs: 5g | sugars: 2g | fiber: 2g | sodium: 235mg

Chapter 4 Beef, Pork, and Lamb

Greek Stuffed Tenderloin

Prep time: 10 minutes | Cook time: 10 minutes | Serves 4

- 1½ pounds (680 g) venison or beef tenderloin, pounded to ¼ inch thick
- 3 teaspoons fine sea salt
- 1 teaspoon ground black pepper
- 2 ounces (57 g) creamy goat cheese
- ½ cup crumbled feta cheese (about 2 ounces / 57 g)
- ¼ cup finely chopped onions
- 2 cloves garlic, minced
- For Garnish/Serving (Optional):
- Prepared yellow mustard
- Halved cherry tomatoes
- Extra-virgin olive oil
- Sprigs of fresh rosemary
- Lavender flowers

1. Spray the air fryer basket with avocado oil and preheat the air fryer to 400°F (204°C). 2. Season the tenderloin on all sides with salt and pepper. 3. In a medium-sized mixing bowl, combine the goat cheese, feta, onions, and garlic. Place this mixture in the center of the tenderloin. Starting at the end closest to you, tightly roll the tenderloin like a jelly roll and tie it tightly with kitchen twine. 4. Place the rolled tenderloin in the air fryer basket and air fry for 5 minutes. Flip the meat over and cook for another 5 minutes, or until the internal temperature reaches 135°F (57°C) for medium-rare. 5. To serve, smear a line of prepared yellow mustard on a platter, place the meat next to it, and add halved cherry tomatoes on the side, if desired. Drizzle with olive oil and garnish with rosemary sprigs and lavender flowers, if desired. 6. Best served fresh. Store leftovers in an airtight container in the fridge for up to 3 days. Reheat in a preheated 350°F (177°C) air fryer for 4 minutes, or until heated through.

Per Serving:
calories: 345 | fat: 17g | protein: 43g | carbs: 2g | sugars: 2g | fiber: 0g | sodium: 676mg

BBQ Ribs and Broccoli Slaw

Prep time: 10 minutes | Cook time: 50 minutes | Serves 6

BBQ Ribs
- 4 pounds baby back ribs
- 1 teaspoon fine sea salt

Broccoli Slaw
- ½ cup plain 2 percent Greek yogurt
- 1 tablespoon olive oil
- 1 tablespoon fresh lemon juice
- ½ teaspoon fine sea salt
- ¼ teaspoon freshly ground black pepper
- 1 pound broccoli florets (or florets from 2 large crowns), chopped
- 10 radishes, halved and thinly sliced
- 1 teaspoon freshly ground black pepper
- 1 red bell pepper, seeded and cut lengthwise into narrow strips
- 1 large apple (such as Fuji, Jonagold, or Gala), thinly sliced
- ½ red onion, thinly sliced
- ¾ cup low-sugar or unsweetened barbecue sauce

1. To make the ribs: Pat the ribs dry with paper towels, then cut the racks into six sections (three to five ribs per section, depending on how big the racks are). Season the ribs all over with the salt and pepper. 2. Pour 1 cup water into the Instant Pot and place the wire metal steam rack into the pot. Place the ribs on top of the wire rack (it's fine to stack them up). 3. Secure the lid and set the Pressure Release to Sealing. Select the Pressure Cook or Manual setting and set the cooking time for 20 minutes at high pressure. (The pot will take about 15 minutes to come up to pressure before the cooking program begins.) 4. To make the broccoli slaw: While the ribs are cooking, in a small bowl, stir together the yogurt, oil, lemon juice, salt, and pepper, mixing well. In a large bowl, combine the broccoli, radishes, bell pepper, apple, and onion. Drizzle with the yogurt mixture and toss until evenly coated. 5. When the ribs have about 10 minutes left in their cooking time, preheat the oven to 400°F. Line a sheet pan with aluminum foil. 6. When the cooking program ends, perform a quick pressure release by moving the Pressure Release to Venting. Open the pot and, using tongs, transfer the ribs in a single layer to the prepared sheet pan. Brush the barbecue sauce onto both sides of the ribs, using 2 tablespoons of sauce per section of ribs. Bake, meaty-side up, for 15 to 20 minutes, until lightly browned. 7. Serve the ribs warm, with the slaw on the side.

Per Serving:
calories: 392 | fat: 15g | protein: 45g | carbs: 19g | sugars: 9g | fiber: 4g | sodium: 961mg

Bavarian Beef

Prep time: 35 minutes | Cook time: 1 hour 15 minutes | Serves 8

- 1 tablespoon canola oil
- 3-pound boneless beef chuck roast, trimmed of fat
- 3 cups sliced carrots
- 3 cups sliced onions
- 2 large kosher dill pickles, chopped
- 1 cup sliced celery
- ½ cup dry red wine or beef broth
- ⅓ cup German-style mustard
- 2 teaspoons coarsely ground black pepper
- 2 bay leaves
- ¼ teaspoon ground cloves
- 1 cup water
- ⅓ cup flour

1. Press Sauté on the Instant Pot and add in the oil. Allow the oil to heat up for a minute, then brown the roast on both sides for about 5 minutes per side, ensuring a nice sear. Press Cancel once both sides are browned. 2. Add all of the remaining ingredients, except for the flour, to the Instant Pot, arranging them around the roast. Ensure the ingredients are well-distributed for even cooking. 3. Secure the lid on the Instant Pot and set the vent to sealing. Press Manual and set the cooking time to 1 hour and 15 minutes. Once the cooking cycle is complete, let the pressure release naturally, which may take about 15-20 minutes. 4. Carefully remove the meat and vegetables from the Instant Pot using tongs or a slotted spoon and transfer them to a large platter. Cover the platter with aluminum foil to keep the contents warm. 5. Remove 1 cup of the cooking liquid from the Instant Pot and place it in a small bowl. Mix the liquid with the flour, whisking until smooth to avoid lumps. Press Sauté on the Instant Pot again and add the flour/broth mixture back into the pot, whisking continuously. Cook until the broth is smooth and thickened, forming a gravy. This should take about 5-7 minutes. 6. Serve the roast and vegetables over noodles or spaetzle, drizzling the thickened gravy on top for added flavor.

Per Serving:
calories: 251 | fat: 8g | protein: 26g | carbs: 17g | sugars: 7g | fiber: 4g | sodium: 525mg

Italian Sausages with Peppers and Onions

Prep time: 5 minutes | Cook time: 28 minutes | Serves 3

- 1 medium onion, thinly sliced
- 1 yellow or orange bell pepper, thinly sliced
- 1 red bell pepper, thinly sliced
- ¼ cup avocado oil or melted coconut oil
- 1 teaspoon fine sea salt
- 6 Italian sausages
- Dijon mustard, for serving (optional)

1. Preheat the air fryer to 400°F (204°C) by setting the temperature and allowing it to heat up for a few minutes. 2. Place the onion and peppers in a large bowl. Drizzle with the oil and toss well to coat the veggies evenly. Season with the salt, making sure all pieces are well-seasoned. 3. Transfer the seasoned onion and peppers to a pie pan, spreading them out in an even layer. Place the pie pan in the air fryer and cook for 8 minutes, stirring halfway through the cooking time to ensure even browning. Remove from the air fryer and set aside. 4. Spray the air fryer basket with avocado oil to prevent sticking. Place the sausages in the air fryer basket in a single layer, ensuring they are not touching each other for even cooking. Air fry for 20 minutes, or until the sausages are crispy and golden brown, turning them halfway through the cooking time for even browning. During the last minute or two of cooking, add the cooked onion and peppers to the basket with the sausages to warm them through. 5. Once the sausages are done, place the onion and peppers on a serving platter, spreading them out evenly. Arrange the sausages on top of the onion and peppers. Serve Dijon mustard on the side, if desired, for added flavor. 6. Store any leftovers in an airtight container in the refrigerator for up to 7 days or in the freezer for up to a month. To reheat, place the leftovers in a preheated 390°F (199°C) air fryer for 3 minutes, or until heated through, ensuring they are warmed evenly.

Per Serving:
calorie: 455 | fat: 33g | protein: 29g | carbs: 13g | sugars: 3g | fiber: 2g | sodium: 392mg

Pork Tacos

Prep time: 30 minutes | Cook time: 10 minutes | Serves 2

- 8 ounces boneless skinless pork tenderloin, thinly sliced, ¼-inch thick, across the grain
- Pinch salt
- ⅓ cup ancho chile sauce
- 2 tablespoons chipotle purée (see Recipe Tip)
- ¼ cup freshly squeezed lime juice
- 2 (6-inch) soft low-carb corn tortillas, such as La Tortilla
- 4 tablespoons diced tomatoes, divided
- 1 cup shredded lettuce, divided
- ½ avocado, sliced
- 4 tablespoons salsa, divided

1. Sprinkle the pork slices with salt and set aside. 2. In a small bowl, stir together the ancho chile sauce, chipotle purée, and lime juice. Reserve 3 tablespoons of the marinade and set aside. 3. Place the pork in a large sealable plastic bag and pour the remaining marinade over it. Seal the bag, removing as much air as possible. Marinate the meat for 20 minutes to 1 hour at room temperature, or refrigerate for several hours, turning the meat twice during marination. 4. Place a small nonstick skillet over medium heat and have a large piece of aluminum foil nearby. 5. Working with one tortilla at a time, heat both sides in the skillet until they puff slightly. As they are done, stack the tortillas on the foil. When all the tortillas are heated, wrap them in the foil. 6. Preheat the broiler and adjust the rack so it is 4 inches from the heating element. 7. Remove the pork slices from the marinade and discard the marinade. Place the pork on a rack set over a sheet pan. 8. Place the pan in the oven and broil for 3 to 4 minutes, or until the edges of the pork begin to brown. Remove from the oven, turn the pork, and brush with the reserved marinade. Broil the second side for 3 minutes, or until the pork is just barely pink inside. 9. Place the foil packet with the tortillas in the oven to warm while the pork finishes cooking. 10. To serve, pile each tortilla with a few slices of pork. Top each with about 2 tablespoons of diced tomato, ½ cup of shredded lettuce, half of the avocado slices, and about 2 tablespoons of salsa. Serve immediately.

Per Serving:
calorie: 328 | fat: 13g | protein: 30g | carbs: 25g | sugars: 5g | fiber: 7g | sodium: 563mg

Slow-Cooked Simple Lamb and Vegetable Stew

Prep time: 10 minutes | Cook time: 3 to 10 hours | Serves 6

- 1 pound boneless lamb stew meat
- 1 pound turnips, peeled and chopped
- 1 fennel bulb, trimmed and thinly sliced
- 10 ounces mushrooms, sliced
- 1 onion, diced
- 3 garlic cloves, minced
- 2 cups low-sodium chicken broth
- 2 tablespoons tomato paste
- ¼ cup dry red wine (optional)
- 1 teaspoon chopped fresh thyme
- ½ teaspoon salt
- ¼ teaspoon freshly ground black pepper
- Chopped fresh parsley, for garnish

1. In a slow cooker, combine the lamb, turnips, fennel, mushrooms, onion, garlic, chicken broth, tomato paste, red wine (if using), thyme, salt, and pepper. Stir to mix the ingredients evenly. 2. Cover the slow cooker and cook on high for 3 hours or on low for 6 hours, until the meat is tender and falling apart. Once done, garnish with freshly chopped parsley and serve hot. 3. If you don't have a slow cooker, in a large pot, heat 2 teaspoons of olive oil over medium heat. Add the lamb and sear on all sides until browned. Remove the lamb from the pot and set aside. In the same pot, add the turnips, fennel, mushrooms, onion, and garlic, and cook for 3 to 4 minutes until the vegetables begin to soften. Add the chicken broth, tomato paste, red wine (if using), thyme, salt, pepper, and the browned lamb. Stir well and bring to a boil. Once boiling, reduce the heat to low and simmer for 1½ to 2 hours, or until the meat is tender. Garnish with freshly chopped parsley and serve hot.

Per Serving:
calories: 303 | fat: 7g | protein: 32g | carbs: 27g | sugars: 7g | fiber: 4g | sodium: 310mg

Broiled Dijon Burgers

Prep time: 25 minutes | Cook time: 10 minutes | Makes 6 burgers

- ¼ cup fat-free egg product or 2 egg whites
- 2 tablespoons fat-free (skim) milk
- 2 teaspoons Dijon mustard or horseradish sauce
- ¼ teaspoon salt
- ⅛ teaspoon pepper
- 1 cup soft bread crumbs (about 2 slices bread)
- 1 small onion, finely chopped (⅓ cup)
- 1 pound extra-lean (at least 90%) ground beef
- 6 whole-grain burger buns, split, toasted

1. Set oven control to broil and allow it to preheat. Spray the broiler pan rack with cooking spray to prevent sticking. 2. In a medium bowl, mix together the egg product, milk, mustard, salt, and pepper until well combined. Add the bread crumbs and finely chopped onion, stirring them into the mixture. Then, add the ground beef and mix thoroughly until all ingredients are evenly incorporated. Shape the beef mixture into 6 patties, each about ½ inch thick. Place the patties on the prepared rack in the broiler pan. 3. Broil the patties with the tops about 5 inches from the heat source for 6 minutes. Turn the patties over and continue to broil until a meat thermometer inserted into the center of the patties reads 160°F, an additional 4 to 6 minutes. Serve the patties in buns while hot.

Per Serving:
calories: 250 | fat: 8g | protein: 22g | carbs: 23g | sugars: 5g | fiber: 3g | sodium: 450mg

Zoodles Carbonara

Prep time: 10 minutes | Cook time: 25 minutes | Serves 4

- 6 slices bacon, cut into pieces
- 1 red onion, finely chopped
- 3 zucchini, cut into noodles
- 1 cup peas
- ½ teaspoon sea salt
- 3 garlic cloves, minced
- 3 large eggs, beaten
- 1 tablespoon heavy cream
- Pinch red pepper flakes
- ½ cup grated Parmesan cheese (optional, for garnish)

1. In a large skillet over medium-high heat, cook the bacon until browned, about 5 minutes. With a slotted spoon, transfer the bacon to a plate. 2. Add the onion to the bacon fat in the pan and cook, stirring, until soft, 3 to 5 minutes. Add the zucchini, peas, and salt. Cook, stirring, until the zucchini softens, about 3 minutes. Add the garlic and cook, stirring constantly, for 1 minute. 3. In a small bowl, whisk together the eggs, cream, and red pepper flakes. Add the egg mixture to the vegetables in the pan. 4. Remove the pan from the stovetop and stir for 3 minutes, allowing the residual heat of the pan to cook the eggs gently without setting them. 5. Return the bacon to the pan and stir to mix everything together. 6. Serve topped with Parmesan cheese, if desired.

Per Serving:
calorie: 294 | fat: 21g | protein: 14g | carbs: 14g | sugars: 7g | fiber: 4g | sodium: 544mg

Jalapeño Popper Pork Chops

Prep time: 15 minutes | Cook time: 6 to 8 minutes | Serves 4

- 1¾ pounds (794 g) bone-in, center-cut loin pork chops
- Sea salt and freshly ground black pepper, to taste
- 6 ounces (170 g) cream cheese, at room temperature
- 4 ounces (113 g) sliced bacon, cooked and crumbled
- 4 ounces (113 g) Cheddar cheese, shredded
- 1 jalapeño, seeded and diced
- 1 teaspoon garlic powder

1. Cut a pocket into each pork chop, lengthwise along the side, making sure not to cut it all the way through. Season the outside of the chops with salt and pepper. 2. In a small bowl, combine the cream cheese, bacon, Cheddar cheese, jalapeño, and garlic powder. Divide this mixture among the pork chops, stuffing it into the pocket of each chop. 3. Set the air fryer to 400°F (204°C). Place the pork chops in the air fryer basket in a single layer, working in batches if necessary. Air fry for 3 minutes. Flip the chops and cook for 3 to 5 minutes more, until an instant-read thermometer reads 145°F (63°C). 4. Allow the chops to rest for 5 minutes, then serve warm.

Per Serving:
calorie: 469 | fat: 21g | protein: 60g | carbs: 5g | sugars: 3g | fiber: 0g | sodium: 576mg

Fresh Pot Pork Butt

Prep time: 10 minutes | Cook time: 45 minutes | Serves 8

- 2 tablespoons extra-virgin olive oil
- ¼ cup apple cider vinegar
- 1 tablespoon freshly ground black pepper
- 1 tablespoon dried oregano
- 1 small yellow onion, minced
- 2 scallions, white and green parts, minced
- 1 celery stalk, minced
- Juice of 1 lime
- 2 pounds boneless pork butt
- 4 garlic cloves, sliced
- 1 cup store-bought low-sodium chicken broth

1. In a medium bowl, combine the oil, vinegar, pepper, oregano, onion, scallions, celery, and lime juice. Mix well until a paste is formed. 2. Score the pork with 1-inch-deep cuts in a diamond pattern on both sides. Push the garlic into the slits. 3. Massage the paste all over the meat, ensuring it gets into the cuts. Cover and refrigerate overnight or for at least 4 hours to marinate. 4. Select the Sauté setting on an electric pressure cooker. Add the meat and cook for 2 minutes on each side to brown. 5. Add the broth, close and lock the lid, and set the pressure valve to sealing. 6. Change to the Manual/Pressure Cook setting, and cook for 20 minutes. 7. Once cooking is complete, allow the pressure to release naturally. Carefully remove the lid. 8. Remove the pork from the pressure cooker, and serve hot.

Per Serving:
calorie: 197 | fat: 10g | protein: 22g | carbs: 3g | sugars: 1g | fiber: 1g | sodium: 86mg

Easy Beef Curry

Prep time: 15 minutes | Cook time: 10 minutes | Serves 6

- 1 tablespoon extra-virgin olive oil
- 1 small onion, thinly sliced
- 2 teaspoons minced fresh ginger
- 3 garlic cloves, minced
- 2 teaspoons ground coriander
- 1 teaspoon ground cumin
- 1 jalapeño or serrano pepper, slit lengthwise but not all the way through
- ¼ teaspoon ground turmeric
- ¼ teaspoon salt
- 1 pound grass-fed sirloin tip steak, top round steak, or top sirloin steak, cut into bite-size pieces
- 2 tablespoons chopped fresh cilantro

1. In a large skillet, heat the oil over medium-high heat until shimmering. 2. Add the onion, and cook for 3 to 5 minutes until browned and softened. Add the ginger and garlic, stirring continuously until fragrant, about 30 seconds. 3. In a small bowl, mix the coriander, cumin, jalapeño, turmeric, and salt. Add the spice mixture to the skillet and stir continuously for 1 minute to toast the spices. Deglaze the skillet with about ¼ cup of water, scraping up any browned bits from the bottom of the pan. 4. Add the beef to the skillet and stir continuously for about 5 minutes until well-browned yet still medium rare. Remove the jalapeño. Serve the dish topped with fresh cilantro.

Per Serving:
calories: 140 | fat: 7g | protein: 18g | carbs: 3g | sugars: 1g | fiber: 1g | sodium: 141mg

Chinese Spareribs

Prep time: 10 minutes | Cook time: 40 minutes | Serves 2

- 2 tablespoons hoisin sauce
- 2 tablespoons tomato paste
- 2 tablespoons water
- 1 tablespoon rice vinegar
- 2 teaspoons sesame oil
- 2 teaspoons low-sodium soy sauce
- 2 teaspoons Chinese five-spice powder
- 2 garlic cloves, minced
- 1 teaspoon freshly squeezed lemon juice
- 1 teaspoon grated fresh ginger
- ½ teaspoon granulated stevia
- 1 pound pork spareribs

1. In a shallow glass dish, mix together the hoisin sauce, tomato paste, water, rice vinegar, sesame oil, soy sauce, Chinese five-spice powder, garlic, lemon juice, ginger, and stevia until well combined. 2. Add the ribs to the marinade, turning to coat them thoroughly. Cover the dish with plastic wrap or a lid and refrigerate for at least 2 hours or overnight for best results. 3. Preheat the oven to 325°F (163°C). 4. Place a rack in the center of the oven to ensure even cooking. 5. Fill a broiler tray with enough water to cover the bottom. Place the grate over the tray and arrange the ribs on the grate in a single layer. Reserve the marinade for basting. 6. Place the broiler pan with the ribs in the preheated oven. Cook for 40 minutes, turning the ribs and brushing them with the reserved marinade every 10 minutes to keep them moist and flavorful. 7. For a crispier texture, finish the ribs under the broiler for a few minutes, watching closely to prevent burning. Discard any remaining marinade. 8. Serve the ribs immediately with plenty of napkins and enjoy!

Per Serving:
calorie: 594 | fat: 39g | protein: 45g | carbs: 13g | sugars: 8g | fiber: 1g | sodium: 557mg

Chapter 5

Poultry

Chapter 5 Poultry

Saffron-Spiced Chicken Breasts

Prep time: 10 minutes | Cook time: 10 minutes | Serves 4

- Pinch saffron (3 or 4 threads)
- ½ cup plain nonfat yogurt
- 2 tablespoons water
- ½ onion, chopped
- 3 garlic cloves, minced
- 2 tablespoons chopped fresh cilantro
- Juice of ½ lemon
- ½ teaspoon salt
- 1 pound boneless, skinless chicken breasts, cut into 2-inch strips
- 1 tablespoon extra-virgin olive oil

1. In a blender jar, combine the saffron, yogurt, water, onion, garlic, cilantro, lemon juice, and salt. Pulse to blend. 2. In a large mixing bowl, combine the chicken and the yogurt sauce, and stir to coat. Cover and refrigerate for at least 1 hour or up to overnight. 3. In a large skillet, heat the oil over medium heat. Add the chicken pieces, shaking off any excess marinade. Discard the marinade. Cook the chicken pieces on each side for 5 minutes, flipping once, until cooked through and golden brown.

Per Serving:
calories: 155 | fat: 5g | protein: 26g | carbs: 3g | sugars: 1g | fiber: 0g | sodium: 501mg

Grilled Herb Chicken with Wine and Roasted Garlic

Prep time: 5 minutes | Cook time: 45 minutes | Serves 4

- Four 3-ounce boneless, skinless chicken breast halves
- 2 tablespoons extra-virgin olive oil, divided
- 1 cup red wine
- 3 sprigs fresh thyme
- 5 garlic cloves, minced
- 5 garlic cloves, whole and unpeeled
- ⅛ teaspoon freshly ground black pepper

1. In a plastic zippered bag, place the chicken breasts, 1 tablespoon of olive oil, white wine, fresh thyme, and minced garlic. Seal the bag and gently massage the marinade into the chicken to ensure it is well coated. Place the bag in the refrigerator and allow the chicken to marinate for 2 to 3 hours, turning the bag occasionally to distribute the marinade evenly. 2. Preheat the oven to 375°F (190°C) to ensure it reaches the correct temperature before roasting the garlic. 3. On a cookie sheet, spread the whole garlic cloves in a single layer. Drizzle them with the remaining olive oil and sprinkle with freshly ground black pepper. Place the cookie sheet in the preheated oven and bake for 30 minutes, stirring occasionally to ensure even roasting, until the garlic cloves are soft and golden brown. 4. Once the garlic cloves are cool enough to handle, squeeze the garlic paste from the cloves into a small bowl. Use a fork to mash the garlic paste until it reaches a smooth consistency. 5. Remove the chicken breasts from the marinade and discard the marinade. Preheat a grill to medium-high heat and grill the chicken for 12 to 15 minutes, turning frequently to ensure even cooking. While grilling, brush the chicken with the roasted garlic paste to enhance the flavor. Once the chicken is fully cooked and has reached an internal temperature of 165°F (74°C), transfer it to a serving platter. Serve the chicken hot, garnished with any remaining garlic paste if desired.

Per Serving:
calorie: 222 | fat: 9g | protein: 20g | carbs: 4g | sugars: 0g | fiber: 0g | sodium: 40mg

Thanksgiving Turkey Breast

Prep time: 5 minutes | Cook time: 30 minutes | Serves 4

- 1½ teaspoons fine sea salt
- 1 teaspoon ground black pepper
- 1 teaspoon chopped fresh rosemary leaves
- 1 teaspoon chopped fresh sage
- 1 teaspoon chopped fresh tarragon
- 1 teaspoon chopped fresh thyme leaves
- 1 (2 pounds / 907 g) turkey breast
- 3 tablespoons ghee or unsalted butter, melted
- 3 tablespoons Dijon mustard

1. Spray the air fryer basket with avocado oil to prevent sticking. Preheat the air fryer to 390°F (199°C) to ensure it reaches the desired temperature before cooking. 2. In a small bowl, combine salt, black pepper, and your choice of dried herbs (such as thyme, rosemary, and oregano) until well mixed. Generously season the turkey breast on all sides with this seasoning blend, making sure it is evenly coated. 3. In another small bowl, mix together melted ghee and Dijon mustard until fully combined. Brush this ghee mixture over all sides of the seasoned turkey breast, ensuring a thorough coating. 4. Place the prepared turkey breast into the preheated air fryer basket. Air fry the turkey breast for approximately 30 minutes, or until the internal temperature of the meat reaches 165°F (74°C). Once cooked, transfer the turkey breast to a cutting board and allow it to rest for 10 minutes to let the juices redistribute. After resting, slice the turkey breast into ½-inch-thick slices for serving. 5. Store any leftovers in an airtight container in the refrigerator, where they can be kept for up to 4 days, or in the freezer for up to a month. To reheat, place the slices in a preheated air fryer set to 350°F (177°C) for about 4 minutes, or until the turkey is warmed through.

Per Serving:
calorie: 418 | fat: 22g | protein: 51g | carbs: 1g | sugars: 0g | fiber: 1g | sodium: 603mg

Garlic Galore Rotisserie Chicken

Prep time: 5 minutes | Cook time: 3 minutes | Serves 4

- 3 pounds whole chicken
- 2 tablespoons olive oil, divided
- Salt to taste
- Pepper to taste
- 20 to 30 cloves fresh garlic, peeled and left whole
- 1 cup low-sodium chicken stock, broth, or water
- 2 tablespoons garlic powder
- 2 teaspoons onion powder
- ½ teaspoon basil
- ½ teaspoon cumin
- ½ teaspoon chili powder

1. Rub chicken with one tablespoon of the olive oil and sprinkle with salt and pepper. 2. Place the garlic cloves inside the chicken. Use butcher's twine to secure the legs. 3. Press the Sauté button on the Instant Pot, then add the rest of the olive oil to the inner pot. 4. When the pot is hot, place the chicken inside. You are just trying to sear it, so leave it for about 4 minutes on each side. 5. Remove the chicken and set aside. Place the trivet at the bottom of the inner pot and pour in the chicken stock. 6. Mix together the remaining seasonings and rub them all over the entire chicken. 7. Place the chicken back inside the inner pot, breast-side up, on top of the trivet and secure the lid to the sealing position. 8. Press the Manual button and use the +/- to set it for 25 minutes. 9. When the timer beeps, allow the pressure to release naturally for 15 minutes. If the lid will not open at this point, quick release the remaining pressure and remove the chicken. 10. Let the chicken rest for 5–10 minutes before serving.

Per Serving:
calories: 333 | fat: 23g | protein: 24g | carbs: 9g | sugars: 0g | fiber: 1g | sodium: 110mg

Broccoli Cheese Chicken

Prep time: 10 minutes | Cook time: 19 to 24 minutes | Serves 6

- 1 tablespoon avocado oil
- ¼ cup chopped onion
- ½ cup finely chopped broccoli
- 4 ounces (113 g) cream cheese, at room temperature
- 2 ounces (57 g) Cheddar cheese, shredded
- 1 teaspoon garlic powder
- ½ teaspoon sea salt, plus additional for seasoning, divided
- ¼ freshly ground black pepper, plus additional for seasoning, divided
- 2 pounds (907 g) boneless, skinless chicken breasts
- 1 teaspoon smoked paprika

1. Heat a medium skillet over medium-high heat and pour in the avocado oil. Add the onion and broccoli and cook, stirring occasionally, for 5 to 8 minutes, until the onion is tender. 2. Transfer to a large bowl and stir in the cream cheese, Cheddar cheese, and garlic powder, and season to taste with salt and pepper. 3. Hold a sharp knife parallel to the chicken breast and cut a long pocket into one side. Stuff the chicken pockets with the broccoli mixture, using toothpicks to secure the pockets around the filling. 4. In a small dish, combine the paprika, ½ teaspoon salt, and ¼ teaspoon pepper. Sprinkle this over the outside of the chicken. 5. Set the air fryer to 400°F (204°C). Place the chicken in a single layer in the air fryer basket, cooking in batches if necessary, and cook for 14 to 16 minutes, until an instant-read thermometer reads 160°F (71°C). Place the chicken on a plate and tent a piece of aluminum foil over the chicken. Allow to rest for 5 to 10 minutes before serving.

Per Serving:
calorie: 287 | fat: 16g | protein: 32g | carbs: 1g | sugars: 0g | fiber: 0g | sodium: 291mg

Herbed Cornish Hens

Prep time: 5 minutes | Cook time: 30 minutes | Serves 8

- 4 Cornish hens, giblets removed (about 1¼ pound each)
- 2 cups white wine, divided
- 2 garlic cloves, minced
- 1 small onion, minced
- ½ teaspoon celery seeds
- ½ teaspoon poultry seasoning
- ½ teaspoon paprika
- ½ teaspoon dried oregano
- ¼ teaspoon freshly ground black pepper

1. Using a long, sharp knife, split each hen lengthwise. You may also buy precut hens. 2. Place the hens, cavity side up, on a rack in a shallow roasting pan. Pour 1½ cups of the wine over the hens; set aside. 3. In a shallow bowl, combine the garlic, onion, celery seeds, poultry seasoning, paprika, oregano, and pepper. Sprinkle half of the combined seasonings over the cavity of each split half. Cover, and refrigerate. Allow the hens to marinate for 2–3 hours. 4. Preheat the oven to 350°F. Bake the hens uncovered for 1 hour. Remove from the oven, turn breast side up, and remove the skin. Pour the remaining ½ cup of wine over the top, and sprinkle with the remaining seasonings. 5. Continue to bake for an additional 25–30 minutes, basting every 10 minutes until the hens are done. Transfer to a serving platter, and serve hot.

Per Serving:
calorie: 383 | fat: 10g | protein: 57g | carbs: 3g | sugars: 1g | fiber: 0g | sodium: 197mg

Chicken Nuggets

Prep time: 10 minutes | Cook time: 15 minutes | Serves 4

- 1 pound (454 g) ground chicken thighs
- ½ cup shredded Mozzarella cheese
- 1 large egg, whisked
- ½ teaspoon salt
- ¼ teaspoon dried oregano
- ¼ teaspoon garlic powder

1. In a large bowl, combine all the ingredients thoroughly. Using approximately 2 tablespoons of the mixture for each nugget, shape the mixture into twenty nugget-sized portions. 2. Place the formed nuggets into the ungreased basket of an air fryer, arranging them in a single layer and working in batches if necessary to avoid overcrowding. Adjust the air fryer temperature to 375°F (191°C) and cook the nuggets for 15 minutes, turning them halfway through the cooking time to ensure even browning. Once cooked, let the nuggets cool for 5 minutes before serving to allow them to firm up and be easier to handle. Enjoy the homemade nuggets warm.

Per Serving:
calorie: 315 | fat: 19g | protein: 30g | carbs: 2g | sugars: 0g | fiber: 0g | sodium: 495mg

Chicken with Spiced Sesame Sauce

Prep time: 20 minutes | Cook time: 8 minutes | Serves 5

- 2 tablespoons tahini (sesame sauce)
- ¼ cup water
- 1 tablespoon low-sodium soy sauce
- ¼ cup chopped onion
- 1 teaspoon red wine vinegar
- 2 teaspoons minced garlic
- 1 teaspoon shredded ginger root (Microplane works best)
- 2 pounds chicken breast, chopped into 8 portions

1. Place the first seven ingredients in the bottom of the inner pot of the Instant Pot. These ingredients typically include a combination of seasonings, aromatics, and possibly a liquid base. 2. Add the coarsely chopped chicken on top of the ingredients in the pot, spreading it out evenly. 3. Secure the lid on the Instant Pot and make sure the vent is set to the sealing position. Select the Manual setting and set the cooking time for 8 minutes. When the cooking time is complete, allow the pressure to release naturally for 10 minutes, then carefully perform a quick release to release any remaining pressure. 4. Open the Instant Pot and remove the ingredients. Use a fork to shred the chicken into bite-sized pieces. Combine the shredded chicken with the other ingredients in the pot, mixing well to create a tasty sandwich filling or sauce. Serve as desired, enjoying the flavorful mixture.

Per Serving:
calorie: 215 | fat: 7g | protein: 35g | carbs: 2g | sugars: 0g | fiber: 0g | sodium: 178mg

Spice-Rubbed Chicken Thighs

Prep time: 10 minutes | Cook time: 25 minutes | Serves 4

- 4 (4-ounce / 113-g) bone-in, skin-on chicken thighs
- ½ teaspoon salt
- ½ teaspoon garlic powder
- 2 teaspoons chili powder
- 1 teaspoon paprika
- 1 teaspoon ground cumin
- 1 small lime, halved

1. Pat the chicken thighs dry with paper towels to remove any excess moisture. Sprinkle the thighs evenly with salt, garlic powder, chili powder, paprika, and cumin, ensuring they are well coated with the seasonings. 2. Squeeze the juice from half a lime over the seasoned chicken thighs, making sure the juice is evenly distributed. Place the thighs into the ungreased basket of an air fryer, arranging them in a single layer without overlapping. Adjust the air fryer temperature to 380ºF (193ºC) and roast the chicken thighs for 25 minutes, turning them halfway through the cooking time to ensure even browning. The thighs should be crispy and browned with an internal temperature of at least 165ºF (74ºC) when done. 3. Once cooked, transfer the chicken thighs to a large serving plate. Drizzle the thighs with the juice from the remaining half of the lime to add a fresh, zesty flavor. Serve the chicken thighs warm, enjoying their crispy texture and flavorful seasoning.

Per Serving:
calorie: 210 | fat: 12g | protein: 23g | carbs: 3g | sugars: 0g | fiber: 1g | sodium: 357mg

Grilled Lemon Mustard Chicken

Prep time: 5 minutes | Cook time: 15 minutes | Serves 6

- Juice of 6 medium lemons
- ½ cup mustard seeds
- 1 tablespoon minced fresh tarragon
- 2 tablespoons freshly ground black pepper
- 4 garlic cloves, minced
- 2 tablespoons extra-virgin olive oil
- Three 8-ounce boneless, skinless chicken breasts, halved

1. In a small mixing bowl, combine the lemon juice, mustard seeds, dried tarragon, black pepper, minced garlic, and oil. Mix well until all the ingredients are thoroughly combined, creating a flavorful marinade. 2. Place the chicken pieces in a baking dish and pour the marinade over them, ensuring each piece is well coated. Cover the baking dish with plastic wrap or a lid and refrigerate overnight to allow the flavors to infuse into the chicken. 3. Preheat the grill to medium heat. Remove the chicken from the refrigerator and place it on the grill. Cook the chicken for 10 to 15 minutes, turning occasionally and basting with the remaining marinade to keep the meat moist and flavorful. The chicken is done when it is fully cooked and has reached an internal temperature of at least 165ºF (74ºC). Serve the chicken hot, enjoying its tender texture and rich flavors.

Per Serving:
calorie: 239 | fat: 11g | protein: 28g | carbs: 8g | sugars: 2g | fiber: 2g | sodium: 54mg

Chicken Patties

Prep time: 15 minutes | Cook time: 12 minutes | Serves 4

- 1 pound (454 g) ground chicken thigh meat
- ½ cup shredded Mozzarella cheese
- 1 teaspoon dried parsley
- ½ teaspoon garlic powder
- ¼ teaspoon onion powder
- 1 large egg
- 2 ounces (57 g) pork rinds, finely ground

1. In a large bowl, mix together ground chicken, shredded Mozzarella cheese, chopped parsley, garlic powder, and onion powder until well combined. Form the mixture into four equal-sized patties. 2. Place the chicken patties in the freezer for 15 to 20 minutes, allowing them to firm up slightly and hold their shape better during cooking. 3. While the patties are chilling, whisk an egg in a medium bowl until well beaten. Place the ground pork rinds into a separate large bowl, preparing them for coating the patties. 4. Once the patties are firm, dip each one into the beaten egg, ensuring it is fully coated. Then, press each patty into the ground pork rinds, covering all sides thoroughly. Place the coated patties into the air fryer basket in a single layer. 5. Set the air fryer temperature to 360ºF (182ºC) and cook the patties for 12 minutes, flipping them halfway through the cooking time to ensure even browning. 6. The patties are done when they are firm and have reached an internal temperature of 165ºF (74ºC). Serve the chicken patties immediately, enjoying their crispy exterior and juicy interior.

Per Serving:
calorie: 394 | fat: 26g | protein: 35g | carbs: 2g | sugars: 0g | fiber: 0g | sodium: 563mg

Garlic Dill Wings

Prep time: 5 minutes | Cook time: 25 minutes | Serves 4

- 2 pounds (907 g) bone-in chicken wings, separated at joints
- ½ teaspoon salt
- ½ teaspoon ground black pepper
- ½ teaspoon onion powder
- ½ teaspoon garlic powder
- 1 teaspoon dried dill

1. In a large bowl, toss the chicken wings with salt, black pepper, onion powder, garlic powder, and dried dill until they are evenly coated with the seasonings. Arrange the seasoned wings in an ungreased air fryer basket in a single layer, ensuring they do not overlap. If necessary, cook in batches to avoid overcrowding. 2. Preheat the air fryer to 400°F (204°C). Place the basket with the wings into the preheated air fryer and cook for 25 minutes. Shake the basket every 7 minutes to ensure the wings cook evenly and become crispy on all sides. The wings are done when they reach an internal temperature of at least 165°F (74°C) and are golden brown and crispy. Serve the wings warm, enjoying their flavorful and crispy texture.

Per Serving:
calorie: 340 | fat: 24g | protein: 27g | carbs: 2g | sugars: 0g | fiber: 0g | sodium: 642mg

Chicken Paprika

Prep time: 5 minutes | Cook time: 35 minutes | Serves 8

- 1 tablespoon extra-virgin olive oil
- 1 large onion, minced
- 1 medium red bell pepper, julienned
- 1 cup sliced fresh mushrooms
- 1 to 2 teaspoons smoked paprika
- 2 tablespoons lemon juice
- teaspoon salt
- ⅛ teaspoon freshly ground black pepper
- Four 8 ounces boneless, skinless chicken breasts, halved
- 8 ounces plain low-fat Greek yogurt

1. Heat the oil in a large skillet over medium heat. Once the oil is hot, add the chopped onion, diced red pepper, and sliced mushrooms. Sauté the vegetables, stirring occasionally, until they are tender and slightly caramelized, about 3 to 4 minutes. 2. Add 1 cup of water to the skillet, followed by paprika, fresh lemon juice, salt, and black pepper. Stir the mixture well to ensure the spices are evenly distributed. Increase the heat to high and bring the mixture to a boil. Once boiling, reduce the heat to medium, and add the chicken pieces to the skillet. Cover the skillet with a lid and let the chicken simmer for 25 to 30 minutes, or until it is fully cooked and no longer pink in the center. 3. Reduce the heat to low, and quickly stir in the Greek yogurt, mixing thoroughly to create a creamy sauce. Continue to cook for an additional 1 to 2 minutes, ensuring the yogurt is well incorporated, but do not let the mixture boil to prevent curdling. Serve the dish hot, enjoying the tender chicken and flavorful sauce.

Per Serving:
calorie: 184 | fat: 5g | protein: 29g | carbs: 4g | sugars: 3g | fiber: 1g | sodium: 209mg

Buttermilk-Ginger Smothered Chicken

Prep time: 30 minutes | Cook time: 20 minutes | Serves 8

- 8 boneless, skinless chicken thighs
- 2 cups low-fat buttermilk
- ½ bunch fresh chives, thinly sliced
- ½ bunch fresh cilantro, thinly sliced
- 2 garlic cloves, minced
- 1 teaspoon ground ginger

1. Preheat the oven to 375°F (190°C) to ensure it reaches the correct temperature before cooking. 2. In a large bowl, combine the chicken pieces with buttermilk, chopped chives, fresh cilantro, minced garlic, and grated ginger. Mix well to ensure the chicken is thoroughly coated with the marinade. Cover the bowl with plastic wrap and place it in the refrigerator to marinate for at least 30 minutes, allowing the flavors to infuse into the chicken. 3. After marinating, transfer the chicken pieces to a Dutch oven, arranging them in a single layer. Cover the Dutch oven with its lid and place it in the preheated oven. Cook the chicken for 20 minutes, or until it is tender and moist on the inside, and caramelized on the outside. 4. Once cooked, remove the Dutch oven from the oven. Serve the chicken hot, enjoying its rich flavor and tender texture.

Per Serving:
calorie: 363 | fat: 8g | protein: 64g | carbs: 4g | sugars: 3g | fiber: 0g | sodium: 188mg

Cast Iron Hot Chicken

Prep time: 10 minutes | Cook time: 40 minutes | Serves 4

- 2 boneless, skinless chicken breasts
- Juice of 2 limes
- 2 garlic cloves, minced
- 1 medium yellow onion, chopped
- 1½ teaspoons cayenne pepper
- 1 teaspoon smoked paprika

1. Preheat the oven to 375°F (190°C), ensuring it reaches the correct temperature before cooking the chicken. 2. In a shallow bowl, place the chicken breasts and squeeze fresh lime juice over them, making sure they are evenly coated. Add minced garlic, finely chopped onion, cayenne pepper, and paprika to the bowl. Use your hands to massage these ingredients into the chicken, ensuring each piece is thoroughly covered with the mixture. 3. Take a cast iron skillet and arrange the chicken breasts in a single, even layer, ensuring the pieces do not overlap for even cooking. 4. Transfer the cast iron skillet with the chicken into the preheated oven and cook for 35 to 40 minutes, or until the chicken is fully cooked. To check for doneness, use a meat thermometer to ensure the internal temperature of the chicken reaches 165°F (74°C). 5. Once cooked, carefully remove the skillet from the oven and let the chicken rest in the skillet for about 5 minutes to allow the juices to redistribute throughout the meat, making it more tender. 6. After resting, divide each chicken breast into two portions and serve.

Per Serving:
calorie: 286 | fat: 4g | protein: 31g | carbs: 6g | sugars: 2g | fiber: 1g | sodium: 64mg

Greek Chicken

Prep time: 25 minutes | Cook time: 20 minutes | Serves 6

- 4 potatoes, unpeeled, quartered
- 2 pounds chicken pieces, trimmed of skin and fat
- 2 large onions, quartered
- 1 whole bulb garlic, cloves minced
- 3 teaspoons dried oregano
- ¾ teaspoons salt
- ½ teaspoons pepper
- 1 tablespoon olive oil
- 1 cup water

1. Preheat the oven to 375°F (190°C), ensuring it reaches the correct temperature before cooking the chicken. 2. In a large bowl, combine the chicken with buttermilk, finely chopped chives, fresh cilantro, minced garlic, and grated ginger. Mix thoroughly to ensure the chicken is well coated with the marinade. Cover the bowl with plastic wrap and refrigerate for at least 30 minutes to allow the flavors to infuse into the chicken. 3. After marinating, transfer the chicken pieces to a Dutch oven, arranging them in a single layer. Cover the Dutch oven with its lid and place it in the preheated oven. Cook the chicken for 20 minutes, or until the interior is tender and the exterior is caramelized. 4. Once cooked, carefully remove the Dutch oven from the oven. Let the chicken rest for a few minutes before serving to allow the juices to redistribute. Serve the chicken hot, enjoying the rich flavors and tender texture.

Per Serving:
calorie: 278 | fat: 6g | protein: 27g | carbs: 29g | sugars: 9g | fiber: 4g | sodium: 358mg

Cilantro Lime Chicken Thighs

Prep time: 15 minutes | Cook time: 22 minutes | Serves 4

- 4 bone-in, skin-on chicken thighs
- 1 teaspoon baking powder
- ½ teaspoon garlic powder
- 2 teaspoons chili powder
- 1 teaspoon cumin
- 2 medium limes
- ¼ cup chopped fresh cilantro

1. Pat the chicken thighs dry with paper towels to remove any excess moisture, then evenly sprinkle baking powder over the thighs. 2. In a small bowl, combine garlic powder, chili powder, and cumin. Sprinkle this spice mixture evenly over the chicken thighs, gently rubbing it both on the surface and under the skin to ensure thorough seasoning. 3. Cut one lime in half and squeeze its juice over the seasoned chicken thighs, ensuring they are well coated with the lime juice. Place the chicken thighs into the air fryer basket in a single layer. 4. Set the air fryer to 380ºF (193ºC) and cook the chicken thighs for 22 minutes, or until they are crispy and fully cooked with an internal temperature of at least 165ºF (74ºC). 5. While the chicken is cooking, cut the other lime into four wedges. Once the chicken is done, garnish the cooked chicken thighs with the lime wedges and fresh cilantro. Serve immediately, enjoying the flavorful and juicy chicken.

Per Serving:
calorie: 293 | fat: 19g | protein: 26g | carbs: 6g | sugars: 1g | fiber: 2g | sodium: 355mg

Chicken Provençal

Prep time: 5 minutes | Cook time: 25 minutes | Serves 4

- 2 tablespoons extra-virgin olive oil
- Two 8-ounce boneless, skinless chicken breasts, halved
- 1 medium garlic clove, minced
- ¼ cup minced onion
- ¼ cup minced green bell pepper
- ½ cup dry white wine
- 1 cup canned diced tomatoes
- ¼ cup pitted Kalamata olives
- ¼ cup finely chopped fresh basil
- ⅛ teaspoon freshly ground black pepper

1. Heat the oil in a skillet over medium heat. Once the oil is hot, add the chicken pieces to the skillet and brown them, cooking for about 3 to 5 minutes until they develop a golden crust on all sides. 2. Add the remaining ingredients to the skillet, stirring to combine them with the chicken. Continue to cook the mixture uncovered over medium heat for 20 minutes, or until the chicken is fully cooked and no longer pink in the center. Stir occasionally to ensure even cooking and prevent sticking. Transfer the cooked chicken and sauce to a serving platter. Season with additional black pepper to taste, if desired, before serving. Enjoy the flavorful and tender chicken hot.

Per Serving:
calorie: 245 | fat: 11g | protein: 26g | carbs: 5g | sugars: 2g | fiber: 2g | sodium: 121mg

Herbed Buttermilk Chicken

Prep time: 5 minutes | Cook time: 25 minutes | Serves 4

- 1½ pounds boneless, skinless chicken breasts
- 4 cups buttermilk
- Pinch kosher salt
- Pinch freshly ground black pepper
- 1 cup thinly sliced yellow onion
- 2 tablespoons canola oil
- ¼ cup Italian seasoning
- 1 lemon, cut into wedges

1. In a large bowl or sealable plastic bag, combine the chicken, buttermilk, salt, and pepper. Cover or seal and refrigerate for at least 1 hour and up to 24 hours. 2. When the chicken is ready to cook, preheat the oven to 425°F. Line a baking sheet with parchment paper. 3. Remove the chicken from the buttermilk brine and pat it dry. Place the chicken on the prepared baking sheet along with the onion, and drizzle everything with the canola oil. Toss together on the baking sheet (this will save you a bowl) to coat the chicken and onion evenly. 4. Bake for 25 minutes or until the chicken is cooked through. (If the chicken is thick, you can cut the breasts in half lengthwise. It will cut down on your cook time by half or less. Check the chicken after it's cooked for 8 minutes if the breasts are thin.) 5. Allow the chicken to rest and sprinkle it and the onions with the Italian seasoning. 6. Serve with a squeeze of lemon juice.

Per Serving:
calorie: 380 | fat: 14g | protein: 47g | carbs: 16g | sugars: 13g | fiber: 1g | sodium: 543mg

Smoky Whole Chicken

Prep time: 20 minutes | Cook time: 21 minutes | Serves 6

- 2 tablespoons extra-virgin olive oil
- 1 tablespoon kosher salt
- 1½ teaspoons smoked paprika
- 1 teaspoon freshly ground black pepper
- ½ teaspoon herbes de Provence
- ¼ teaspoon cayenne pepper
- 1 (3½ pounds) whole chicken, rinsed and patted dry, giblets removed
- 1 large lemon, halved
- 6 garlic cloves, peeled and crushed with the flat side of a knife
- 1 large onion, cut into 8 wedges, divided
- 1 cup Chicken Bone Broth, low-sodium store-bought chicken broth, or water
- 2 large carrots, each cut into 4 pieces
- 2 celery stalks, each cut into 4 pieces

1. In a small bowl, combine the olive oil, salt, paprika, pepper, herbes de Provence, and cayenne. 2. Place the chicken on a cutting board and rub the olive oil mixture under the skin and all over the outside. Stuff the cavity with the lemon halves, garlic cloves, and 3 to 4 wedges of onion. 3. Pour the broth into the electric pressure cooker. Add the remaining onion wedges, carrots, and celery. Insert a wire rack or trivet on top of the vegetables. 4. Place the chicken, breast-side up, on the rack. 5. Close and lock the lid of the pressure cooker. Set the valve to sealing. 6. Cook on high pressure for 21 minutes. 7. When the cooking is complete, hit Cancel and allow the pressure to release naturally for 15 minutes, then quick release any remaining pressure. 8. Once the pin drops, unlock and remove the lid. 9. Carefully remove the chicken to a clean cutting board. Remove the skin and cut the chicken into pieces or shred/chop the meat, and serve.

Per Serving:
calorie: 362 | fat: 9g | protein: 60g | carbs: 8g | sugars: 3g | fiber: 2g | sodium: 611mg

Turkey and Quinoa Caprese Casserole

Prep time: 10 minutes | Cook time: 35 minutes | Serves 8

- ⅔ cup quinoa
- 1⅓ cups water
- Nonstick cooking spray
- 2 teaspoons extra-virgin olive oil
- 1 pound lean ground turkey
- ¼ cup chopped red onion
- ½ teaspoon salt
- 1 (15-ounce can) fire-roasted tomatoes, drained
- 4 cups spinach leaves, finely sliced
- 3 garlic cloves, minced
- ¼ cup sliced fresh basil
- ¼ cup chicken or vegetable broth
- 2 large ripe tomatoes, sliced
- 4 ounces mozzarella cheese, thinly sliced

1. In a small pot, combine the quinoa and water. Bring the mixture to a boil over high heat, then reduce the heat to low. Cover the pot and simmer for 10 minutes. After 10 minutes, turn off the heat and let the quinoa sit, covered, for an additional 5 minutes to absorb any remaining water. 2. Preheat the oven to 400°F (200°C). Spray a baking dish with nonstick cooking spray to prevent sticking. 3. In a large skillet, heat the oil over medium heat. Add the ground turkey, chopped onion, and a pinch of salt. Cook, breaking up the turkey with a spoon, until the turkey is fully cooked and crumbled, and the onion is tender. 4. Add the diced tomatoes, fresh spinach, minced garlic, and chopped basil to the skillet. Stir in the chicken broth and the cooked quinoa, mixing well to combine all ingredients. Transfer the mixture to the prepared baking dish, spreading it out evenly. Arrange the tomato slices and cheese slices on top of the quinoa mixture. 5. Bake the dish in the preheated oven for 15 minutes, or until the cheese is melted and bubbly, and the tomatoes are softened. Remove from the oven and let it sit for a few minutes before serving hot. Enjoy the flavorful combination of turkey, quinoa, vegetables, and melted cheese.

Per Serving:
calories: 218 | fat: 9g | protein: 18g | carbs: 17g | sugars: 3g | fiber: 3g | sodium: 340mg

Wine-Poached Chicken with Herbs and Vegetables

Prep time: 5 minutes | Cook time: 1 hour | Serves 8

- 4 quarts low-sodium chicken broth
- 2 cups dry white wine
- 4 large bay leaves
- 4 sprigs fresh thyme
- ¼ teaspoon freshly ground black pepper
- 4-pound chicken, giblets removed, washed and patted dry
- ½ pound carrots, peeled and julienned
- ½ pound turnips, peeled and julienned
- ½ pound parsnips, peeled and julienned
- 4 small leeks, washed and trimmed

1. In a large stockpot, combine chicken broth, white wine, bay leaves, fresh thyme, a dash of salt (optional), and black pepper. Let the mixture simmer over medium heat while you prepare the chicken. 2. Stuff the cavity of the chicken with one-third of the chopped carrots, turnips, and parsnips. After stuffing, truss the chicken by tying the legs together with kitchen twine to ensure it cooks evenly. Carefully add the stuffed chicken to the simmering stockpot, ensuring it is fully submerged. Cover the stockpot and poach the chicken over low heat for 30 minutes. 3. After 30 minutes, add the remaining carrots, turnips, parsnips, and the sliced leeks to the stockpot. Continue to simmer the chicken and vegetables for an additional 25 to 30 minutes, or until the chicken is fully cooked and the juices run clear when pierced with a fork. 4. Once the chicken is cooked, carefully remove the chicken and vegetables from the stockpot and place them on a serving platter. Carve the chicken, removing the skin if desired, and arrange the sliced meat on the platter. Surround the chicken with the poached vegetables and serve hot, enjoying the tender, flavorful chicken and aromatic vegetables.

Per Serving:
calorie: 476 | fat: 13g | protein: 57g | carbs: 24g | sugars: 6g | fiber: 4g | sodium: 387mg

Spice-Rubbed Turkey Breast

Prep time: 5 minutes | Cook time: 45 to 55 minutes | Serves 10

- 1 tablespoon sea salt
- 1 teaspoon paprika
- 1 teaspoon onion powder
- 1 teaspoon garlic powder
- ½ teaspoon freshly ground black pepper
- 4 pounds (1.8 kg) bone-in, skin-on turkey breast
- 2 tablespoons unsalted butter, melted

1. In a small bowl, combine salt, paprika, onion powder, garlic powder, and black pepper, mixing them thoroughly until evenly blended. 2. Sprinkle the seasoning mixture generously over all sides of the turkey breast, ensuring it is well coated. Brush the turkey with some of the melted butter, covering as much surface area as possible. 3. Preheat the air fryer to 350°F (177°C). Place the seasoned turkey breast in the air fryer basket with the skin-side down. Roast the turkey in the air fryer for 25 minutes. 4. After 25 minutes, carefully flip the turkey breast and brush it with the remaining melted butter. Continue cooking for an additional 20 to 30 minutes, or until an instant-read thermometer inserted into the thickest part of the turkey breast reads 160°F (71°C). 5. Once the turkey breast reaches the desired temperature, remove it from the air fryer. Tent a piece of aluminum foil loosely over the turkey and allow it to rest for about 5 minutes. This resting period will help the juices redistribute, resulting in a more tender and flavorful turkey. After resting, carve and serve the turkey as desired.

Per Serving:
calorie: 331 | fat: 12g | protein: 49g | carbs: 2g | sugars: 0g | fiber: 1g | sodium: 2235mg

Jerk Chicken Kebabs

Prep time: 10 minutes | Cook time: 14 minutes | Serves 4

- 8 ounces (227 g) boneless, skinless chicken thighs, cut into 1-inch cubes
- 2 tablespoons jerk seasoning
- 2 tablespoons coconut oil
- ½ medium red bell pepper, seeded and cut into 1-inch pieces
- ¼ medium red onion, peeled and cut into 1-inch pieces
- ½ teaspoon salt

1. Place the chicken pieces in a medium bowl and sprinkle them with jerk seasoning. Add the melted coconut oil and toss the chicken to coat it evenly on all sides. 2. Take eight 6-inch skewers and start building them by alternating pieces of chicken, bell pepper, and onion. Aim for about three repetitions of each ingredient per skewer to ensure a balanced mix. 3. Lightly sprinkle salt over the assembled skewers. Place the skewers into an ungreased air fryer basket, making sure they are in a single layer and not overcrowded. Set the air fryer to 370°F (188°C) and cook the skewers for 14 minutes, turning them halfway through the cooking time. The chicken should be golden brown and have an internal temperature of at least 165°F (74°C) when done. Serve the skewers warm, enjoying the flavorful combination of jerk-seasoned chicken and vegetables.

Per Serving:
calorie: 257 | fat: 17g | protein: 21g | carbs: 6g | sugars: 2g | fiber: 2g | sodium: 338mg

Greek Chicken Stuffed Peppers

Prep time: 5 minutes | Cook time: 30 minutes | Serves 4

- 2 large red bell peppers
- 2 teaspoons extra-virgin olive oil, divided
- ½ cup uncooked brown rice or quinoa
- 4 (4-ounce) boneless, skinless chicken breasts
- ¼ teaspoon garlic powder
- ¼ teaspoon onion powder
- ⅛ teaspoon dried thyme
- ½ teaspoon dried oregano
- ½ cup crumbled feta

1. Cut the bell peppers in half and remove the seeds. 2. In a large skillet, heat 1 teaspoon of olive oil over low heat. When hot, place the bell pepper halves cut-side up in the skillet. Cover and cook for 20 minutes. 3. Cook the rice according to the package instructions. 4. Meanwhile, cut the chicken into 1-inch pieces. 5. In a medium skillet, heat the remaining 1 teaspoon of olive oil over medium-low heat. When hot, add the chicken. 6. Season the chicken with garlic powder, onion powder, thyme, and oregano. 7. Cook for 5 minutes, stirring occasionally, until cooked through. 8. In a large bowl, combine the cooked rice and chicken. Scoop one-quarter of the chicken and rice mixture into each pepper half, cover, and cook for 10 minutes over low heat. 9. Top each pepper half with 2 tablespoons of crumbled feta.

Per Serving:
calorie: 311 | fat: 11g | protein: 32g | carbs: 20g | sugars: 4g | fiber: 3g | sodium: 228mg

Herbed Whole Turkey Breast

Prep time: 10 minutes | Cook time: 30 minutes | Serves 12

- 3 tablespoons extra-virgin olive oil
- 1½ tablespoons herbes de Provence or poultry seasoning
- 2 teaspoons minced garlic
- 1 teaspoon lemon zest (from 1 small lemon)
- 1 tablespoon kosher salt
- 1½ teaspoons freshly ground black pepper
- 1 (6 pounds) bone-in, skin-on whole turkey breast, rinsed and patted dry

1. In a small bowl, whisk together the olive oil, herbes de Provence, minced garlic, lemon zest, salt, and black pepper. 2. Rub the outside of the turkey and under the skin with the olive oil mixture, ensuring it is well coated. 3. Pour 1 cup of water into the electric pressure cooker and insert a wire rack or trivet into the pot. 4. Place the seasoned turkey on the rack, skin-side up, making sure it is positioned securely. 5. Close and lock the lid of the pressure cooker, setting the valve to sealing. 6. Cook on high pressure for 30 minutes. 7. When the cooking cycle is complete, hit Cancel. Allow the pressure to release naturally for 20 minutes, then perform a quick release for any remaining pressure. 8. Once the pressure pin drops, unlock and remove the lid carefully. 9. Transfer the turkey to a cutting board with caution. Remove the skin, slice the turkey, and serve.

Per Serving:
calorie: 389 | fat: 19g | protein: 50g | carbs: 1g | sugars: 0g | fiber: 0g | sodium: 582mg

Creamy Nutmeg Chicken

Prep time: 20 minutes | Cook time: 10 minutes | Serves 6

- 1 tablespoon canola oil
- 6 boneless chicken breast halves, skin and visible fat removed
- ¼ cup chopped onion
- ¼ cup minced parsley
- 2 (10¾-ounce) cans 98% fat-free, reduced-sodium cream of mushroom soup
- ½ cup fat-free sour cream
- ½ cup fat-free milk
- 1 tablespoon ground nutmeg
- ¼ teaspoon sage
- ¼ teaspoon dried thyme
- ¼ teaspoon crushed rosemary

1. Press the Sauté button on the Instant Pot and add the canola oil. Once the oil is hot, place the chicken pieces in the pot and brown them on both sides. After browning, remove the chicken and place it on a plate. 2. In the remaining oil in the Instant Pot, sauté the chopped onion and parsley until the onions are tender and translucent. Press the Cancel button on the Instant Pot, then return the browned chicken to the pot. 3. In a separate bowl, mix together the remaining ingredients (specify ingredients if needed) until well combined. Pour this mixture over the chicken in the Instant Pot. 4. Secure the lid of the Instant Pot and set the vent to the sealing position. Select Manual mode and set the cooking time to 10 minutes. 5. Once the cooking time is complete, allow the pressure to release naturally. When the pressure has fully released, carefully remove the lid and serve the chicken hot, enjoying the tender and flavorful dish.

Per Serving:
calories: 264 | fat: 8g | protein: 31g | carbs: 15g | sugars: 5g | fiber: 1g | sodium: 495mg

Herb-Roasted Turkey and Vegetables

Prep time: 20 minutes | Cook time: 2 hours | Serves 6

- 2 teaspoons minced garlic
- 1 tablespoon chopped fresh parsley
- 1 teaspoon chopped fresh thyme
- 1 teaspoon chopped fresh rosemary
- 2 pounds boneless, skinless whole turkey breast
- 3 teaspoons extra-virgin olive oil, divided
- Sea salt
- Freshly ground black pepper
- 2 sweet potatoes, peeled and cut into 2-inch chunks
- 2 carrots, peeled and cut into 2-inch chunks
- 2 parsnips, peeled and cut into 2-inch chunks
- 1 sweet onion, peeled and cut into eighths

1. Preheat the oven to 350°F. 2. Line a large roasting pan with aluminum foil and set it aside. 3. In a small bowl, mix together the garlic, parsley, thyme, and rosemary. 4. Place the turkey breast in the roasting pan and rub it all over with 1 teaspoon of olive oil. 5. Rub the garlic-herb mixture all over the turkey and season lightly with salt and pepper. 6. Place the turkey in the oven and roast for 30 minutes. 7. While the turkey is roasting, toss the sweet potatoes, carrots, parsnips, onion, and the remaining 2 teaspoons of olive oil in a large bowl. 8. Remove the turkey from the oven and arrange the vegetables around it. 9. Roast until the turkey is cooked through (170°F internal temperature) and the vegetables are lightly caramelized, about 1 ½ hours.

Per Serving:
calorie: 267 | fat: 4g | protein: 35g | carbs: 25g | sugars: 8g | fiber: 5g | sodium: 379mg

Ground Turkey Tetrazzini

Prep time: 5 minutes | Cook time: 20 minutes | Serves 6

- 1 tablespoon extra-virgin olive oil
- 2 garlic cloves, minced
- 1 yellow onion, diced
- 8 ounces cremini or button mushrooms, sliced
- ½ teaspoon fine sea salt
- ¼ teaspoon freshly ground black pepper
- 1 pound 93 percent lean ground turkey
- 1 teaspoon poultry seasoning
- 6 ounces whole-grain extra-broad egg-white pasta (such as No Yolks brand) or whole-wheat elbow pasta
- 2 cups low-sodium chicken broth
- 1½ cups frozen green peas, thawed
- 3 cups baby spinach
- Three ¾-ounce wedges Laughing Cow creamy light Swiss cheese, or 2 tablespoons Neufchâtel cheese, at room temperature
- ⅓ cup grated Parmesan cheese
- 1 tablespoon chopped fresh flat-leaf parsley

1. Select the Sauté setting on the Instant Pot and heat the oil and garlic for 2 minutes, until the garlic is bubbling but not browned. Add the onion, mushrooms, salt, and pepper and sauté for about 5 minutes, until the mushrooms have wilted and begun to give up their liquid. Add the turkey and poultry seasoning and sauté, using a wooden spoon or spatula to break up the meat as it cooks, for about 4 minutes more, until cooked through and no streaks of pink remain. 2. Stir in the pasta. Pour in the broth and use the spoon or spatula to nudge the pasta into the liquid as much as possible. It's fine if some pieces are not completely submerged. 3. Secure the lid and set the Pressure Release to Sealing. Press the Cancel button to reset the cooking program, then select the Pressure Cook or Manual setting and set the cooking time for 5 minutes at high pressure. (The pot will take about 5 minutes to come up to pressure before the cooking program begins.) 4. When the cooking program ends, let the pressure release naturally for 5 minutes, then move the Pressure Release to Venting to release any remaining steam. Open the pot and stir in the peas, spinach, Laughing Cow cheese, and Parmesan. Let stand for 2 minutes, then stir the mixture once more. 5. Ladle into bowls or onto plates and sprinkle with the parsley. Serve right away.

Per Serving:
calories: 321 | fat: 11g | protein: 26g | carbs: 35g | sugars: 4g | fiber: 5g | sodium: 488mg

Spicy Chicken Cacciatore

Prep time: 20 minutes | Cook time: 1 hour | Serves 6

- 1 (2-pound) chicken
- ¼ cup all-purpose flour
- Sea salt
- Freshly ground black pepper
- 2 tablespoons extra-virgin olive oil
- 3 slices bacon, chopped
- 1 sweet onion, chopped
- 2 teaspoons minced garlic
- 4 ounces button mushrooms, halved
- 1 (28-ounce) can low-sodium stewed tomatoes
- ½ cup red wine
- 2 teaspoons chopped fresh oregano
- Pinch red pepper flakes

1. Cut the chicken into pieces: 2 drumsticks, 2 thighs, 2 wings, and 4 breast pieces. 2. Dredge the chicken pieces in the flour and season each piece with salt and pepper. 3. Place a large skillet over medium-high heat and add the olive oil. 4. Brown the chicken pieces on all sides, about 20 minutes in total. Transfer the chicken to a plate. 5. Add the chopped bacon to the skillet and cook until crispy, about 5 minutes. With a slotted spoon, transfer the cooked bacon to the same plate as the chicken. 6. Pour off most of the oil from the skillet, leaving just a light coating. Sauté the onion, garlic, and mushrooms in the skillet until tender, about 4 minutes. 7. Stir in the tomatoes, wine, oregano, and red pepper flakes. 8. Bring the sauce to a boil. Return the chicken and bacon, plus any accumulated juices from the plate, to the skillet. 9. Reduce the heat to low and simmer until the chicken is tender, about 30 minutes.

Per Serving:
calorie: 330 | fat: 14g | protein: 35g | carbs: 14g | sugars: 7g | fiber: 4g | sodium: 196mg

Teriyaki Chicken and Broccoli

Prep time: 5 minutes | Cook time: 20 minutes | Serves 4

For The Sauce
- ½ cup water
- 2 tablespoons low-sodium soy sauce
- 2 tablespoons honey
- 1 tablespoon rice vinegar
- ¼ teaspoon garlic powder
- Pinch ground ginger
- 1 tablespoon cornstarch

For The Entrée
- 1 tablespoon sesame oil
- 4 (4 ounces) boneless, skinless chicken breasts, cut into bite-size cubes
- 1 (12 ounces) bag frozen broccoli
- 1 (12 ounces) bag frozen cauliflower rice

Make The Sauce: 1. In a small saucepan, whisk together the water, soy sauce, honey, rice vinegar, garlic powder, and ginger. Add the cornstarch and whisk until it is fully incorporated. 2. Over medium heat, bring the teriyaki sauce to a boil. Let the sauce boil for 1 minute to thicken. Remove the sauce from the heat and set aside. Make The Entrée 1. Heat a large skillet over medium-low heat. When hot, add the oil and the chicken. Cook for 5 to 7 minutes, until the chicken is cooked through, stirring as needed. 2. Steam the broccoli and cauliflower rice in the microwave according to the package instructions. 3. Divide the cauliflower rice into four equal portions. Put one-quarter of the broccoli and chicken over each portion and top with the teriyaki sauce.

Per Serving:
calorie: 256 | fat: 7g | protein: 30g | carbs: 20g | sugars: 11g | fiber: 4g | sodium: 347mg

Baked Chicken Dijon

Prep time: 25 minutes | Cook time: 40 minutes | Serves 6

- 3 cups uncooked bow-tie (farfalle) pasta (6 ounces)
- 2 cups frozen broccoli cuts (from 12 ounces bag)
- 2 cups cubed cooked chicken
- ⅓ cup diced roasted red bell peppers (from 7 ounces jar)
- 1 can (10¾ ounces) condensed cream of chicken or cream of mushroom soup
- ⅓ cup reduced-sodium chicken broth (from 32 ounces carton)
- 3 tablespoons Dijon mustard
- 1 tablespoon finely chopped onion
- ½ cup shredded Parmesan cheese

1. Preheat the oven to 375°F (190°C). Spray a 2½-quart casserole dish with cooking spray to prevent sticking. 2. Cook the pasta according to the package directions. Add the broccoli to the boiling pasta water for the last 2 minutes of the cooking time. Drain the pasta and broccoli together once they are cooked. 3. In the prepared casserole dish, mix the cooked chicken and roasted red peppers until evenly distributed. In a small bowl, combine the condensed soup, chicken broth, Dijon mustard, and finely chopped onion, mixing well. Pour this mixture over the chicken and roasted peppers in the casserole dish, stirring to combine. 4. Add the cooked pasta and broccoli to the casserole, stirring everything together until well mixed. Sprinkle the top with shredded cheese. 5. Cover the casserole dish with a lid or aluminum foil. Bake in the preheated oven for about 30 minutes, or until the center is hot and the cheese is melted and bubbly. Serve the casserole hot, enjoying the comforting blend of flavors and textures.

Per Serving:
calories: 290 | fat: 9g | protein: 24g | carbs: 29g | sugars: 2g | fiber: 3g | sodium: 770mg

Chapter 6

Fish and Seafood

Chapter 6 Fish and Seafood

Bacon-Wrapped Scallops

Prep time: 5 minutes | Cook time: 10 minutes | Serves 4

- 8 (1-ounce / 28-g) sea scallops, cleaned and patted dry
- 8 slices sugar-free bacon
- ¼ teaspoon salt
- ¼ teaspoon ground black pepper

1. Wrap each scallop in a slice of bacon and secure it with a toothpick, ensuring the bacon is snug around the scallop. Sprinkle the wrapped scallops lightly with salt and pepper to season. 2. Place the bacon-wrapped scallops in a single layer in the ungreased basket of an air fryer, making sure they are not touching each other. Adjust the air fryer temperature to 360°F (182°C) and cook for 10 minutes. The scallops should be opaque and firm, with an internal temperature of 135°F (57°C) when done. 3. Once cooked, carefully remove the scallops from the air fryer and transfer them to a serving plate. Serve the bacon-wrapped scallops warm, enjoying their tender texture and savory flavor.

Per Serving:
calories: 251 | fat: 21g | protein: 13g | carbs: 2g | sugars: 0g | fiber: 0g | sodium: 612mg

Tarragon Cod in a Packet

Prep time: 10 minutes | Cook time: 20 minutes | Serves 2

- 1 tablespoon extra-virgin olive oil, divided
- 1 small zucchini, thinly sliced
- 1 cup sliced fresh mushrooms
- 2 (6-ounce) cod fillets, rinsed
- ½ red onion, thinly sliced
- Juice of 1 lemon
- ¼ cup low-sodium vegetable broth
- 1 teaspoon dried tarragon
- Dash salt
- Dash freshly ground black pepper
- 1 (6.5-ounce) jar marinated quartered artichoke hearts, drained
- 6 black olives, halved and pitted

1. Preheat the oven to 450°F. 2. Fold 2 (12-by-24-inch) aluminum foil sheets in half widthwise into 2 (12-by-12-inch) squares. 3. Brush ½ teaspoon of olive oil in the center of each foil square. 4. In the middle of each square, layer, in this order, half of the zucchini slices, ½ cup of mushrooms, 1 cod fillet, and half of the onion slices. 5. Sprinkle each packet with 1 of the remaining 2 teaspoons of olive oil, half of the lemon juice, 2 tablespoons of vegetable broth, and ½ teaspoon of tarragon. Season with salt and pepper. 6. Top with half of the artichokes and 6 black olive halves. 7. Fold and seal the foil into airtight packets. Place the packets in a baking dish and into the preheated oven. Bake for 20 minutes. 8. Carefully avoiding the steam that will be released, open a packet and check that the fish is cooked. It should be opaque and flake easily. To test for doneness, poke the tines of a fork into the thickest portion of the fish at a 45-degree angle. Gently twist the fork and pull up some of the fish. If the fish resists flaking, return it to the oven for another 2 minutes then test again. Fish cooks very quickly, so be careful not to overcook it. 9. With a spatula, lift the fish and vegetables onto individual serving plates. Pour any liquid left in the foil over each serving. 10. Enjoy!

Per Serving:
calories: 296 | fat: 10g | protein: 35g | carbs: 19g | sugars: 5g | fiber: 10g | sodium: 428mg

Ginger-Glazed Salmon and Broccoli

Prep time: 10 minutes | Cook time: 15 minutes | Serves 4

- Nonstick cooking spray
- 1 tablespoon low-sodium tamari or gluten-free soy sauce
- Juice of 1 lemon
- 1 tablespoon honey
- 1 (1-inch) piece fresh ginger, grated
- 1 garlic clove, minced
- 1 pound salmon fillet
- ¼ teaspoon salt, divided
- ⅛ teaspoon freshly ground black pepper
- 2 broccoli heads, cut into florets
- 1 tablespoon extra-virgin olive oil

1. Preheat the oven to 400°F (200°C). Spray a baking sheet with nonstick cooking spray to prevent sticking. 2. In a small bowl, mix together the tamari, lemon juice, honey, grated ginger, and minced garlic until well combined. Set the mixture aside. 3. Place the salmon fillets skin-side down on the prepared baking sheet. Season the salmon with ⅛ teaspoon of salt and freshly ground black pepper. 4. In a large mixing bowl, toss the broccoli florets with olive oil until they are evenly coated. Season the broccoli with the remaining ⅛ teaspoon of salt. Arrange the broccoli in a single layer on the baking sheet next to the salmon. 5. Bake in the preheated oven for 15 to 20 minutes, or until the salmon flakes easily with a fork and the broccoli is tender and slightly crispy. 6. While the salmon and broccoli are baking, heat a small pan over medium heat. Pour in the tamari-ginger mixture and bring it to a simmer. Cook for 1 to 2 minutes, stirring occasionally, until the sauce just begins to thicken. 7. Once the salmon and broccoli are done, remove them from the oven. Drizzle the tamari-ginger sauce over the salmon fillets. Serve immediately, enjoying the flavorful salmon and perfectly roasted broccoli.

Per Serving:
calories: 238 | fat: 11g | protein: 25g | carbs: 11g | sugars: 6g | fiber: 2g | sodium: 334mg

Shrimp Étouffée

Prep time: 20 minutes | Cook time: 30 minutes | Serves 4 to 6

- 2 cups store-bought low-sodium vegetable broth, divided
- ¼ cup whole-wheat flour
- 1 small onion, finely chopped
- 2 celery stalks including leaves, finely chopped
- 1 medium green bell pepper, finely chopped
- 1 medium poblano pepper, finely chopped
- 3 garlic cloves, minced
- 1 tablespoon Creole seasoning
- 2 pounds medium shrimp, shelled and deveined
- ⅓ cup finely chopped chives, for garnish

1. In a Dutch oven, bring ½ cup of broth to a simmer over medium heat. 2. Stir in the flour and reduce the heat to low. Cook, stirring often, for 5 minutes, or until a thick paste is formed. 3. Add another ½ cup of broth, along with the chopped onion, diced celery, bell pepper, diced poblano pepper, and minced garlic. Cook for 2 to 5 minutes, or until the vegetables have softened. 4. Gradually add the seasoning and the remaining 1 cup of broth, ¼ cup at a time, stirring constantly to ensure the mixture is well combined. 5. Add the shrimp to the Dutch oven and cook for about 5 minutes, or until the shrimp are just opaque and cooked through. 6. Serve the shrimp and vegetable mixture with the vegetable of your choice. Garnish with freshly chopped chives and enjoy.

Per Serving:
calories: 164 | fat: 1g | protein: 32g | carbs: 8g | sugars: 2g | fiber: 1g | sodium: 500mg

Asian Salmon in a Packet

Prep time: 10 minutes | Cook time: 20 minutes | Serves 2

For the sauce
- 1 tablespoon extra-virgin olive oil, divided
- 1 teaspoon grated fresh ginger

For the salmon packets
- 1 teaspoon extra-virgin olive oil, divided
- 1 cup cooked brown rice, divided
- 2 cups coarsely chopped bok choy, divided
- 1 small red bell pepper, sliced, divided
- ½ cup sliced shiitake mushrooms, divided
- 2 (6-ounce) salmon steaks, rinsed
- 2 scallions, chopped, divided
- 1 garlic clove, minced
- 2 tablespoons low-sodium soy sauce
- 2 teaspoons dark sesame oil

To make the sauce: 1. In a small bowl, whisk together the olive oil, ginger, garlic, soy sauce, and sesame oil. Set aside. To make the salmon packets 1. Preheat the oven to 450°F. 2. Fold 2 (12-by-24-inch) aluminum foil sheets in half widthwise into 2 (12-by-12-inch) squares. 3. Brush ½ teaspoon of the olive oil in the center of each foil square. 4. Spread ½ cup of the rice in the center of each square. 5. Over the rice in each packet, layer 1 cup of bok choy, half of the red bell pepper slices, ¼ cup of mushrooms, 1 salmon steak, and half of the scallions. 6. Pour half of the sauce over each. 7. Fold and seal the foil into airtight packets. Place the packets in a baking dish and into the preheated oven. Bake for 20 minutes. 8. Carefully avoiding the steam that will be released, open a packet and check that the fish is cooked. It should be opaque and flake easily. To test for doneness, poke the tines of a fork into the thickest portion of the fish at a 45-degree angle. Gently twist the fork and pull up some of the fish. If the fish resists flaking, return it to the oven for another 2 minutes then test again. Fish cooks very quickly, so be careful not to overcook it. 9. Transfer the contents of the packets to serving plates or bowls. 10. Enjoy!

Per Serving:
calories: 491 | fat: 22g | protein: 41g | carbs: 31g | sugars: 4g | fiber: 5g | sodium: 595mg

Salmon with Provolone Cheese

Prep time: 5 minutes | Cook time: 15 minutes | Serves 4

- 1 pound (454 g) salmon fillet, chopped
- 2 ounces (57 g) Provolone, grated
- 1 teaspoon avocado oil
- ¼ teaspoon ground paprika

1. Sprinkle the salmon fillets with avocado oil, ensuring they are evenly coated. Place the fillets in the air fryer basket in a single layer. 2. Sprinkle the salmon fillets with ground paprika, ensuring even coverage. Top each fillet with a slice of Provolone cheese. 3. Set the air fryer to 360°F (182°C) and cook the salmon for 15 minutes, or until the fish is cooked through and the cheese is melted and bubbly. Serve immediately, enjoying the flavorful, cheesy salmon fillets.

Per Serving:
calorie: 200 | fat: 12g | protein: 20g | carbs: 1g | sugars: 0g | fiber: 0g | sodium: 180mg

Spicy Corn and Shrimp Salad in Avocado

Prep time: 10 minutes | Cook time: 0 minutes | Serves 2

- ¼ cup mayonnaise
- 1 teaspoon sriracha (or to taste)
- ½ teaspoon lemon zest
- ¼ teaspoon sea salt
- 4 ounces cooked baby shrimp
- ½ cup cooked and cooled corn kernels
- ½ red bell pepper, seeded and chopped
- 1 avocado, halved lengthwise

1. In a medium bowl, combine the mayonnaise, sriracha, lemon zest, and a pinch of salt. Mix well until the ingredients are fully blended. 2. Add the cooked shrimp, corn kernels, and diced bell pepper to the bowl. Stir the mixture until the shrimp and vegetables are evenly coated with the mayonnaise-sriracha sauce. 3. Cut the avocados in half and remove the pits. Spoon the shrimp mixture into the avocado halves, filling each cavity generously. Serve immediately, enjoying the fresh and zesty flavors.

Per Serving:
calories: 354 | fat: 25g | protein: 17g | carbs: 21g | sugars: 2g | fiber: 9g | sodium: 600mg

Salmon Florentine

Prep time: 10 minutes | Cook time: 30 minutes | Serves 4

- 1 teaspoon extra-virgin olive oil
- ½ sweet onion, finely chopped
- 1 teaspoon minced garlic
- 3 cups baby spinach
- 1 cup kale, tough stems removed, torn into 3-inch pieces
- Sea salt
- Freshly ground black pepper
- 4 (5-ounce) salmon fillets
- Lemon wedges, for serving

1. Preheat the oven to 350°F (175°C). 2. Place a large skillet over medium-high heat and add the oil. 3. Sauté the chopped onion and minced garlic in the skillet until they are softened and translucent, about 3 minutes. 4. Add the spinach and kale to the skillet and continue to sauté until the greens wilt, about 5 minutes. 5. Remove the skillet from the heat and season the wilted greens with salt and pepper to taste. 6. Nestle the salmon fillets into the greens, ensuring they are partially covered by the mixture. Transfer the skillet to the preheated oven and bake the salmon until it is opaque and cooked through, about 20 minutes. 7. Serve the salmon immediately with a squeeze of fresh lemon juice for added brightness and flavor. Enjoy the dish hot.

Per Serving:
calories: 211 | fat: 8g | protein: 30g | carbs: 5g | sugars: 2g | fiber: 1g | sodium: 129mg

Whole Veggie-Stuffed Trout

Prep time: 10 minutes | Cook time: 25 minutes | Serves 2

- Nonstick cooking spray
- 2 (8-ounce) whole trout fillets, dressed (cleaned but with bones and skin intact)
- 1 tablespoon extra-virgin olive oil
- ¼ teaspoon salt
- ⅛ teaspoon freshly ground black pepper
- ½ red bell pepper, seeded and thinly sliced
- 1 small onion, thinly sliced
- 2 or 3 shiitake mushrooms, sliced
- 1 poblano pepper, seeded and thinly sliced
- 1 lemon, sliced

1. Preheat the oven to 425°F (220°C). Spray a baking sheet with nonstick cooking spray to prevent sticking. 2. Rub both trout, inside and out, with olive oil, ensuring they are evenly coated. Season the fish generously with salt and pepper, both inside and out. 3. In a large bowl, combine the diced bell pepper, chopped onion, sliced mushrooms, and diced poblano pepper. Stuff half of this vegetable mixture into the cavity of each fish. Place 2 or 3 lemon slices on top of the vegetable mixture inside each fish cavity for added flavor. 4. Arrange the stuffed fish side by side on the prepared baking sheet. Roast in the preheated oven for 25 minutes, or until the fish is cooked through and flakes easily with a fork, and the vegetables are tender. Serve the roasted trout hot, enjoying the flavorful combination of fish and vegetables.

Per Serving:
calories: 452 | fat: 22g | protein: 49g | carbs: 14g | sugars: 2g | fiber: 3g | sodium: 357mg

Lobster Fricassee

Prep time: 5 minutes | Cook time: 20 minutes | Serves 4

- 2 cups shelled lobster meat
- 1 tablespoon extra-virgin olive oil
- ¾ pound mushrooms, sliced
- 1 small onion, minced
- ½ cup fat-free milk
- ¼ cup flour
- ¼ teaspoon paprika
- ¼ teaspoon salt
- ⅛ teaspoon freshly ground black pepper
- 2 cups cooked whole-wheat pasta
- ¼ cup finely chopped parsley

1. Cut the lobster meat into bite-size pieces. In a saucepan, heat the oil over medium heat. Add the sliced mushrooms and chopped onion, and sauté for 5 to 6 minutes until the vegetables are softened and lightly browned. 2. In a small bowl, whisk together the milk and flour, whisking quickly to eliminate any lumps. Pour the milk mixture into the saucepan with the mushrooms and onions, mixing thoroughly. Continue cooking for 3 to 5 minutes, stirring constantly, until the sauce thickens. 3. Add the bite-size lobster pieces, paprika, salt, and pepper to the saucepan. Continue cooking for 5 to 10 minutes, stirring occasionally, until the lobster is heated through and well coated with the sauce. 4. Spread the cooked pasta onto a serving platter. Spoon the lobster and sauce mixture over the top of the pasta, ensuring even coverage. Garnish with chopped parsley to serve, enjoying the rich and flavorful dish.

Per Serving:
calories: 248 | fat: 5g | protein: 22g | carbs: 31g | sugars: 5g | fiber: 5g | sodium: 523mg

Lemon Pepper Salmon

Prep time: 5 minutes | Cook time: 20 minutes | Serves 4

- Avocado oil cooking spray
- 20 Brussels sprouts, halved lengthwise
- 4 (4-ounce) skinless salmon fillets
- ½ teaspoon garlic powder
- ½ teaspoon freshly ground black pepper
- ¼ teaspoon salt
- 2 teaspoons freshly squeezed lemon juice

1. Heat a large skillet over medium-low heat. When hot, coat the cooking surface with cooking spray, and put the Brussels sprouts cut-side down in the skillet. Cover and cook for 5 minutes. 2. Meanwhile, season both sides of the salmon with the garlic powder, pepper, and salt. 3. Flip the Brussels sprouts, and move them to one side of the skillet. Add the salmon and cook, uncovered, for 4 to 6 minutes. 4. Check the Brussels sprouts. When they are tender, remove them from the skillet and set them aside. 5. Flip the salmon fillets. Cook for 4 to 6 more minutes, or until the salmon is opaque and flakes easily with a fork. Remove the salmon from the skillet, and let it rest for 5 minutes. 6. Divide the Brussels sprouts into four equal portions and add 1 salmon fillet to each portion. Sprinkle the lemon juice on top and serve.

Per Serving:
calories: 163 | fat: 7g | protein: 23g | carbs: 1g | sugars: 0g | fiber: 0g | sodium: 167mg

Teriyaki Salmon

Prep time: 30 minutes | Cook time: 12 minutes | Serves 4

- 4 (6-ounce / 170-g) salmon fillets
- ½ cup soy sauce
- ¼ cup packed light brown sugar
- 2 teaspoons rice vinegar
- 1 teaspoon minced garlic
- ¼ teaspoon ground ginger
- 2 teaspoons olive oil
- ½ teaspoon salt
- ¼ teaspoon freshly ground black pepper
- Oil, for spraying

1. Place the salmon in a small pan, skin-side up. 2. In a small bowl, whisk together soy sauce, brown sugar, rice vinegar, minced garlic, grated ginger, olive oil, salt, and black pepper until well combined. 3. Pour the mixture over the salmon, ensuring it is evenly coated, and let it marinate for about 30 minutes. 4. Line the air fryer basket with parchment paper and spray lightly with oil. Place the marinated salmon in the prepared basket, skin-side down. Depending on the size of your air fryer, you may need to work in batches. 5. Air fry the salmon at 400°F (204°C) for 6 minutes. Brush the salmon with more marinade, then cook for another 6 minutes, or until the internal temperature reaches 145°F (63°C). Serve immediately, enjoying the flavorful and tender salmon.

Per Serving:
calories: 319 | fat: 14g | protein: 37g | carbs: 8g | sugars: 6g | fiber: 1g | sodium: 762mg

Crab Cakes with Honeydew Melon Salsa

Prep time: 30 minutes | Cook time: 10 minutes | Serves 4

For the Salsa
- 1 cup finely chopped honeydew melon
- 1 scallion, white and green parts, finely chopped
- 1 red bell pepper, seeded, finely chopped

For the Crab Cakes
- 1 pound lump crabmeat, drained and picked over
- ¼ cup finely chopped red onion
- ¼ cup panko bread crumbs
- 1 tablespoon chopped fresh parsley
- 1 teaspoon chopped fresh thyme
- Pinch sea salt
- Pinch freshly ground black pepper

- 1 teaspoon lemon zest
- 1 egg
- ¼ cup whole-wheat flour
- Nonstick cooking spray

To Make the Salsa 1. In a small bowl, stir together the melon, scallion, bell pepper, and thyme. 2. Season the salsa with salt and pepper and set aside. To Make the Crab Cakes 1. In a medium bowl, mix together the crab, onion, bread crumbs, parsley, lemon zest, and egg until very well combined. 2. Divide the crab mixture into 8 equal portions and form them into patties about ¾-inch thick. 3. Chill the crab cakes in the refrigerator for at least 1 hour to firm them up. 4. Dredge the chilled crab cakes in the flour until lightly coated, shaking off any excess flour. 5. Place a large skillet over medium heat and lightly coat it with cooking spray. 6. Cook the crab cakes until they are golden brown, turning once, about 5 minutes per side. 7. Serve warm with the salsa.

Per Serving:
calories: 222 | fat: 3g | protein: 29g | carbs: 18g | sugars: 6g | fiber: 2g | sodium: 504mg

Salmon with Brussels Sprouts

Prep time: 5 minutes | Cook time: 20 minutes | Serves 4

- 2 tablespoons unsalted butter, divided
- 20 Brussels sprouts, halved lengthwise
- 4 (4-ounce) skinless salmon fillets
- ½ teaspoon salt
- ¼ teaspoon garlic powder

1. Heat a medium skillet over medium-low heat. When hot, melt 1 tablespoon of butter in the skillet, then add the Brussels sprouts, placing them cut-side down. Cook for 10 minutes, allowing them to caramelize. 2. Season both sides of the salmon fillets with salt and garlic powder. 3. Heat another medium skillet over medium-low heat. When hot, melt the remaining 1 tablespoon of butter in the skillet, then add the seasoned salmon fillets. Cover the skillet and cook the salmon for 6 to 8 minutes, or until the salmon is opaque and flakes easily with a fork. 4. Meanwhile, flip the Brussels sprouts and cover the skillet. Continue cooking for an additional 10 minutes, or until the Brussels sprouts are tender. 5. Divide the cooked Brussels sprouts into four equal portions and place one salmon fillet on each portion. Serve immediately, enjoying the perfectly cooked salmon and caramelized Brussels sprouts.

Per Serving:
calories: 236 | fat: 11g | protein: 27g | carbs: 9g | sugars: 2g | fiber: 4g | sodium: 400mg

Tilapia with Pecans

Prep time: 20 minutes | Cook time: 16 minutes | Serves 5

- 2 tablespoons ground flaxseeds
- 1 teaspoon paprika
- Sea salt and white pepper, to taste
- 1 teaspoon garlic paste
- 2 tablespoons extra-virgin olive oil
- ½ cup pecans, ground
- 5 tilapia fillets, sliced into halves

1. Combine the ground flaxseeds, paprika, salt, white pepper, garlic paste, olive oil, and ground pecans in a Ziploc bag. Add the fish fillets to the bag and shake well to coat them evenly with the mixture. 2. Lightly spritz the air fryer basket with cooking spray. Place the coated fish fillets in the preheated air fryer at 400°F (204°C) and cook for 10 minutes. Turn the fillets over and cook for an additional 6 minutes. Depending on the size of your air fryer, you may need to work in batches. 3. Once cooked, serve the fish fillets with lemon wedges, if desired. Enjoy!

Per Serving:
calorie: 344 | fat: 23g | protein: 28g | carbs: 6g | sugars: 1g | fiber: 4g | sodium: 81mg

Roasted Salmon with Salsa Verde

Prep time: 5 minutes | Cook time: 25 minutes | Serves 4

- Nonstick cooking spray
- 8 ounces tomatillos, husks removed
- ½ onion, quartered
- 1 jalapeño or serrano pepper, seeded
- 1 garlic clove, unpeeled
- 1 teaspoon extra-virgin olive oil
- ½ teaspoon salt, divided
- 4 (4-ounce) wild-caught salmon fillets
- ¼ teaspoon freshly ground black pepper
- ¼ cup chopped fresh cilantro
- Juice of 1 lime

1. Preheat the oven to 425°F (220°C). Spray a baking sheet with nonstick cooking spray to prevent sticking. 2. In a large bowl, toss the tomatillos, chopped onion, sliced jalapeño, garlic cloves, olive oil, and ¼ teaspoon of salt until everything is evenly coated. Arrange the vegetables in a single layer on the prepared baking sheet and roast in the preheated oven for about 10 minutes, or until they are just softened. Once done, transfer the roasted vegetables to a dish or plate and set them aside. 3. Arrange the salmon fillets skin-side down on the same baking sheet. Season the fillets with the remaining ¼ teaspoon of salt and freshly ground black pepper. Bake the salmon for 12 to 15 minutes, or until the fish is firm and flakes easily with a fork. 4. While the salmon is baking, peel the roasted garlic and place it in a blender or food processor along with the other roasted vegetables. Add a scant ¼ cup of water to the blender and process the mixture until smooth. 5. Add the fresh cilantro and lime juice to the blender and process again until the salsa verde is smooth and well combined. Serve the baked salmon fillets topped with the homemade salsa verde, enjoying the vibrant flavors and fresh ingredients.

Per Serving:
calories: 199 | fat: 9g | protein: 23g | carbs: 6g | sugars: 3g | fiber: 2g | sodium: 295mg

Quinoa Pilaf with Salmon and Asparagus

Prep time: 30 minutes | Cook time: 15 minutes | Serves 4

- 1 cup uncooked quinoa
- 6 cups water
- 1 vegetable bouillon cube
- 1 pound salmon fillets
- 2 teaspoons butter or margarine
- 20 stalks fresh asparagus, cut diagonally into 2-inch pieces (2 cups)
- 4 medium green onions, sliced (¼ cup)
- 1 cup frozen sweet peas (from 1 pound bag), thawed
- ½ cup halved grape tomatoes
- ½ cup vegetable or chicken broth
- 1 teaspoon lemon-pepper seasoning
- 2 teaspoons chopped fresh or ½ teaspoon dried dill weed

1. Rinse quinoa thoroughly by placing in a fine-mesh strainer and holding under cold running water until water runs clear; drain well. 2. In 2-quart saucepan, heat 2 cups of the water to boiling over high heat. Add quinoa; reduce heat to low. Cover; simmer 10 to 12 minutes or until water is absorbed. 3. Meanwhile, in 12-inch skillet, heat remaining 4 cups water and the bouillon cube to boiling over high heat. Add salmon, skin side up; reduce heat to low. Cover; simmer 10 to 12 minutes or until fish flakes easily with fork. Transfer with slotted spoon to plate; let cool. Discard water. Remove skin from salmon; break into large pieces. 4. Meanwhile, rinse and dry skillet. Melt butter in skillet over medium heat. Add asparagus; cook 5 minutes, stirring frequently. Stir in onions; cook 1 minute, stirring frequently. Stir in peas, tomatoes and broth; cook 1 minute. 5. Gently stir quinoa, salmon, lemon-pepper seasoning and dill weed into asparagus mixture. Cover; cook about 2 minutes or until hot.

Per Serving:
calories: 380 | fat: 12g | protein: 32g | carbs: 37g | sugars: 7g | fiber: 6g | sodium: 600mg

Parmesan Mackerel with Coriander

Prep time: 10 minutes | Cook time: 7 minutes | Serves 2

- 12 ounces (340 g) mackerel fillet
- 2 ounces (57 g) Parmesan, grated
- 1 teaspoon ground coriander
- 1 tablespoon olive oil

1. Sprinkle the mackerel fillet with olive oil, ensuring it is evenly coated, and place it in the air fryer basket. 2. Top the fish with ground coriander and a generous amount of grated Parmesan cheese. 3. Cook the fish in the air fryer at 390°F (199°C) for 7 minutes, or until the fish is cooked through and the cheese is golden and crispy. Serve immediately.

Per Serving:
calorie: 400 | fat: 25g | protein: 40g | carbs: 2g | sugars: 0g | fiber: 0g | sodium: 500mg

Charcuterie Dinner For One

Prep time: 5 minutes | Cook time: 10 to 12 minutes | Serves 1

- 1 (6 ounces [170 g]) salmon fillet
- Cooking oil spray, as needed
- 1 ounce (28 g) fresh mozzarella cheese slices or balls
- ½ cup (60 g) thinly sliced cucumbers
- ¼ cup (50 g) plain nonfat Greek yogurt
- 1 ounce (28 g) grain-free or whole-grain crackers

1. Preheat the oven to 400°F (204°C). Line a medium baking sheet with parchment paper. 2. Lightly spray the salmon fillet with the cooking oil spray and place the salmon on the prepared baking sheet. Bake the salmon for 10 to 12 minutes, or until it has browned slightly on top. 3. Meanwhile, assemble the mozzarella cheese, sliced cucumbers, yogurt, and crackers on a serving plate. 4. Once the salmon is cooked, transfer it to the plate with the other assembled ingredients and serve immediately.

Per Serving:
calorie: 517 | fat: 29g | protein: 47g | carbs: 16g | sugars: 5g | fiber: 1g | sodium: 418mg

Scallops and Asparagus Skillet

Prep time: 10 minutes | Cook time: 15 minutes | Serves 4

- 3 teaspoons extra-virgin olive oil, divided
- 1 pound asparagus, trimmed and cut into 2-inch segments
- 1 tablespoon butter
- 1 pound sea scallops
- ¼ cup dry white wine
- Juice of 1 lemon
- 2 garlic cloves, minced
- ¼ teaspoon freshly ground black pepper

1. In a large skillet, heat 1½ teaspoons of oil over medium heat. 2. Add the asparagus and sauté for 5 to 6 minutes until just tender, stirring regularly. Remove from the skillet and cover with aluminum foil to keep warm. 3. Add the remaining 1½ teaspoons of oil and the butter to the skillet. When the butter is melted and sizzling, place the scallops in a single layer in the skillet. Cook for about 3 minutes on one side until nicely browned. Use tongs to gently loosen and flip the scallops, and cook on the other side for another 3 minutes until browned and cooked through. Remove and cover with foil to keep warm. 4. In the same skillet, combine the wine, lemon juice, garlic, and pepper. Bring to a simmer for 1 to 2 minutes, stirring to mix in any browned pieces left in the pan. 5. Return the asparagus and the cooked scallops to the skillet to coat with the sauce. Serve warm.

Per Serving:
calories: 252 | fat: 7g | protein: 26g | carbs: 15g | sugars: 3g | fiber: 2g | sodium: 493mg

Ginger-Garlic Cod Cooked in Paper

Prep time: 10 minutes | Cook time: 15 minutes | Serves 4

- 1 chard bunch, stemmed, leaves and stems cut into thin strips
- 1 red bell pepper, seeded and cut into strips
- 1 pound cod fillets cut into 4 pieces
- 1 tablespoon grated fresh ginger
- 3 garlic cloves, minced
- 2 tablespoons white wine vinegar
- 2 tablespoons low-sodium tamari or gluten-free soy sauce
- 1 tablespoon honey

1. Preheat the oven to 425°F (220°C). 2. Cut four pieces of parchment paper, each about 16 inches wide. Lay the four pieces out on a large workspace to prepare the packets. 3. On each piece of parchment paper, arrange a small pile of chard leaves and stems, topped with several strips of bell pepper. Place a piece of cod on top of the vegetables. 4. In a small bowl, mix together the grated ginger, minced garlic, vinegar, tamari, and honey until well combined. Spoon one-fourth of the mixture over each piece of cod, ensuring the fish is evenly coated. 5. Fold the parchment paper over the fish and vegetables so the edges overlap. Fold the edges over several times to create a secure packet that will hold in the steam during baking. Carefully place the packets on a large baking sheet. 6. Bake the packets in the preheated oven for 12 minutes. Once done, carefully open the packets, allowing steam to escape. Serve the cod and vegetables immediately, enjoying the flavorful and aromatic dish straight from the parchment.

Per Serving:
calories: 118 | fat: 1g | protein: 19g | carbs: 9g | sugars: 6g | fiber: 1g | sodium: 715mg

Easy Tuna Patties

Prep time: 5 minutes | Cook time: 10 minutes | Serves 4

- 1 pound canned tuna, drained
- 1 cup whole-wheat bread crumbs
- 2 large eggs, beaten
- ½ onion, grated
- 1 tablespoon chopped fresh dill
- Juice and zest of 1 lemon
- 3 tablespoons extra-virgin olive oil
- ½ cup tartar sauce, for serving

1. In a large bowl, combine the canned tuna, bread crumbs, beaten eggs, finely chopped onion, chopped fresh dill, lemon juice, and lemon zest. Mix thoroughly until all ingredients are well incorporated. Form the mixture into 4 equal-sized patties and place them in the refrigerator to chill for 10 minutes, allowing them to firm up. 2. In a large nonstick skillet over medium-high heat, heat the olive oil until it shimmers. Carefully add the chilled tuna patties to the skillet and cook until they are browned and crispy on both sides, about 4 to 5 minutes per side. Use a spatula to flip the patties gently, ensuring they hold together. 3. Once the patties are cooked through and golden brown, remove them from the skillet and place them on a serving plate. Serve the tuna patties hot, topped with tartar sauce, and enjoy.

Per Serving:
calories: 473 | fat: 25g | protein: 34g | carbs: 27g | sugars: 4g | fiber: 2g | sodium: 479mg

Oregano Tilapia Fingers

Prep time: 15 minutes | Cook time: 9 minutes | Serves 4

- 1 pound (454 g) tilapia fillet
- ½ cup coconut flour
- 2 eggs, beaten
- ½ teaspoon ground paprika
- 1 teaspoon dried oregano
- 1 teaspoon avocado oil

1. Cut the tilapia fillets into finger-sized pieces, ensuring they are roughly uniform in size for even cooking. Sprinkle each piece generously with ground paprika and dried oregano, making sure the seasoning coats all sides of the fish fingers evenly. 2. Crack the eggs into a shallow bowl and beat them until well mixed. Place the coconut flour in another shallow bowl. Dip each seasoned tilapia finger into the beaten eggs, allowing any excess egg to drip off, and then coat them thoroughly in the coconut flour, pressing gently to ensure the flour adheres to all sides. 3. Lightly spray or drizzle the coated fish fingers with avocado oil to help them crisp up in the air fryer. Place the fish fingers in a single layer in the air fryer basket, ensuring they are not touching or overlapping. Set the air fryer to 370°F (188°C) and cook the tilapia fingers for 9 minutes, or until they are golden brown and cooked through. Serve immediately while hot and crispy.

Per Serving:
calorie: 250 | fat: 9g | protein: 30g | carbs: 10g | sugars: 1g | fiber: 5g | sodium: 150mg

Crab-Stuffed Avocado Boats

Prep time: 5 minutes | Cook time: 7 minutes | Serves 4

- 2 medium avocados, halved and pitted
- 8 ounces (227 g) cooked crab meat
- ¼ teaspoon Old Bay seasoning
- 2 tablespoons peeled and diced yellow onion
- 2 tablespoons mayonnaise

1. Scoop out the avocado flesh from each avocado half, leaving about ½ inch around the edges to form a sturdy shell. Chop the scooped-out avocado into small pieces.2. In a medium bowl, combine the crab meat, Old Bay seasoning, finely chopped onion, mayonnaise, and the chopped avocado. Mix well to ensure all ingredients are evenly distributed. Place about ¼ of the crab mixture into each avocado shell, filling them generously.3. Place the filled avocado boats into the ungreased air fryer basket. Adjust the air fryer temperature to 350°F (177°C) and cook for 7 minutes. The avocados will be browned on top, and the mixture will be bubbling when done. Serve the warm avocado boats immediately and enjoy!

Per Serving:
calories: 226 | fat: 17g | protein: 12g | carbs: 10g | sugars: 1g | fiber: 7g | sodium: 239mg

Avo-Tuna with Croutons

Prep time: 10 minutes | Cook time: 0 minutes | Serves 3

- 2 (5-ounce) cans chunk-light tuna, drained
- 2 tablespoons low-fat mayonnaise
- ½ teaspoon freshly ground black pepper
- 3 avocados, halved and pitted
- 6 tablespoons packaged croutons

1. In a medium bowl, combine the tuna, mayonnaise, and pepper, mixing well until thoroughly combined.2. Cut the avocados in half and remove the pits. Scoop some of the avocado flesh out to create a larger cavity. Top each avocado half with the tuna mixture, then sprinkle croutons on top for added crunch. Serve immediately and enjoy!

Per Serving:
calories: 441 | fat: 32g | protein: 23g | carbs: 22g | sugars: 2g | fiber: 14g | sodium: 284mg

Peppercorn-Crusted Baked Salmon

Prep time: 5 minutes | Cook time: 20 minutes | Serves 4

- Nonstick cooking spray
- ½ teaspoon freshly ground black pepper
- ¼ teaspoon salt
- Zest and juice of ½ lemon
- ¼ teaspoon dried thyme
- 1 pound salmon fillet

1. Preheat the oven to 425°F (220°C). Spray a baking sheet with nonstick cooking spray.2. In a small bowl, combine black pepper, salt, lemon zest, lemon juice, and chopped fresh thyme. Stir the mixture well to combine.3. Place the salmon fillet on the prepared baking sheet, skin-side down. Spread the seasoning mixture evenly over the top of the fillet, ensuring it is well coated.4. Bake the salmon in the preheated oven for 15 to 20 minutes, depending on the thickness of the fillet, until the flesh flakes easily with a fork. Serve the salmon hot and enjoy.

Per Serving:
calories: 163 | fat: 7g | protein: 23g | carbs: 1g | sugars: 0g | fiber: 0g | sodium: 167mg

Baked Garlic Scampi

Prep time: 5 minutes | Cook time: 10 minutes | Serves 4

- 1 tablespoon extra-virgin olive oil
- ¼ teaspoon salt
- 7 garlic cloves, crushed
- 2 tablespoons chopped fresh parsley, divided
- 1 pound large shrimp, shelled (with tails left on) and deveined
- Juice and zest of 1 lemon
- 2 cups baby arugula

1. Preheat the oven to 350°F (175°C). Grease a 13-x-9-x-2-inch baking pan with olive oil. In a medium bowl, mix together the salt, minced garlic, and 1 tablespoon of chopped parsley, then set the mixture aside.2. Arrange the shrimp in a single layer in the prepared baking pan and bake, uncovered, for 3 minutes. Turn the shrimp over, and sprinkle them with lemon zest, lemon juice, and the remaining 1 tablespoon of chopped parsley. Continue to bake for an additional 1–2 minutes, or until the shrimp are bright pink and tender.3. Remove the shrimp from the oven. Arrange the arugula on a serving platter and top with the baked shrimp. Spoon the garlic mixture over the shrimp and arugula, and serve immediately.

Per Serving:
calories: 140 | fat: 4g | protein: 23g | carbs: 3g | sugars: 1g | fiber: 0g | sodium: 285mg

Grilled Rosemary Swordfish

Prep time: 5 minutes | Cook time: 15 minutes | Serves 4

- 2 scallions, thinly sliced
- 2 tablespoons extra-virgin olive oil
- 2 tablespoons white wine vinegar
- 1 teaspoon fresh rosemary, finely chopped
- 4 swordfish steaks (1 pound total)

1. In a small bowl, combine the chopped scallions, olive oil, vinegar, and finely chopped rosemary. Mix well to create a marinade. Place the swordfish steaks in a shallow dish and pour the marinade over them, ensuring they are evenly coated. Let the steaks marinate for 30 minutes, turning them occasionally to absorb the flavors.2. Preheat the grill to medium-high heat. Remove the swordfish steaks from the marinade, allowing any excess to drip off, and place them on the grill. Grill the steaks for 5–7 minutes per side, brushing occasionally with the reserved marinade, until the fish is cooked through and has grill marks.3. Transfer the grilled swordfish steaks to a serving platter. Serve immediately, enjoying the flavorful and juicy fish.

Per Serving:
calories: 225 | fat: 14g | protein: 22g | carbs: 0g | sugars: 0g | fiber: 0g | sodium: 92mg

Roasted Salmon with Honey-Mustard Sauce

Prep time: 5 minutes | Cook time: 20 minutes | Serves 4

- Nonstick cooking spray
- 2 tablespoons whole-grain mustard
- 1 tablespoon honey
- 2 garlic cloves, minced
- ¼ teaspoon salt
- ¼ teaspoon freshly ground black pepper
- 1 pound salmon fillet

1. Preheat the oven to 425°F (220°C). Spray a baking sheet with nonstick cooking spray to prevent the salmon from sticking. 2. In a small bowl, whisk together the mustard, honey, minced garlic, salt, and black pepper until well combined and smooth. 3. Place the salmon fillet on the prepared baking sheet, skin-side down. Spoon the mustard-honey sauce onto the salmon, using the back of the spoon to spread it evenly over the entire surface of the fillet. 4. Roast the salmon in the preheated oven for 15 to 20 minutes, depending on the thickness of the fillet. The salmon is done when the flesh flakes easily with a fork and has reached an internal temperature of 145°F (63°C). Serve the roasted salmon hot, enjoying the flavorful glaze and tender, juicy fish.

Per Serving:
calories: 186 | fat: 7g | protein: 23g | carbs: 6g | sugars: 4g | fiber: 0g | sodium: 312mg

Grilled Fish with Jicama Salsa

Prep time: 15 minutes | Cook time: 10 minutes | Serves 6

Jicama Salsa
- 2 cups chopped peeled jicama (¾ pound)
- 1 medium cucumber, peeled, chopped (1 cup)
- 1 medium orange, peeled, chopped (¾ cup)
- 1 tablespoon chopped fresh cilantro or parsley
- ½ teaspoon chili powder
- ¼ teaspoon salt
- 1 tablespoon lime juice

Fish
- 1½ pounds swordfish, tuna or marlin steaks, ¾ to 1 inch thick
- 2 tablespoons olive or canola oil
- 1 tablespoon lime juice
- ¼ teaspoon salt
- ⅛ teaspoon crushed red pepper

1. In a medium bowl, mix the salsa ingredients. Cover the bowl and refrigerate for at least 2 hours to allow the flavors to blend. 2. If the fish steaks are large, cut them into 6 serving pieces. In a shallow glass or plastic dish, or a heavy-duty resealable food-storage plastic bag, mix the oil, lime juice, salt, and red pepper. Add the fish to the marinade, turning to coat it thoroughly. Cover the dish or seal the bag, and refrigerate for 30 minutes. 3. Prepare a charcoal or gas grill for direct heat. Remove the fish from the marinade, reserving the marinade. Place the fish on the grill, about 5 to 6 inches from medium heat. Grill the fish for about 10 minutes, turning once and brushing 2 or 3 times with the reserved marinade, until the fish flakes easily with a fork. Discard any remaining marinade. Serve the grilled fish with the chilled salsa. Enjoy!

Per Serving:
calories: 200 | fat: 10g | protein: 20g | carbs: 7g | sugars: 2g | fiber: 3g | sodium: 250mg

Lemon Butter Cod with Asparagus

Prep time: 5 minutes | Cook time: 15 minutes | Serves 4

- ½ cup uncooked brown rice or quinoa
- 4 (4-ounce) cod fillets
- ¼ teaspoon salt
- ¼ teaspoon freshly ground black pepper
- ¼ teaspoon garlic powder
- 24 asparagus spears
- 2 tablespoons unsalted butter
- 1 tablespoon freshly squeezed lemon juice

1. Cook the rice according to the package instructions. 2. Meanwhile, season both sides of the cod fillets with salt, pepper, and garlic powder. 3. Cut the bottom 1½ inches from the asparagus and discard. 4. Heat a large skillet over medium-low heat. When hot, melt the butter in the skillet, then arrange the cod and asparagus in a single layer. 5. Cover the skillet and cook for 8 minutes, or until the cod is cooked through and the asparagus is tender. 6. Divide the cooked rice, cod fillets, and asparagus into four equal portions. Drizzle each portion with fresh lemon juice to finish and serve immediately.

Per Serving:
calories: 236 | fat: 7g | protein: 23g | carbs: 19g | sugars: 1g | fiber: 1g | sodium: 210mg

Sea Bass with Ginger Sauce

Prep time: 5 minutes | Cook time: 15 minutes | Serves 2

- Two 4-ounce sea bass filets
- 1 tablespoon extra-virgin olive oil
- 2 tablespoons minced fresh ginger
- 2 garlic cloves, minced
- ⅓ cup minced scallions
- 4 teaspoons chopped cilantro
- 1 tablespoon light soy sauce

1. In a medium steamer, add water and bring it to a boil. Arrange the fish fillets on the steamer rack in a single layer, ensuring they are not overlapping. Cover the steamer and steam the fillets for 6–8 minutes, or until the fish is opaque and flakes easily with a fork. 2. While the fish is steaming, heat the oil in a small skillet over medium-high heat. Once the oil is hot, add the finely chopped ginger and minced garlic. Sauté for 2–3 minutes, stirring frequently, until the ginger and garlic are fragrant and lightly golden. 3. Carefully transfer the steamed fish fillets to a serving platter. Drizzle the hot ginger-garlic oil evenly over the fillets. Garnish the fish with thinly sliced scallions, fresh cilantro leaves, and a splash of soy sauce. Serve immediately, enjoying the delicate flavors and tender texture of the steamed fish.

Per Serving:
calories: 207 | fat: 11g | protein: 22g | carbs: 5g | sugars: 2g | fiber: 1g | sodium: 202mg

Chapter 7
Snacks and Appetizers

Chapter 7 Snacks and Appetizers

Cucumber Pâté

Prep time: 10 minutes | Cook time: 20 minutes | Serves 12

- 1 large cucumber, peeled, seeded, and quartered
- 1 small green bell pepper, seeded and quartered
- 3 stalks celery, quartered
- 1 medium onion, quartered
- 1 cup low-fat cottage cheese
- ½ cup plain nonfat Greek yogurt
- 1 package unflavored gelatin
- ¼ cup boiling water
- ¼ cup cold water

1. Begin by spraying a 5-cup mold or a 1½-quart mixing bowl with nonstick cooking spray to ensure easy removal of the mixture later. 2. In a food processor, place the cucumber, green pepper, celery, and onion. Pulse the vegetables until they are coarsely chopped. Transfer the chopped vegetables to a separate bowl and set aside. 3. Rinse out the food processor, then add the cottage cheese and yogurt. Blend these ingredients until the mixture is smooth and creamy. 4. In a medium bowl, dissolve the gelatin in the boiling water, stirring constantly until fully dissolved. Slowly add the cold water to the gelatin mixture, stirring to combine. Next, add the coarsely chopped vegetables and the blended cottage cheese mixture to the gelatin, mixing thoroughly to ensure all ingredients are well incorporated. 5. Pour the combined mixture into the prepared mold, smoothing the top if necessary. Place the mold in the refrigerator and let it chill overnight or until the mixture is firm. When ready to serve, carefully invert the mold onto a serving plate and gently remove the mold. Surround the pâté with an assortment of crackers, and serve immediately.

Per Serving:
calorie: 57 | fat: 2g | protein: 6g | carbs: 3g | sugars: 2g | fiber: 1g | sodium: 107mg

Blood Sugar–Friendly Nutty Trail Mix

Prep time: 5 minutes | Cook time: 0 minutes | Serves 4

- ¼ cup (31 g) raw shelled pistachios
- ¼ cup (30 g) raw pecans
- ¼ cup (43 g) raw almonds
- ¼ cup (38 g) raisins
- ¼ cup (45 g) dairy-free dark chocolate chips

1. In a medium bowl, combine the pistachios, pecans, almonds, raisins, and chocolate chips. Stir the mixture well to ensure an even distribution of all the ingredients. 2. Once thoroughly mixed, divide the trail mix into four equal portions. You can use small containers or resealable bags to keep the portions separate and easy to grab for a quick snack.

Per Serving:
calorie: 234 | fat: 17g | protein: 5g | carbs: 21g | sugars: 15g | fiber: 4g | sodium: 6mg

Green Goddess White Bean Dip

Prep time: 1 minutes | Cook time: 45 minutes | Makes 3 cups

- 1 cup dried navy, great Northern, or cannellini beans
- 4 cups water
- 2 teaspoons fine sea salt
- 3 tablespoons fresh lemon juice
- ¼ cup extra-virgin olive oil, plus 1 tablespoon
- ¼ cup firmly packed fresh flat-leaf parsley leaves
- 1 bunch chives, chopped
- Leaves from 2 tarragon sprigs
- Freshly ground black pepper

1. Combine the beans, water, and 1 teaspoon of the salt in the Instant Pot and stir to dissolve the salt. 2. Secure the lid and set the Pressure Release to Sealing. Select the Bean/Chili, Pressure Cook, or Manual setting and set the cooking time for 30 minutes at high pressure if using navy or Great Northern beans or 40 minutes at high pressure if using cannellini beans. (The pot will take about 15 minutes to come up to pressure before the cooking program begins.) 3. When the cooking program ends, let the pressure release naturally for 15 minutes, then move the Pressure Release to Venting to release any remaining steam. Open the pot and scoop out and reserve ½ cup of the cooking liquid. Wearing heat-resistant mitts, lift out the inner pot and drain the beans in a colander. 4. In a food processor or blender, combine the beans, ½ cup cooking liquid, lemon juice, ¼ cup olive oil, ½ teaspoon parsley, chives, tarragon, remaining 1 teaspoon salt, and ½ teaspoon pepper. Process or blend on medium speed, stopping to scrape down the sides of the container as needed, for about 1 minute, until the mixture is smooth. 5. Transfer the dip to a serving bowl. Drizzle with the remaining 1 tablespoon olive oil and sprinkle with a few grinds of pepper. The dip will keep in an airtight container in the refrigerator for up to 1 week. Serve at room temperature or chilled.

Per Serving:
calorie: 70 | fat: 5g | protein: 3g | carbs: 8g | sugars: 1g | fiber: 4g | sodium: 782mg

Cinnamon Toasted Pumpkin Seeds

Prep time: 5 minutes | Cook time: 45 minutes | Serves 4

- 1 cup pumpkin seeds
- 2 tablespoons canola oil
- 1 teaspoon cinnamon
- 2 (1-gram) packets stevia
- ¼ teaspoon sea salt

1. Preheat the oven to 300°F (150°C). This lower temperature allows the pumpkin seeds to roast slowly, enhancing their flavor and ensuring they become crisp without burning. 2. In a mixing bowl, combine the pumpkin seeds with the oil, ground cinnamon, stevia, and a pinch of salt. Toss the seeds thoroughly to ensure they are evenly coated with the seasoning mixture. 3. Spread the seasoned pumpkin seeds in a single, even layer on a rimmed baking sheet. This allows for even roasting and prevents overcrowding, which can lead to uneven cooking. Bake the seeds in the preheated oven for about 45 minutes, stirring once or twice during the cooking process to promote even browning. Keep an eye on the seeds towards the end of the baking time to ensure they become nicely browned and fragrant without burning. Once done, remove the baking sheet from the oven and let the seeds cool before serving or storing. Enjoy as a crunchy, flavorful snack.

Per Serving:
calorie: 233 | fat: 21g | protein: 9g | carbs: 5g | sugars: 0g | fiber: 2g | sodium: 151mg

Candied Pecans

Prep time: 5 minutes | Cook time: 20 minutes | Serves 10

- 4 cups raw pecans
- 1½ teaspoons liquid stevia
- ½ cup plus 1 tablespoon water, divided
- 1 teaspoon vanilla extract
- 1 teaspoon cinnamon
- ¼ teaspoon nutmeg
- ⅛ teaspoon ground ginger
- ⅛ teaspoon sea salt

1. Place the raw pecans, liquid stevia, 1 tablespoon of water, vanilla extract, ground cinnamon, ground nutmeg, ground ginger, and sea salt into the inner pot of the Instant Pot. Ensure all ingredients are well distributed and the pecans are evenly coated with the seasoning. 2. Press the Sauté button on the Instant Pot and sauté the pecans along with the other ingredients until the pecans start to soften, stirring frequently to prevent sticking and ensure even cooking. 3. Once the pecans are softened, pour in ½ cup of water and secure the lid of the Instant Pot in the locked position. Set the vent to the sealing position to prepare for pressure cooking. 4. Press the Manual button and set the Instant Pot to cook on high pressure for 15 minutes. This will further infuse the flavors into the pecans and soften them to the desired consistency. 5. While the pecans are cooking, preheat your oven to 350°F (175°C) to get it ready for the final baking step. 6. When the cooking time is complete, turn off the Instant Pot and carefully perform a quick release to release the pressure. This will stop the cooking process immediately. 7. Carefully remove the pecans from the Instant Pot and spread them evenly onto a greased, lined baking sheet. This will prevent sticking and ensure easy cleanup. 8. Place the baking sheet in the preheated oven and bake the pecans for 5 minutes or less, checking frequently to avoid burning. The goal is to achieve a slight crispiness and enhance the flavor without overcooking. Once done, remove the baking sheet from the oven and let the pecans cool before serving or storing. Enjoy your deliciously spiced pecans as a snack or topping.

Per Serving:
calories: 275 | fat: 28g | protein: 4g | carbs: 6g | sugars: 2g | fiber: 4g | sodium: 20mg

Lemony White Bean Puree

Prep time: 10 minutes | Cook time: 0 minutes | Makes 4 cups

- 1 (15-ounce) can white beans, drained and rinsed
- 1 small onion, coarsely chopped
- 1 garlic clove, minced
- Zest and juice of 1 lemon
- ½ teaspoon herbs de Provence
- 3 tablespoons extra-virgin olive oil, divided
- 1 tablespoon chopped fresh parsley

1. Place the beans, chopped onion, minced garlic, lemon zest, lemon juice, and fresh herbs into a food processor. Pulse the mixture until it becomes smooth, ensuring all ingredients are well blended. While the food processor is running, slowly stream in 2 tablespoons of extra-virgin olive oil. If the mixture appears too thick, gradually add water, a little at a time, until you reach the desired consistency. 2. Once the mixture is smooth and well combined, transfer the puree to a medium serving bowl. Drizzle the remaining 1 tablespoon of extra-virgin olive oil over the top of the puree, and garnish with freshly chopped parsley for added flavor and presentation. 3. Serve the bean puree with your favorite vegetables or flatbread. This dish pairs well with a variety of dippable items like carrot sticks, cucumber slices, or warm pita bread. Store any leftovers in an airtight container and keep in the refrigerator for up to 4 days, ensuring it stays fresh and flavorful.

Per Serving:
calorie: 121 | fat: 5g | protein: 5g | carbs: 15g | sugars: 1g | fiber: 3g | sodium: 4mg

Guacamole with Jicama

Prep time: 5 minutes | Cook time: 0 minutes | Serves 4

- 1 avocado, cut into cubes
- Juice of ½ lime
- 2 tablespoons finely chopped red onion
- 2 tablespoons chopped fresh cilantro
- 1 garlic clove, minced
- ¼ teaspoon sea salt
- 1 cup sliced jicama

1. In a small bowl, combine the diced avocado, lime juice, finely chopped onion, chopped cilantro, minced garlic, and salt. Mash the mixture lightly with a fork until you achieve a chunky yet combined texture. 2. Serve the avocado mixture with sliced jicama for dipping. Enjoy!

Per Serving:
calorie: 97 | fat: 7g | protein: 1g | carbs: 8g | sugars: 1g | fiber: 5g | sodium: 151mg

Chapter 7 Snacks and Appetizers

Turkey Rollups with Veggie Cream Cheese

Prep time: 10 minutes | Cook time: 0 minutes | Serves 2

- ¼ cup cream cheese, at room temperature
- 2 tablespoons finely chopped red onion
- 2 tablespoons finely chopped red bell pepper
- 1 tablespoon chopped fresh chives
- 1 teaspoon Dijon mustard
- 1 garlic clove, minced
- ¼ teaspoon sea salt
- 6 slices deli turkey

1. In a small bowl, combine the cream cheese, finely chopped red onion, diced bell pepper, chopped chives, mustard, minced garlic, and a pinch of salt. Mix thoroughly until all ingredients are well incorporated and the mixture is smooth and creamy. 2. Lay out the turkey slices on a flat surface. Evenly spread a layer of the cream cheese mixture over each slice of turkey. Once covered, carefully roll up each turkey slice, starting from one end and rolling tightly to enclose the filling.

Per Serving:
calorie: 146 | fat: 1g | protein: 24g | carbs: 8g | sugars: 6g | fiber: 1g | sodium: 572mg

Crab-Filled Mushrooms

Prep time: 5 minutes | Cook time: 25 minutes | Serves 10

- 20 large fresh mushroom caps
- 6 ounces canned crabmeat, rinsed, drained, and flaked
- ½ cup crushed whole-wheat crackers
- 2 tablespoons chopped fresh parsley
- 2 tablespoons finely chopped green onion
- ⅛ teaspoon freshly ground black pepper
- ¼ cup chopped pimiento
- 3 tablespoons extra-virgin olive oil
- 10 tablespoons wheat germ

1. Preheat your oven to 350 °F (175°C). Clean the mushrooms by gently dusting off any dirt on the caps using a mushroom brush or a paper towel. Remove the stems carefully to create space for the stuffing. 2. In a small mixing bowl, combine the crabmeat, crushed crackers, chopped parsley, finely chopped onion, and a pinch of pepper. Mix these ingredients thoroughly until well combined. 3. Arrange the cleaned mushroom caps in a 13-x-9-x-2-inch baking dish with the crown side down, creating little cups. Spoon some of the crabmeat filling into each mushroom cap, pressing down slightly to ensure the filling stays in place. Place a small piece of pimiento on top of the filling in each mushroom cap for added color and flavor. 4. Drizzle olive oil evenly over the stuffed mushroom caps, then sprinkle each cap with ½ tablespoon of wheat germ. This will add a nice crunch and a boost of nutrition. Bake the stuffed mushrooms in the preheated oven for 15–17 minutes, or until the mushrooms are tender and the filling is heated through. Once done, carefully transfer the stuffed mushrooms to a serving platter. Serve them hot and enjoy.

Per Serving:
calorie: 113 | fat: 6g | protein: 7g | carbs: 9g | sugars: 1g | fiber: 2g | sodium: 77mg

Guacamole

Prep time: 5 minutes | Cook time: 5 minutes | Serves 8

- 2 large (8½ ounces) ripe avocados, peeled, pits removed, and mashed
- ½ cup chopped onion
- 2 medium jalapeño peppers, seeded and chopped
- 2 tablespoons minced fresh parsley
- 2 tablespoons fresh lime juice
- ⅛ teaspoon freshly ground black pepper
- 2 medium tomatoes, finely chopped
- 1 medium garlic clove, minced
- 1 tablespoon extra-virgin olive oil
- ½ teaspoon salt

1. In a large mixing bowl, combine all the ingredients, ensuring they are thoroughly blended. Use a spatula or a spoon to mix everything together until the mixture is uniform and well incorporated.

Per Serving:
calorie: 107 | fat: 9g | protein: 1g | carbs: 7g | sugars: 2g | fiber: 4g | sodium: 152mg

Low-Sugar Blueberry Muffins

Prep time: 5 minutes | Cook time: 20 to 25 minutes | Makes 12 muffins

- 2 large eggs
- 1½ cups (144 g) almond flour
- 1 cup (80 g) gluten-free rolled oats
- ½ cup (120 ml) pure maple syrup
- ½ cup (120 ml) avocado oil
- 1 teaspoon baking powder
- 1 teaspoon ground cinnamon
- ½ teaspoon pure vanilla extract
- ½ teaspoon pure almond extract
- 1 cup (150 g) fresh or frozen blueberries

1. Preheat the oven to 350°F (177°C). Line a 12-well muffin pan with paper liners or spray the wells with cooking oil spray to prevent the muffins from sticking. 2. In a blender, combine the eggs, almond flour, oats, maple syrup, oil, baking powder, ground cinnamon, vanilla extract, and almond extract. Blend the ingredients on high for 20 to 30 seconds until the mixture is smooth and homogeneous. 3. Pour the blended batter into a large mixing bowl. Gently fold in the fresh blueberries, making sure they are evenly distributed throughout the batter without crushing them. 4. Using a spoon or a scoop, divide the batter evenly among the 12 muffin wells, filling each about three-quarters full. This ensures even baking and nicely rounded muffin tops. 5. Place the muffin pan in the preheated oven and bake for 20 to 25 minutes, or until a toothpick inserted into the center of a muffin comes out clean. The muffins should be golden brown and firm to the touch. 6. Once baked, let the muffins rest in the pan for 5 minutes to set. Then, transfer them to a cooling rack to cool completely. Enjoy your freshly baked blueberry muffins warm or at room temperature.

Per Serving:
calorie: 240 | fat: 18g | protein: 5g | carbs: 19g | sugars: 10g | fiber: 3g | sodium: 19mg

Chicken Kabobs

Prep time: 5 minutes | Cook time: 20 minutes | Serves 6

- 1 pound boneless, skinless chicken breast
- 3 tablespoons light soy sauce
- One 1-inch cube of fresh ginger root, finely chopped
- 3 tablespoons extra-virgin olive oil
- 3 tablespoons dry vermouth
- 1 large clove garlic, finely chopped
- 12 watercress sprigs
- 2 large lemons, cut into wedges

1. Begin by cutting the chicken into 1-inch cubes, ensuring they are all uniformly sized for even cooking. Place these chicken cubes in a shallow bowl, spreading them out so they can absorb the marinade properly. 2. In a separate small bowl, mix together the soy sauce, freshly grated ginger root, vegetable oil, vermouth, and minced garlic. Stir the mixture well to combine all the flavors. Once mixed, pour this marinade over the chicken cubes in the shallow bowl. Cover the bowl with plastic wrap or a lid and let the chicken marinate in the refrigerator for at least 1 hour. For a deeper flavor, you can let it marinate overnight. 3. After marinating, prepare the skewers. If using wooden skewers, soak them in water for at least 30 minutes to prevent them from burning during cooking. Thread the marinated chicken cubes onto 12 metal or soaked wooden skewers, ensuring the pieces are evenly spaced. Preheat your grill or broiler to medium-high heat. Place the skewers about 6 inches from the heat source and cook for approximately 8 minutes, turning them frequently to ensure even cooking on all sides. 4. Once the chicken is cooked through and has a nice char, remove the skewers from the grill or broiler. Arrange them neatly on a serving platter. Garnish the platter with fresh watercress and lemon wedges for a burst of color and added flavor. Serve the skewers hot, with additional soy sauce on the side for those who may want extra seasoning.

Per Serving:
calorie: 187 | fat: 10g | protein: 18g | carbs: 4g | sugars: 2g | fiber: 1g | sodium: 158mg

Smoky Spinach Hummus with Popcorn Chips

Prep time: 10 minutes | Cook time: 0 minutes | Serves 12

- 1 can (15 ounces) chickpeas (garbanzo beans), drained, liquid reserved
- 1 cup chopped fresh spinach leaves
- 2 tablespoons lemon juice
- 2 tablespoons sesame tahini paste (from 16 ounces. jar)
- 2 teaspoons smoked Spanish paprika
- 1 teaspoon ground cumin
- ½ teaspoon salt
- 2 tablespoons chopped red bell pepper, if desired
- 6 ounces popcorn snack chips

1. In a food processor, place the chickpeas along with ¼ cup of the reserved liquid from the chickpeas. Add fresh spinach, freshly squeezed lemon juice, tahini paste, paprika, ground cumin, and salt. Cover the food processor and process the mixture for about 30 seconds, using quick on-and-off motions to ensure even blending. Stop occasionally to scrape down the sides of the processor to make sure all ingredients are well incorporated. 2. If the mixture is too thick, add more of the reserved chickpea liquid, one tablespoon at a time. Continue covering and processing with quick on-and-off motions until the mixture is smooth and reaches your desired dipping consistency. Once smooth, transfer the hummus to a serving bowl. Garnish the hummus with finely chopped bell pepper for a burst of color and added flavor. Serve the prepared hummus with popcorn snack chips for a delightful and healthy snack.

Per Serving:
calories: 140 | fat: 4g | protein: 4g | carbs: 22g | sugars: 0g | fiber: 3g | sodium: 270mg

Homemade Sun-Dried Tomato Salsa

Prep time: 5 minutes | Cook time: 0 minutes | Serves 4

- ½ (15 ounces [425 g]) can no-salt-added diced tomatoes, drained
- 6 tablespoons (20 g) julienned sun-dried tomatoes (see Tip)
- 1½ cups (330 g) canned artichoke hearts, drained
- 1 clove garlic
- ⅛ cup (3 g) fresh basil leaves
- 1 teaspoon balsamic vinegar
- 2 tablespoons (30 ml) olive oil
- Sea salt, as needed
- Black pepper, as needed

1. In a food processor or blender, combine the diced tomatoes, sun-dried tomatoes, artichoke hearts, minced garlic, fresh basil leaves, balsamic vinegar, olive oil, sea salt, and black pepper. Process or blend the ingredients until you reach your desired consistency, whether that's a chunky texture or a smooth puree. Adjust seasoning to taste before serving.

Per Serving:
calorie: 131 | fat: 7g | protein: 2g | carbs: 13g | sugars: 3g | fiber: 4g | sodium: 279mg

Zucchini Hummus Dip with Red Bell Peppers

Prep time: 10 minutes | Cook time: 0 minutes | Serves 4

- 2 zucchini, chopped
- 3 garlic cloves
- 2 tablespoons extra-virgin olive oil
- 2 tablespoons tahini
- Juice of 1 lemon
- ½ teaspoon sea salt
- 1 red bell pepper, seeded and cut into sticks

1. In a blender or food processor, combine the chopped zucchini, minced garlic, olive oil, tahini, freshly squeezed lemon juice, and a pinch of salt. Blend the mixture until it becomes smooth and creamy, ensuring all the ingredients are well incorporated. 2. Transfer the smooth zucchini dip to a serving bowl. Serve it with sliced red bell pepper strips for dipping, providing a fresh and crunchy complement to the creamy dip. Enjoy this healthy and flavorful snack!

Per Serving:
calorie: 136 | fat: 11g | protein: 3g | carbs: 8g | sugars: 4g | fiber: 2g | sodium: 309mg

Southern Boiled Peanuts

Prep time: 5 minutes | Cook time: 1 hour 20 minutes | Makes 8 cups

1 pound raw jumbo peanuts in the shell
3 tablespoons fine sea salt

1. Remove the inner pot from the Instant Pot and add the peanuts to it. Cover the peanuts with water and use your hands to agitate them, loosening any dirt. Drain the peanuts in a colander, rinse out the pot, and return the peanuts to it. Return the inner pot to the Instant Pot housing. 2. Add the salt and 9 cups water to the pot and stir to dissolve the salt. Select a salad plate just small enough to fit inside the pot and set it on top of the peanuts to weight them down, submerging them all in the water. 3. Secure the lid and set the Pressure Release to Sealing. Select the Steam setting and set the cooking time for 1 hour at low pressure. (The pot will take about 20 minutes to come up to pressure before the cooking program begins.) 4. When the cooking program ends, let the pressure release naturally (this will take about 1 hour). Open the pot and, wearing heat-resistant mitts, remove the inner pot from the housing. Let the peanuts cool to room temperature in the brine (this will take about 1½ hours). 5. Serve at room temperature or chilled. Transfer the peanuts with their brine to an airtight container and refrigerate for up to 1 week.

Per Serving:
calories: 306 | fat: 17g | protein: 26g | carbs: 12g | sugars: 2g | fiber: 4g | sodium: 303mg

Vietnamese Meatball Lollipops with Dipping Sauce

Prep time: 30 minutes | Cook time: 20 minutes | Serves 12

Meatballs
- 1¼ pounds lean (at least 90%) ground turkey
- ¼ cup chopped water chestnuts (from 8 ounces can), drained
- ¼ cup chopped fresh cilantro
- 1 tablespoon cornstarch
- 2 tablespoons fish sauce
- ½ teaspoon pepper
- 3 cloves garlic, finely chopped

Dipping Sauce
- ¼ cup water
- ¼ cup reduced-sodium soy sauce
- 2 tablespoons packed brown sugar
- 2 tablespoons chopped fresh chives or green onions
- 2 tablespoons lime juice
- 2 cloves garlic, finely chopped
- ½ teaspoon crushed red pepper
- About 24 (6-inch) bamboo skewers

1. Preheat your oven to 400°F (200°C). Line a cookie sheet with aluminum foil and spray it with cooking spray, or you can use nonstick foil for easy cleanup. 2. In a large mixing bowl, combine all the ingredients for the meatballs, ensuring they are well mixed to distribute the flavors evenly. Once the mixture is well combined, shape it into meatballs that are about 1¼ inches in diameter. Place these meatballs on the prepared cookie sheet, spacing them about 1 inch apart to ensure they cook evenly. Bake the meatballs in the preheated oven for 20 minutes, turning them halfway through the cooking time. Use a meat thermometer to check that the internal temperature of the meatballs has reached at least 165°F (74°C) to ensure they are fully cooked. 3. While the meatballs are baking, prepare the dipping sauce. In a 1-quart saucepan, combine all the ingredients for the dipping sauce and heat over low heat. Stir the mixture occasionally until the sugar is completely dissolved and the sauce is well blended. Once ready, set the sauce aside and keep it warm. 4. After the meatballs are cooked, remove them from the oven and allow them to cool slightly. Insert bamboo skewers into the meatballs for easy serving. Arrange the skewered meatballs on a serving plate. Serve them hot, accompanied by the warm dipping sauce on the side for a delicious appetizer or snack.

Per Serving:
calorie: 80 | fat: 2g | protein: 10g | carbs: 5g | sugars: 3g | fiber: 0g | sodium: 440mg

Vegetable Kabobs with Mustard Dip

Prep time: 35 minutes | Cook time: 10 minutes | Serves 9

Dip
- ⅔ cup plain fat-free yogurt
- ⅓ cup fat-free sour cream
- 1 tablespoon finely chopped fresh parsley
- 1 teaspoon onion powder
- 1 teaspoon garlic salt
- 1 tablespoon Dijon mustard

Kabobs
- 1 medium bell pepper, cut into 6 strips, then cut into thirds
- 1 medium zucchini, cut diagonally into ½-inch slices
- 1 package (8 ounces) fresh whole mushrooms
- 9 large cherry tomatoes
- 2 tablespoons olive or vegetable oil

1. In a small bowl, mix together all the dip ingredients until well combined. Cover the bowl with plastic wrap or a lid and refrigerate for at least 1 hour to allow the flavors to meld. 2. Preheat your gas or charcoal grill to medium heat. On 5 (12-inch) metal skewers, thread the vegetables, ensuring that each skewer holds only one type of vegetable (use 2 skewers for the mushrooms to ensure they cook evenly). Leave a small space between each piece to ensure even cooking. Brush all the vegetables lightly with oil to prevent sticking and enhance grilling. 3. Place the skewers of bell pepper and zucchini on the preheated grill. Cover the grill and cook for 2 minutes. Then, add the skewers of mushrooms and tomatoes to the grill. Cover the grill again and cook for an additional 4 to 5 minutes, carefully turning the skewers every 2 minutes, until all the vegetables are tender and slightly charred. 4. Once the vegetables are cooked through, transfer them from the skewers to a serving plate. Serve the grilled vegetables hot, accompanied by the chilled dip from the refrigerator. Enjoy your delicious and healthy grilled vegetable dish!

Per Serving:
calories: 60 | fat: 4g | protein: 2g | carbs: 6g | sugars: 3g | fiber: 1g | sodium: 180mg

Creamy Spinach Dip

Prep time: 13 minutes | Cook time: 5 minutes | Serves 11

- 8 ounces low-fat cream cheese
- 1 cup low-fat sour cream
- ½ cup finely chopped onion
- ½ cup no-sodium vegetable broth
- 5 cloves garlic, minced
- ½ teaspoon salt
- ¼ teaspoon black pepper
- 10 ounces frozen spinach
- 12 ounces reduced-fat shredded Monterey Jack cheese
- 12 ounces reduced-fat shredded Parmesan cheese

1. Place the cream cheese, sour cream, finely chopped onion, vegetable broth, minced garlic, salt, pepper, and fresh spinach into the inner pot of the Instant Pot. Ensure the ingredients are evenly distributed for consistent cooking. 2. Secure the lid of the Instant Pot and make sure the vent is set to the sealing position. Select the Bean/Chili setting and set it to cook on high pressure for 5 minutes. This will help blend the flavors and soften the ingredients. 3. Once the cooking time is complete, carefully perform a manual release to release the pressure. Open the lid once the pressure has fully released and it is safe to do so. 4. Add the shredded cheeses (such as mozzarella, cheddar, or Parmesan) to the pot. Mix everything well until the cheeses are fully melted and the mixture is creamy and well combined. Adjust the seasoning if necessary. Serve the creamy spinach dip hot, with your favorite bread, crackers, or vegetables for dipping. Enjoy!

Per Serving:
calorie: 274 | fat: 18g | protein: 19g | carbs: 10g | sugars: 3g | fiber: 1g | sodium: 948mg

Creamy Apple-Cinnamon Quesadilla

Prep time: 15 minutes | Cook time: 10 minutes | Serves 4

- 1 tablespoon granulated sugar
- ½ teaspoon ground cinnamon
- ¼ cup reduced-fat cream cheese (from 8 ounces container)
- 1 tablespoon packed brown sugar
- 2 whole wheat tortillas (8 inch)
- ½ small apple, cut into ¼-inch slices (½ cup)
- Cooking spray

1. In a small bowl, mix the granulated sugar and ¼ teaspoon of the cinnamon; set this mixture aside for later use. In another small bowl, combine the cream cheese, brown sugar, and the remaining ¼ teaspoon of cinnamon. Mix these ingredients with a spoon until they are well blended and smooth. 2. Spread the cream cheese mixture evenly over the surface of two tortillas. Arrange the apple slices on top of the cream cheese mixture on one of the tortillas. Place the second tortilla on top, with the cheese side facing down to create a sandwich. Spray both sides of the assembled quesadilla with cooking spray, then sprinkle the top with the reserved cinnamon-sugar mixture. 3. Heat a 10-inch nonstick skillet over medium heat. Once the skillet is hot, add the quesadilla. Cook for 2 to 3 minutes, or until the bottom is golden brown and crisp. Carefully turn the quesadilla over and cook for another 2 to 3 minutes, or until the other side is also golden brown and crisp. 4. Remove the quesadilla from the skillet and place it on a cutting board. Let it stand for 2 to 3 minutes to set slightly. Using a sharp knife or pizza cutter, cut the quesadilla into 8 wedges. Serve warm and enjoy!

Per Serving:
calories: 110 | fat: 3g | protein: 3g | carbs: 19g | sugars: 9g | fiber: 2g | sodium: 170mg

Monterey Jack Cheese Quiche Squares

Prep time: 10 minutes | Cook time: 15 minutes | Serves 12

- 4 egg whites
- 1 cup plus 2 tablespoons low-fat cottage cheese
- ¼ cup plus 2 tablespoons flour
- ¾ teaspoon baking powder
- 1 cup shredded reduced-fat Monterey Jack cheese
- ½ cup diced green chilies
- 1 red bell pepper, diced
- 1 cup lentils, cooked
- 1 tablespoon extra-virgin olive oil
- Parsley sprigs

1. Preheat the oven to 350 °F (175°C). 2. In a medium bowl, beat the egg whites and cottage cheese together for about 2 minutes, until the mixture is smooth and well combined. 3. Add the flour and baking powder to the egg mixture, and continue to beat until the batter is smooth. Stir in the shredded cheese, chopped green chilies, diced red pepper, and cooked lentils, mixing until all ingredients are evenly distributed. 4. Lightly coat a 9-inch-square baking pan with olive oil to prevent sticking. Pour the egg mixture into the prepared pan, spreading it out evenly. 5. Bake in the preheated oven for 30–35 minutes, or until the quiche is firm and a toothpick inserted into the center comes out clean. 6. Remove the quiche from the oven and let it cool for 10 minutes to make cutting easier. Once cooled, cut the quiche into 12 equal squares and transfer them to a serving platter. Garnish with fresh parsley sprigs for a touch of color and flavor, and serve warm. Enjoy!

Per Serving:
calorie: 104 | fat: 6g | protein: 8g | carbs: 4g | sugars: 0g | fiber: 0g | sodium: 215mg

Creamy Cheese Dip

Prep time: 5 minutes | Cook time: 5 minutes | Serves 40

- 1 cup plain fat-free yogurt, strained overnight in cheesecloth over a bowl set in the refrigerator
- 1 cup fat-free ricotta cheese
- 1 cup low-fat cottage cheese

1. Combine all the ingredients in a food processor. Process the mixture until it becomes smooth and creamy, ensuring all ingredients are well blended. 2. Transfer the smooth cream cheese mixture into a covered container. Place the container in the refrigerator to chill until ready to use. This cream cheese can be stored in the refrigerator for up to 1 week, maintaining its freshness and flavor.

Per Serving:
calorie: 21 | fat: 1g | protein: 2g | carbs: 1g | sugars: 1g | fiber: 0g | sodium: 81mg

Chapter 7 Snacks and Appetizers

Ginger and Mint Dip with Fruit

Prep time: 20 minutes | Cook time: 0 minutes | Serves 6

Dip
- 1¼ cups plain fat-free yogurt
- ¼ cup packed brown sugar
- 2 teaspoons chopped fresh mint leaves
- 2 teaspoons grated gingerroot
- ½ teaspoon grated lemon peel

Fruit Skewers
- 12 bamboo skewers (6 inch)
- 1 cup fresh raspberries
- 2 cups melon cubes (cantaloupe and/or honeydew)

1. In a small bowl, mix the dip ingredients with a whisk until smooth. Cover the bowl and refrigerate for at least 15 minutes to allow the flavors to blend. 2. On each skewer, alternately thread 3 raspberries and 2 melon cubes. Serve the skewers with the prepared dip. Enjoy!

Per Serving:
calories: 100 | fat: 0g | protein: 3g | carbs: 20g | sugars: 17g | fiber: 2g | sodium: 50mg

Ground Turkey Lettuce Cups

Prep time: 5 minutes | Cook time: 30 minutes | Serves 8

- 3 tablespoons water
- 2 tablespoons soy sauce, tamari, or coconut aminos
- 3 tablespoons fresh lime juice
- 2 teaspoons Sriracha, plus more for serving
- 2 tablespoons cold-pressed avocado oil
- 2 teaspoons toasted sesame oil
- 4 garlic cloves, minced
- 1-inch piece fresh ginger, peeled and minced
- 2 carrots, diced
- 2 celery stalks, diced
- 1 yellow onion, diced
- 2 pounds 93 percent lean ground turkey
- ½ teaspoon fine sea salt
- Two 8-ounce cans sliced water chestnuts, drained and chopped
- 1 tablespoon cornstarch
- 2 hearts romaine lettuce or 2 heads butter lettuce, leaves separated
- ½ cup roasted cashews (whole or halves and pieces), chopped
- 1 cup loosely packed fresh cilantro leaves

1. In a small bowl, combine the water, soy sauce, 2 tablespoons of the lime juice, and the Sriracha and mix well. Set aside. 2. Select the Sauté setting on the Instant Pot and heat the avocado oil, sesame oil, garlic, and ginger for 2 minutes, until the garlic is bubbling but not browned. Add the carrots, celery, and onion and sauté for about 3 minutes, until the onion begins to soften. 3. Add the turkey and salt and sauté, using a wooden spoon or spatula to break up the meat as it cooks, for about 5 minutes, until cooked through and no streaks of pink remain. Add the water chestnuts and soy sauce mixture and stir to combine, working quickly so not too much steam escapes. 4. Secure the lid and set the Pressure Release to Sealing. Press the Cancel button to reset the cooking program, then select the Pressure Cook or Manual setting and set the cooking time for 5 minutes at high pressure. (The pot will take about 10 minutes to come up to pressure before the cooking program begins.) 5. When the cooking program ends, perform a quick pressure release by moving the Pressure Release to Venting, or let the pressure release naturally. Open the pot. 6. In a small bowl, stir together the remaining 1 tablespoon lime juice and the cornstarch, add the mixture to the pot, and stir to combine. Press the Cancel button to reset the cooking program, then select the Sauté setting. Let the mixture come to a boil and thicken, stirring often, for about 2 minutes, then press the Cancel button to turn off the pot. 7. Spoon the turkey mixture onto the lettuce leaves and sprinkle the cashews and cilantro on top. Serve right away, with additional Sriracha at the table.

Per Serving:
calories: 127 | fat: 7g | protein: 6g | carbs: 10g | sugars: 2g | fiber: 3g | sodium: 392mg

Roasted Carrot and Herb Spread

Prep time: 20 minutes | Cook time: 1 hour | Serves 16

- 1 pound ready-to-eat baby-cut carrots
- 1 dark orange sweet potato, peeled, cut into 1-inch pieces (2½ cups)
- 1 small onion, cut into 8 wedges, separated
- 2 tablespoons olive oil
- 1 clove garlic, finely chopped
- 1 tablespoon chopped fresh or 1 teaspoon dried thyme leaves
- ¼ teaspoon salt
- ⅛ teaspoon freshly ground pepper
- Assorted whole-grain crackers or vegetable chips

1. Preheat the oven to 350°F (175°C). Spray a 15x10x1-inch baking pan with cooking spray to prevent sticking. Place the chopped carrots, cubed sweet potato, and sliced onion in the prepared pan. Drizzle the vegetables with olive oil, ensuring they are evenly coated. Sprinkle the vegetables with minced garlic, fresh or dried thyme, salt, and pepper. Stir the mixture well to distribute the seasonings evenly. 2. Bake the vegetables uncovered in the preheated oven for about 1 hour, stirring occasionally to ensure even cooking. Continue baking until the vegetables are tender and have a slight caramelization. 3. Once the vegetables are tender, remove the pan from the oven and let them cool slightly. Transfer the roasted vegetable mixture to a food processor. Cover and process the mixture until it is smooth and well blended. Spoon the blended vegetable mixture into a serving bowl. Serve the warm spread immediately with crackers, or cover and refrigerate until ready to serve. Enjoy the spread chilled or at room temperature, depending on your preference.

Per Serving:
calories: 90 | fat: 4g | protein: 1g | carbs: 12g | sugars: 3g | fiber: 2g | sodium: 125mg

Spinach and Artichoke Dip

Prep time: 5 minutes | Cook time: 4 minutes | Serves 11

- 8 ounces low-fat cream cheese
- 10-ounce box frozen spinach
- ½ cup no-sodium chicken broth
- 14-ounce can artichoke hearts, drained
- ½ cup low-fat sour cream
- ½ cup low-fat mayo
- 3 cloves of garlic, minced
- 1 teaspoon onion powder
- 16 ounces reduced-fat shredded Parmesan cheese
- 8 ounces reduced-fat shredded mozzarella

1. Put all the ingredients, except the Parmesan cheese and the mozzarella cheese, into the inner pot of the Instant Pot. Ensure the ingredients are evenly distributed in the pot. 2. Secure the lid of the Instant Pot and set the vent to the sealing position. Select the Manual setting and set it to high pressure for 4 minutes. 3. Once the cooking time is complete, perform a quick release of the steam by carefully turning the vent to the venting position. 4. As soon as the steam has been fully released and it is safe to open the lid, stir in the Parmesan cheese and mozzarella cheese. Mix well until the cheeses are fully melted and the dish is creamy and well combined. Serve immediately and enjoy!

Per Serving:
calories: 288 | fat: 18g | protein: 19g | carbs: 15g | sugars: 3g | fiber: 3g | sodium: 1007mg

Chapter 7 Snacks and Appetizers

Chapter 8: Vegetables and Sides

Chapter 8 Vegetables and Sides

Chunky Red Pepper and Tomato Sauce

Prep time: 5 minutes | Cook time: 40 minutes | Makes 2½ cups

- 3 large red bell peppers, halved lengthwise, seeded, pressed open to flatten
- 2 tablespoons extra-virgin olive oil, plus additional for brushing the peppers
- 1 medium onion, minced
- 1½ teaspoons dried basil
- 1 teaspoon dried rosemary
- ½ teaspoon dried oregano
- ½ teaspoon salt
- ½ cup low-sodium vegetable broth
- 2 cups water
- ½ cup tomato purée
- 1 tablespoon tomato paste
- 2 teaspoons white wine vinegar
- 2 tablespoons chopped fresh basil leaves

1. Preheat the broiler to high. 2. Brush the red bell peppers with olive oil. Place them under the broiler, skin-side up. Cook for about 10 minutes, or until lightly charred. Transfer the peppers to a cutting board, stacking one on top of the other to create steam. Let sit for 10 minutes. Remove as much charred skin as possible. Slice into strips. 3. In a large skillet set over medium-high heat, heat the remaining 2 tablespoons of olive oil. 4. Add the red pepper strips, onion, basil, rosemary, oregano, and salt. Cook for 5 minutes, stirring. 5. Add the vegetable broth. Cook for about 15 minutes more, or until the mixture reduces to a sauce. 6. Add the water, tomato purée, and tomato paste. Reduce the heat to low. Simmer for 25 minutes. 7. Transfer the mixture to a food processor. Purée until smooth, but with some texture remaining. 8. Place the skillet back over low heat. Return the sauce to the skillet. Barely simmer for 1 to 2 minutes to rewarm. Stir in the white wine vinegar and basil. Serve warm. 9. Refrigerate any remaining sauce. Serve chilled or rewarmed, as desired.

Per Serving:
calories: 246 | fat: 15g | protein: 4g | carbs: 26g | sugars: 16g | fiber: 8g | sodium: 641mg

Blooming Onion

Prep time: 10 minutes | Cook time: 10 minutes | Serves 8

- 2 Vidalia onions, peeled
- 1 cup whole-wheat flour
- 1 cup chickpea flour
- 2 tablespoons paprika
- 1 teaspoon ground cumin
- 1 teaspoon Creole seasoning
- 1 cup low-fat buttermilk
- 2 medium egg whites

1. Cut off the top of each onion, then cut each onion vertically until you almost reach the base, taking care not to cut all the way through. Rotate each onion, and make 4 to 6 more vertical cuts to create blooming flowers. 2. In a mixing bowl, use a fork to combine the whole-wheat flour, chickpea flour, paprika, cumin, and Creole seasoning. 3. In another bowl, whisk the buttermilk and egg whites together. 4. Soak the onions in the buttermilk-egg mixture for 60 to 90 seconds, then dredge in the flour mixture. Dunk again in the buttermilk-egg mixture, and place the coated onion in the basket of an air fryer. 5. Set the air fryer to 390°F, close, and cook for 10 minutes. 6. Serve with a plate of greens.

Per Serving:
calories: 135 | fat: 2g | protein: 7g | carbs: 23g | sugars: 4g | fiber: 4g | sodium: 82mg

Classic Oven-Roasted Carrots

Prep time: 10 minutes | Cook time: 15 minutes | Serves 4

- 1½ pounds (680 g) large carrots, trimmed and washed
- Avocado oil spray, as needed
- ¼ teaspoon sea salt
- 1 tablespoon (3 g) dried rosemary

1. Preheat the oven to 400°F (204°C) and line a large baking sheet with parchment paper. 2. Arrange the carrots on the prepared baking sheet, ensuring they are spaced at least ½ inch (13 mm) apart. 3. Spray the carrots generously with avocado oil spray, then sprinkle them evenly with sea salt and rosemary. 4. Roast the carrots in the preheated oven for approximately 15 minutes, or until they reach a fork-tender consistency.

Per Serving:
calorie: 72 | fat: 1g | protein: 2g | carbs: 17g | sugars: 8g | fiber: 5g | sodium: 263mg

Garlic Roasted Radishes

Prep time: 5 minutes | Cook time: 15 minutes | Serves 2 to 4

- 1 pound radishes, halved
- 1 tablespoon canola oil
- Pinch kosher salt
- 4 garlic cloves, thinly sliced
- ¼ cup chopped fresh dill

1. Preheat the oven to 425°F and line a baking sheet with parchment paper. 2. In a medium bowl, coat the radishes evenly with canola oil and salt. Spread them out on the prepared baking sheet and roast for 10 minutes. After 10 minutes, remove the baking sheet from the oven, add the garlic to the radishes, mix well, and return to the oven for an additional 5 minutes. 3. Once roasted, adjust the seasoning of the radishes as desired. Serve them topped with fresh dill on a serving plate or as a side dish. 4. Any leftovers can be stored in an airtight container in the refrigerator for 3 to 4 days.

Per Serving:
calories: 75 | fat: 5g | protein: 1g | carbs: 8g | sugars: 4g | fiber: 3g | sodium: 420mg

Dandelion Greens with Sweet Onion

Prep time: 15 minutes | Cook time: 15 minutes | Serves 4

- 1 tablespoon extra-virgin olive oil
- 1 Vidalia onion, thinly sliced
- 2 garlic cloves, minced
- ½ cup store-bought low-sodium vegetable broth
- 2 bunches dandelion greens, roughly chopped
- Freshly ground black pepper

1. Heat olive oil in a large skillet over low heat. 2. Add onion and garlic to the skillet, stirring constantly to avoid burning the garlic, and cook until the onion turns translucent, about 2 to 3 minutes. 3. Pour in the broth and add the greens, stirring frequently. Cook for 5 to 7 minutes until the greens are wilted and tender. 4. Season the dish with pepper to taste and serve it warm.

Per Serving:
calories: 53 | fat: 4g | protein: 1g | carbs: 5g | sugars: 1g | fiber: 1g | sodium: 39mg

Sautéed Garlicky Mushrooms

Prep time: 10 minutes | Cook time: 12 minutes | Serves 4

- 1 tablespoon butter
- 2 teaspoons extra-virgin olive oil
- 2 pounds button mushrooms, halved
- 2 teaspoons minced fresh garlic
- 1 teaspoon chopped fresh thyme
- Sea salt
- Freshly ground black pepper

1. Heat a large skillet over medium-high heat and melt the butter with olive oil. 2. Sauté the mushrooms in the skillet, stirring occasionally, until they become lightly caramelized and tender, which usually takes about 10 minutes. 3. Stir in the garlic and thyme, continuing to sauté for an additional 2 minutes. 4. Season the mushrooms with salt and pepper to taste before serving.

Per Serving:
calories: 88 | fat: 5g | protein: 5g | carbs: 10g | sugars: 6g | fiber: 3g | sodium: 189mg

Fried Zucchini Salad

Prep time: 10 minutes | Cook time: 5 to 7 minutes | Serves 4

- 2 medium zucchini, thinly sliced
- 5 tablespoons olive oil, divided
- ¼ cup chopped fresh parsley
- 2 tablespoons chopped fresh mint
- Zest and juice of ½ lemon
- 1 clove garlic, minced
- ¼ cup crumbled feta cheese
- Freshly ground black pepper, to taste

1. Preheat the air fryer to 400ºF (204ºC). 2. In a large bowl, toss the zucchini slices with 1 tablespoon of the olive oil. 3. Working in batches if necessary, arrange the zucchini slices in an even layer in the air fryer basket. Pausing halfway through the cooking time to shake the basket, air fry for 5 to 7 minutes until soft and lightly browned on each side. 4. Meanwhile, in a small bowl, combine the remaining 4 tablespoons olive oil, parsley, mint, lemon zest, lemon juice, and garlic. 5. Arrange the zucchini on a plate and drizzle with the dressing. Sprinkle the feta and black pepper on top. Serve warm or at room temperature.

Per Serving:
calories: 190 | fat: 19g | protein: 3g | carbs: 4g | sugars: 2g | fiber: 1g | sodium: 131mg

Not Slow-Cooked Collards

Prep time: 10 minutes | Cook time: 20 minutes | Serves 4

- 1 cup store-bought low-sodium vegetable broth, divided
- ½ onion, thinly sliced
- 2 garlic cloves, thinly sliced
- 1 large bunch collard greens, including stems, roughly chopped
- 1 medium tomato, chopped
- 1 teaspoon ground cumin
- ½ teaspoon freshly ground black pepper

1. In a Dutch oven, bring ½ cup of broth to a simmer over medium heat. 2. Add the onion and garlic to the simmering broth. Sauté them for 3 to 5 minutes, or until they become translucent. 3. Stir in the collard greens, tomato, cumin, pepper, and the remaining ½ cup of broth. Mix gently to combine all ingredients. 4. Reduce the heat to low and let the mixture simmer, uncovered, for 15 minutes, allowing the flavors to meld together.

Per Serving:
calories: 27 | fat: 0g | protein: 1g | carbs: 5g | sugars: 3g | fiber: 1g | sodium: 53mg

Green Beans with Garlic and Onion

Prep time: 5 minutes | Cook time: 12 minutes | Serves 8

- 1 pound fresh green beans, trimmed and cut into 2-inch pieces
- 1 tablespoon extra-virgin olive oil
- 1 small onion, chopped
- 1 large garlic clove, minced
- 1 tablespoon white vinegar
- ¼ cup Parmigiano-Reggiano cheese
- ⅛ teaspoon freshly ground black pepper

1. Steam the beans for approximately 7 minutes or until they reach a tender texture. Set them aside once done. 2. In a skillet, warm the oil over low heat. Add the onion and garlic, and sauté them for about 4 to 5 minutes until the onion turns translucent. 3. Transfer the steamed beans to a serving bowl. Add the sautéed onion mixture and vinegar, tossing everything together well. Sprinkle with cheese and pepper to taste, and serve promptly.

Per Serving:
calories: 43 | fat: 3g | protein: 1g | carbs: 4g | sugars: 1g | fiber: 1g | sodium: 30mg

Roasted Delicata Squash

Prep time: 10 minutes | Cook time: 20 minutes | Serves 4

- 1 (1 to 1½ pounds) delicata squash, halved, seeded, cut into ½-inch-thick strips
- 1 tablespoon extra-virgin olive oil
- ½ teaspoon dried thyme
- ¼ teaspoon salt
- ¼ teaspoon freshly ground black pepper

1. Preheat your oven to 400°F (200°C) and line a baking sheet with parchment paper. 2. In a large mixing bowl, toss the squash strips with olive oil, thyme, salt, and pepper until evenly coated. Spread them out in a single layer on the prepared baking sheet. 3. Roast the squash in the preheated oven for 10 minutes, then flip the strips over. Roast for an additional 10 minutes or until the squash is tender and lightly browned.

Per Serving:
calories: 79 | fat: 4g | protein: 1g | carbs: 12g | sugars: 3g | fiber: 2g | sodium: 123mg

Broccoli Salad

Prep time: 5 minutes | Cook time: 7 minutes | Serves 4

- 2 cups fresh broccoli florets, chopped
- 1 tablespoon olive oil
- ¼ teaspoon salt
- ⅛ teaspoon ground black pepper
- ¼ cup lemon juice, divided
- ¼ cup shredded Parmesan cheese
- ¼ cup sliced roasted almonds

1. Start by tossing broccoli in a large bowl with olive oil, salt, and pepper. Drizzle 2 tablespoons of lemon juice over the broccoli and mix well to coat evenly. 2. Transfer the seasoned broccoli into the ungreased air fryer basket. Adjust the air fryer temperature to 350°F (177°C) and set the timer for 7 minutes, remembering to shake the basket halfway through cooking for even browning. The broccoli should have golden edges when done. 3. Once cooked, transfer the broccoli to a large serving bowl. Drizzle the remaining lemon juice over the top and sprinkle with Parmesan cheese and almonds. Serve the warm and flavorful broccoli immediately.

Per Serving:
calorie: 100 | fat: 7g | protein: 5g | carbs: 7g | sugars: 2g | fiber: 3g | sodium: 260mg

Sautéed Mixed Vegetables

Prep time: 20 minutes | Cook time: 8 minutes | Serves 4

- 2 teaspoons extra-virgin olive oil
- 2 carrots, peeled and sliced
- 4 cups broccoli florets
- 4 cups cauliflower florets
- 1 red bell pepper, seeded and cut into long strips
- 1 cup green beans, trimmed
- Sea salt
- Freshly ground black pepper

1. Heat olive oil in a large skillet over medium heat. 2. Sauté carrots, broccoli, and cauliflower in the skillet until they reach a tender-crisp texture, approximately 6 minutes. 3. Add bell pepper and green beans to the skillet and sauté for an additional 2 minutes. 4. Season the vegetables with salt and pepper to taste, and serve them hot.

Per Serving:
calories: 97 | fat: 3g | protein: 5g | carbs: 15g | sugars: 5g | fiber: 6g | sodium: 211mg

Zucchini Fritters

Prep time: 10 minutes | Cook time: 10 minutes | Serves 4

- 2 zucchini, grated (about 1 pound / 454 g)
- 1 teaspoon salt
- ¼ cup almond flour
- ¼ cup grated Parmesan cheese
- 1 large egg
- ¼ teaspoon dried thyme
- ¼ teaspoon ground turmeric
- ¼ teaspoon freshly ground black pepper
- 1 tablespoon olive oil
- ½ lemon, sliced into wedges

1. Begin by preheating your air fryer to 400ºF (204ºC). Cut a piece of parchment paper to fit slightly smaller than the bottom of the air fryer. 2. Place the zucchini in a large colander and sprinkle it with salt. Allow it to sit for 5 to 10 minutes to release excess moisture. Squeeze the zucchini to remove as much liquid as possible, then transfer it to a large mixing bowl. Add almond flour, Parmesan cheese, egg, thyme, turmeric, and black pepper to the bowl. Gently stir until the mixture is thoroughly combined. 3. Shape the mixture into 8 patties and arrange them on the parchment paper in the air fryer basket. Lightly brush the tops of the patties with olive oil. Air fry the patties for 10 minutes, pausing halfway through to turn them, until they are golden brown and cooked through. 4. Serve the zucchini patties warm, accompanied by lemon wedges for a refreshing touch.

Per Serving:
calorie: 140 | fat: 9g | protein: 8g | carbs: 9g | sugars: 3g | fiber: 3g | sodium: 520mg

Bacon-Wrapped Asparagus

Prep time: 10 minutes | Cook time: 10 minutes | Serves 4

- 8 slices reduced-sodium bacon, cut in half
- 16 thick (about 1 pound / 454 g) asparagus spears, trimmed of woody ends

1. Start by preheating the air fryer to 350ºF (177ºC). 2. Take a half piece of bacon and wrap it around the center of each stalk of asparagus. 3. Arrange the bacon-wrapped asparagus in a single layer in the air fryer basket, seam-side down. Depending on the size of your air fryer, you may need to work in batches. 4. Air fry the bacon-wrapped asparagus for approximately 10 minutes, or until the bacon is crisp and the asparagus stalks are tender. Adjust the cooking time as needed based on your air fryer's performance and the thickness of the bacon.

Per Serving:
calories: 146 | fat: 10g | protein: 12g | carbs: 4g | sugars: 2g | fiber: 2g | sodium: 502mg

Sherried Peppers with Bean Sprouts

Prep time: 5 minutes | Cook time: 8 minutes | Serves 4

- 1 green bell pepper, julienned
- 1 red bell pepper, julienned
- 2 cups canned, drained bean sprouts
- 2 teaspoons light soy sauce
- 1 tablespoon dry sherry
- 1 teaspoon red wine vinegar

1. Heat a large skillet over medium heat and combine peppers, bean sprouts, soy sauce, and sherry. Mix well and cover the skillet. Cook for 5–7 minutes until the vegetables are just tender. 2. Stir in the vinegar, then remove the skillet from the heat. Serve the dish hot and enjoy.

Per Serving:
calories: 34 | fat: 1g | protein: 2g | carbs: 6g | sugars: 4g | fiber: 2g | sodium: 131mg

"Honey" Mustard Sauce

Prep time: 5 minutes | Cook time: 0 minutes | Makes ½ cup

- ½ cup plain nonfat Greek yogurt
- 1 tablespoon apple cider vinegar
- 1 teaspoon dry mustard
- ¾ teaspoon garlic powder
- ⅛ teaspoon paprika
- 1 tablespoon granulated stevia

1. Combine yogurt, apple cider vinegar, dry mustard, garlic powder, paprika, and stevia in a small bowl. Whisk the ingredients together until smooth and well combined. 2. Refrigerate the mixture until it is ready to be used.

Per Serving:
calories: 101 | fat: 0g | protein: 7g | carbs: 17g | sugars: 15g | fiber: 1g | sodium: 81mg

Snow Peas with Sesame Seeds

Prep time: 5 minutes | Cook time: 5 minutes | Serves 6

- 2 cups water
- 1 pound trimmed fresh snow peas
- 3 tablespoons sesame seeds
- 1 tablespoon chopped shallots
- ¼ teaspoon salt
- ⅛ teaspoon freshly ground black pepper
- 1 teaspoon ground ginger

1. In a saucepan, bring water to a boil over high heat. Add the snow peas and immediately turn off the heat. Let the snow peas sit in the hot water for 1 minute, then drain them and rinse under cold running water to stop the cooking process. This blanching method helps the snow peas retain their vibrant green color and crisp texture. 2. Meanwhile, in a skillet over medium heat, toast the sesame seeds for about 1 minute until they become fragrant and lightly browned. Add the blanched snow peas, sliced shallots, salt, pepper, and grated ginger to the skillet. Continue sautéing for 1 to 2 minutes, stirring constantly, until the snow peas are coated with sesame seeds and the flavors have melded together. 3. Remove the snow peas from the skillet and transfer to a serving dish. Serve immediately as a delicious and vibrant side dish.

Per Serving:
calories: 59 | fat: 3g | protein: 3g | carbs: 7g | sugars: 3g | fiber: 3g | sodium: 104mg

Fennel and Chickpeas

Prep time: 10 minutes | Cook time: 20 minutes | Serves 6

- 1 tablespoon extra-virgin olive oil
- 1 small fennel bulb, trimmed and cut into ¼-inch-thick slices
- 1 sweet onion, thinly sliced
- 1 (15½-ounce) can sodium-free chickpeas, rinsed and drained
- 1 cup low-sodium chicken broth
- 2 teaspoons chopped fresh thyme
- ¼ teaspoon sea salt
- ¼ teaspoon freshly ground black pepper
- 1 tablespoon butter

1. Heat oil in a large saucepan over medium-high heat. 2. Sauté the fennel and onion in the hot oil until they are tender and lightly browned, which usually takes about 10 minutes. 3. Add the chickpeas, broth, thyme, salt, and pepper to the saucepan. 4. Cover and simmer the mixture, stirring occasionally, for approximately 10 minutes until the liquid reduces by about half. 5. Remove the saucepan from the heat and stir in the butter until melted and combined. 6. Serve the dish hot, ready to enjoy.

Per Serving:
calories: 132 | fat: 6g | protein:5 g | carbs: 17g | sugars: 6g | fiber: 4g | sodium: 239mg

Roasted Peppers and Eggplant

Prep time: 5 minutes | Cook time: 20 minutes | Serves 2

- Extra-virgin olive oil cooking spray
- 1 small eggplant, halved and sliced
- 1 red bell pepper, cut into thick strips
- 1 yellow bell pepper, cut into thick strips
- 1 red onion, sliced
- 2 garlic cloves, quartered
- 1 tablespoon extra-virgin olive oil
- Salt, to season
- Freshly ground black pepper, to season
- ½ cup chopped fresh basil

1. Preheat the oven to 350°F (175°C). 2. Coat a nonstick baking dish with cooking spray. 3. In the prepared baking dish, combine the eggplant, red bell pepper, yellow bell pepper, onion, and garlic. Drizzle olive oil over the vegetables and toss thoroughly to coat. Spray any exposed surfaces with cooking spray. 4. Place the baking dish in the preheated oven and bake for 20 minutes, turning the vegetables once halfway through cooking to ensure even roasting. 5. Remove the roasted vegetables from the oven and transfer them to a serving dish. Season with salt and pepper to taste. 6. Garnish the dish with fresh basil before serving.

Per Serving:
calories: 185 | fat: 11g | protein: 4g | carbs: 23g | sugars: 12g | fiber: 10g | sodium: 651mg

Balsamic Brussels Sprouts

Prep time: 5 minutes | Cook time: 12 minutes | Serves 4

- 2 cups trimmed and halved fresh Brussels sprouts
- 2 tablespoons olive oil
- ¼ teaspoon salt
- ¼ teaspoon ground black pepper
- 2 tablespoons balsamic vinegar
- 2 slices cooked sugar-free bacon, crumbled

1. In a large bowl, toss Brussels sprouts with olive oil, then season generously with salt and pepper. Transfer the seasoned Brussels sprouts to the ungreased air fryer basket. Set the temperature to 375ºF (191ºC) and cook for 12 minutes, shaking the basket halfway through cooking. The Brussels sprouts should be tender and nicely browned when done. 2. Once cooked, transfer the Brussels sprouts to a large serving dish. Drizzle them with balsamic vinegar and sprinkle crispy bacon over the top. Serve the dish warm and enjoy.

Per Serving:
calories: 97 | fat: 8g | protein: 2g | carbs: 5g | sugars: 2g | fiber: 2g | sodium: 180mg

Garlic Herb Radishes

Prep time: 10 minutes | Cook time: 10 minutes | Serves 4

- 1 pound (454 g) radishes
- 2 tablespoons unsalted butter, melted
- ½ teaspoon garlic powder
- ½ teaspoon dried parsley
- ¼ teaspoon dried oregano
- ¼ teaspoon ground black pepper

1. Start by removing the roots from the radishes and cutting them into quarters. 2. In a small bowl, combine butter and your preferred seasonings. Toss the radish quarters in the herb butter mixture until evenly coated, then place them into the air fryer basket. 3. Adjust the air fryer temperature to 350ºF (177ºC) and set the timer for 10 minutes. 4. Halfway through the cooking time, give the radishes a toss in the air fryer basket to ensure even cooking. Continue cooking until the edges of the radishes begin to turn brown and they are tender. 5. Serve the radishes warm as a delicious side dish.

Per Serving:
calories: 57 | fat: 4g | protein: 1g | carbs: 5g | sugars: 3g | fiber: 2g | sodium: 27mg

Chinese Asparagus

Prep time: 5 minutes | Cook time: 5 minutes | Serves 4

- 1 pound asparagus
- ½ cup plus 1 tablespoon water, divided
- 1 tablespoon light soy sauce
- 1 tablespoon rice vinegar
- 2 teaspoons cornstarch
- 1 tablespoon canola oil
- 2 teaspoons grated fresh ginger
- 1 scallion, minced

1. Prepare the asparagus by trimming off the tough ends and cutting the stalks diagonally into 2-inch pieces. 2. In a small bowl, mix together ½ cup water, soy sauce, and rice vinegar. Set aside. 3. In a separate measuring cup, combine cornstarch with 1 tablespoon of water and set it aside. 4. Heat oil in a wok or skillet over medium-high heat. Add ginger and scallions, stir-frying for about 30 seconds. Then add the asparagus and continue stir-frying for a few more seconds. Pour in the broth mixture, bring it to a boil, cover, and let it simmer for 3–5 minutes until the asparagus is just tender. 5. Stir in the cornstarch mixture and cook until the sauce thickens. Serve the stir-fried asparagus hot and enjoy.

Per Serving:
calories: 73 | fat: 4g | protein: 3g | carbs: 7g | sugars: 3g | fiber: 3g | sodium: 64mg

Roasted Lemon and Garlic Broccoli

Prep time: 10 minutes | Cook time: 25 minutes | Serves 8

- 2 large broccoli heads, cut into florets
- 3 garlic cloves, minced
- 2 tablespoons extra-virgin olive oil
- ¼ teaspoon salt
- ¼ teaspoon freshly ground black pepper
- 2 tablespoons freshly squeezed lemon juice

1. Begin by preheating your oven to 425°F (218°C). 2. On a rimmed baking sheet, toss the broccoli and garlic with olive oil until evenly coated. Season generously with salt and pepper. 3. Roast the broccoli in the preheated oven, tossing occasionally, for 25 to 30 minutes or until the broccoli is tender and nicely browned. 4. Once roasted, drizzle the broccoli with lemon juice to taste, and serve it immediately while still warm and flavorful.

Per Serving:
calories: 30 | fat: 2g | protein: 1g | carbs: 3g | sugars: 1g | fiber: 1g | sodium: 84mg

Horseradish Mashed Cauliflower

Prep time: 5 minutes | Cook time: 10 minutes | Serves 4

- 1 large head cauliflower (about 3 pounds), cut into small florets
- ½ cup skim milk
- 2 tablespoons prepared horseradish
- ¼ teaspoon sea salt
- 2 teaspoons chopped fresh chives

1. Place a large pot of water over high heat and bring it to a vigorous boil. 2. Blanch the cauliflower in the boiling water until it reaches tenderness, approximately 5 minutes. 3. Drain the cauliflower thoroughly and transfer it to a food processor. 4. Add the milk and horseradish to the cauliflower in the food processor. Purée the mixture until it achieves a smooth and thick consistency, approximately 2 minutes, or alternatively, mash it manually with a potato masher. 5. Transfer the mashed cauliflower to a serving bowl and season generously with salt. 6. Serve the dish immediately, garnishing it with freshly chopped chives.

Per Serving:
calories: 102 | fat: 1g | protein: 8g | carbs: 19g | sugars: 9g | fiber: 7g | sodium: 292mg

Roasted Eggplant

Prep time: 15 minutes | Cook time: 15 minutes | Serves 4

- 1 large eggplant
- 2 tablespoons olive oil
- ¼ teaspoon salt
- ½ teaspoon garlic powder

1. Begin by removing the top and bottom from the eggplant, then slice it into ¼-inch-thick rounds. 2. Brush the eggplant slices with olive oil and sprinkle them with salt and garlic powder to taste. Place the seasoned slices into the air fryer basket. 3. Adjust the air fryer temperature to 390ºF (199ºC) and set the timer for 15 minutes to ensure they cook evenly. 4. Once done, serve the air-fried eggplant slices immediately while they are hot and crispy.

Per Serving:
calories: 98 | fat: 7g | protein: 2g | carbs: 8g | sugars: 3g | fiber: 3g | sodium: 200mg

Spaghetti Squash

Prep time: 5 minutes | Cook time: 7 minutes | Serves 4

- 1 spaghetti squash (about 2 pounds)

1. Begin by cutting the spaghetti squash in half crosswise and using a large spoon to scoop out the seeds. 2. Pour 1 cup of water into the electric pressure cooker and place a wire rack or trivet inside. 3. Arrange the squash halves on the rack with the cut-sides facing up. 4. Close and lock the lid of the pressure cooker, ensuring the valve is set to sealing. 5. Cook the squash on high pressure for 7 minutes. 6. Once cooking is complete, press Cancel and perform a quick release of the pressure. 7. After the pressure valve drops, unlock and carefully remove the lid. 8. Use tongs to take the squash out of the pot and transfer it to a plate. Allow it to cool slightly before using a fork to scrape the squash into strands. Discard the skin and serve the spaghetti squash as desired.

Per Serving:
calories: 121 | fat: 2g | protein: 2g | carbs: 28g | sugars: 11g | fiber: 6g | sodium: 68mg

Artichokes Parmesan

Prep time: 5 minutes | Cook time: 20 minutes | Serves 6

- ½ cup dried whole-wheat bread crumbs
- 2 tablespoons grated Parmigiano-Reggiano cheese
- ⅛ teaspoon freshly ground black pepper
- 9 ounces frozen artichoke hearts, thawed
- 2 tablespoons extra-virgin olive oil, divided
- 2 medium tomatoes, diced

1. Start by preheating your oven to 425 °F (218 °C). 2. In a small bowl, mix together the bread crumbs, cheese, and black pepper until well combined. 3. Arrange the artichoke hearts in a 1-quart casserole dish. Sprinkle the tomatoes evenly over the artichokes. Season with salt, if desired. 4. Sprinkle the prepared bread crumb mixture evenly over the vegetables in the casserole dish. 5. Bake in the preheated oven for 15–20 minutes or until the topping becomes lightly browned and crispy.

Per Serving:
calories: 78 | fat: 5g | protein: 2g | carbs:7 g | sugars: 1g | fiber: 2g | sodium: 67mg

Sautéed Spinach and Tomatoes

Prep time: 5 minutes | Cook time: 10 minutes | Serves 4

- 1 tablespoon extra-virgin olive oil
- 1 cup cherry tomatoes, halved
- 3 spinach bunches, trimmed
- 2 garlic cloves, minced
- ¼ teaspoon salt

1. Heat oil in a large skillet over medium heat until it shimmers and is evenly distributed across the pan. 2. Add the tomatoes to the skillet and cook them for approximately 2 minutes, or until their skins start to blister and split, releasing their juices. 3. Gradually add the spinach to the skillet in batches, allowing each batch to wilt slightly before adding more. Stir continuously for about 3 to 4 minutes, until all the spinach is tender and cooked down. 4. Add minced garlic to the skillet and toss it with the spinach and tomatoes until it becomes fragrant, which should take around 30 seconds. 5. Drain any excess liquid from the pan and season the dish with salt, stirring well to combine all the flavors. Serve the spinach and tomato mixture immediately as a delicious side dish or as part of a meal.

Per Serving:
calories: 52 | fat: 4g | protein: 2g | carbs: 4g | sugars: 1g | fiber: 2g | sodium: 183mg

Cauliflower with Lime Juice

Prep time: 10 minutes | Cook time: 7 minutes | Serves 4

- 2 cups chopped cauliflower florets
- 2 tablespoons coconut oil, melted
- 2 teaspoons chili powder
- ½ teaspoon garlic powder
- 1 medium lime
- 2 tablespoons chopped cilantro

1. Begin by tossing cauliflower florets with coconut oil in a large bowl. Sprinkle them evenly with chili powder and garlic powder until well coated. Transfer the seasoned cauliflower into the air fryer basket. 2. Adjust the air fryer temperature to 350ºF (177ºC) and set the timer for 7 minutes to cook the cauliflower until tender and beginning to turn golden around the edges. 3. Once cooked, transfer the cauliflower to a serving bowl. 4. Cut a lime into quarters and squeeze the juice over the cauliflower. Garnish with fresh cilantro for added flavor. Serve the dish warm and enjoy!

Per Serving:
calorie: 80 | fat: 7g | protein: 1g | carbs: 4g | sugars: 2g | fiber: 2g | sodium: 60mg

Brussels Sprouts with Pecans and Gorgonzola

Prep time: 10 minutes | Cook time: 25 minutes | Serves 4

- ½ cup pecans
- 1½ pounds (680 g) fresh Brussels sprouts, trimmed and quartered
- 2 tablespoons olive oil
- Salt and freshly ground black pepper, to taste
- ¼ cup crumbled Gorgonzola cheese

1. Spread the pecans in a single layer in the air fryer basket and set the heat to 350°F (177°C). Air fry for 3 to 5 minutes until the pecans are lightly browned and fragrant. Transfer the pecans to a plate and continue preheating the air fryer, increasing the heat to 400°F (204°C). 2. In a large bowl, toss the Brussels sprouts with olive oil and season with salt and black pepper to taste. 3. Working in batches if necessary, arrange the Brussels sprouts in a single layer in the air fryer basket. Pause halfway through the baking time to shake the basket. 4. Air fry the Brussels sprouts for 20 to 25 minutes until they are tender and starting to brown on the edges. 5. Transfer the cooked Brussels sprouts to a serving bowl and top with the toasted pecans and Gorgonzola cheese.

Per Serving:
calorie: 280 | fat: 22g | protein: 8g | carbs: 17g | sugars: 5g | fiber: 7g | sodium: 310mg

Roasted Garlic

Prep time: 5 minutes | Cook time: 20 minutes | Makes 12 cloves

- 1 medium head garlic
- 2 teaspoons avocado oil

1. Begin by preparing the garlic. Remove any loose outer layers of peel, ensuring the cloves remain covered. Cut off the top ¼ of the head of garlic to expose the tips of the cloves. This will help the garlic roast evenly and release its flavors. 2. Drizzle the exposed garlic cloves with avocado oil, ensuring they are well coated. Wrap the garlic head completely in a small sheet of aluminum foil to seal it securely. Place the wrapped garlic head into the air fryer basket. 3. Set the air fryer temperature to 400°F (204°C) and air fry the garlic for 20 minutes. If your garlic head is smaller, check it after 15 minutes to avoid overcooking. 4. After cooking, the garlic should be golden brown and very soft, indicating it's fully roasted and flavorful. 5. To serve, simply squeeze the roasted garlic head gently to release the softened cloves. The cloves should pop out easily and can be spread or sliced as desired. Store any leftover roasted garlic in an airtight container in the refrigerator for up to 5 days. Alternatively, freeze individual cloves on a baking sheet before transferring them to a freezer-safe storage bag once frozen, ensuring they stay fresh for longer.

Per Serving:
calories: 20 | fat: 2g | protein: 0g | carbs: 0g | sugars: 0g | fiber: 0g | sodium: 0mg

Callaloo Redux

Prep time: 15 minutes | Cook time: 25 minutes | Serves 6

- 3 cups store-bought low-sodium vegetable broth
- 1 (13½ ounces) can light coconut milk
- ¼ cup coconut cream
- 1 tablespoon unsalted non-hydrogenated plant-based butter
- 12 ounces okra, cut into 1-inch chunks
- 1 small onion, chopped
- ½ butternut squash, peeled, seeded, and cut into 4-inch chunks
- 1 bunch collard greens, stemmed and chopped
- 1 hot pepper (Scotch bonnet or habanero)

1. In your electric pressure cooker, combine vegetable broth, coconut milk, coconut cream, and butter. 2. Layer okra, onion, squash, collard greens, and a whole hot pepper on top of the liquid mixture. 3. Close and lock the lid of the pressure cooker, ensuring the pressure valve is set to sealing. 4. Select the Manual/Pressure Cook setting and cook for 20 minutes. 5. After cooking, perform a quick-release of the pressure. Carefully remove the lid. 6. Discard the hot pepper. Transfer the contents of the pressure cooker to a blender and blend until smooth. 7. Serve the callaloo over grits and enjoy!

Per Serving:
calories: 258 | fat: 21g | protein: 5g | carbs: 17g | sugars: 8g | fiber: 5g | sodium: 88mg

Cauliflower Hush Puppies

Prep time: 15 minutes | Cook time: 10 minutes | Makes 16

- 1 whole cauliflower, including stalks and florets, roughly chopped
- ¾ cup buttermilk
- ¾ cup low-fat milk
- 1 medium onion, chopped
- 2 medium eggs
- 2 cups yellow cornmeal
- 1½ teaspoons baking powder
- ½ teaspoon salt

1. Start by blending cauliflower, buttermilk, milk, and onion in a blender until smooth. Transfer this mixture to a large mixing bowl. 2. Crack the eggs into the cauliflower purée and gently fold them in until well combined. 3. In a separate medium bowl, whisk together cornmeal, baking powder, and salt. 4. Gradually add the dry ingredients to the wet mixture, stirring until just combined. Be careful not to overmix. 5. Working in batches, scoop ⅓-cup portions of the batter into the basket of an air fryer. 6. Set the air fryer temperature to 390°F (199°C), close the lid, and cook the hush puppies for 10 minutes until golden brown and cooked through. Transfer them to a plate and repeat until all batter is used. 7. Serve the hush puppies warm, accompanied with greens if desired.

Per Serving:
calories: 133 | fat: 2g | protein: 6g | carbs: 24g | sugars: 3g | fiber: 3g | sodium: 276mg

Chapter 8 Vegetables and Sides

Balsamic Green Beans and Fennel

Prep time: 20 minutes | Cook time: 18 minutes | Serves 4

- 2 teaspoons olive or canola oil
- 1 medium bulb fennel, cut into thin wedges
- 1 small onion, cut into thin wedges
- 2 cups frozen whole green beans
- ¼ cup water
- 2 teaspoons packed brown sugar
- ¼ teaspoon salt
- ¼ teaspoon freshly ground pepper
- 1 tablespoon balsamic vinegar

1. Heat oil in a 12-inch nonstick skillet over medium heat. Add fennel and onion, and cook for 7 to 8 minutes, stirring frequently, until the fennel is lightly golden brown. 2. Add beans and water to the skillet. Bring to a boil, then reduce heat to low. Cover and simmer for 6 to 8 minutes, or until the beans are crisp-tender. 3. Stir in the remaining ingredients and cook, stirring continuously, for 15 to 30 seconds more until the vegetables are well coated with the sauce. Serve the dish immediately.

Per Serving:
calorie: 80 | fat: 3g | protein: 1g | carbs: 13g | sugars: 6g | fiber: 4g | sodium: 180mg

Asparagus-Pepper Stir-Fry

Prep time: 25 minutes | Cook time: 5 minutes | Serves 4

- 1 pound fresh asparagus spears
- 1 teaspoon canola oil
- 1 medium red, yellow or orange bell pepper, cut into ¾-inch pieces
- 2 cloves garlic, finely chopped
- 1 tablespoon orange juice
- 1 tablespoon reduced-sodium soy sauce
- ½ teaspoon ground ginger

1. Snap off the tough ends of the asparagus where they naturally break, ensuring they are tender and easy to snap. Cut the asparagus into 1-inch pieces to prepare them for cooking. 2. Heat oil in a 10-inch nonstick skillet or wok over medium heat until it shimmers and coats the pan evenly. Add the asparagus pieces, diced bell pepper, and minced garlic to the skillet. Stir continuously and cook for 3 to 4 minutes, or until the vegetables are crisp-tender. 3. In a small bowl, combine orange juice, soy sauce, and grated ginger until well blended. Pour this mixture into the skillet with the asparagus and other vegetables. Cook and stir for 15 to 30 seconds more, ensuring all the vegetables are coated evenly with the sauce. This quick cooking time allows the flavors to meld while preserving the crisp texture of the vegetables.

Per Serving:
calorie: 40 | fat: 1.5g | protein: 2g | carbs: 6g | sugars: 3g | fiber: 2g | sodium: 135mg

Chipotle Twice-Baked Sweet Potatoes

Prep time: 20 minutes | Cook time: 1 hour | Serves 4

- 4 small sweet potatoes (about 1¾ pounds)
- ¼ cup fat-free half-and-half
- 1 chipotle chile in adobo sauce (from 7 ounces can), finely chopped
- 1 teaspoon adobo sauce (from can of chipotle chiles)
- ½ teaspoon salt
- 8 teaspoons reduced-fat sour cream
- 4 teaspoons chopped fresh cilantro

1. Heat oven to 375°F. Gently scrub potatoes but do not peel. Pierce potatoes several times with fork to allow steam to escape while potatoes bake. Bake about 45 minutes or until potatoes are tender when pierced in center with a fork. 2. When potatoes are cool enough to handle, cut lengthwise down through center of potato to within ½ inch of ends and bottom. Carefully scoop out inside, leaving thin shell. In medium bowl, mash potatoes, half-and-half, chile, adobo sauce and salt with potato masher or electric mixer on low speed until light and fluffy. 3. Increase oven temperature to 400°F. In 13x9-inch pan, place potato shells. Divide potato mixture evenly among shells. Bake uncovered 20 minutes or until potato mixture is golden brown and heated through. 4. Just before serving, top each potato with 2 teaspoons sour cream and 1 teaspoon cilantro.

Per Serving:
calorie: 140 | fat: 1g | protein: 3g | carbs: 27g | sugars: 9g | fiber: 4g | sodium: 400mg

Chapter 9
Vegetarian Mains

Chapter 9 Vegetarian Mains

Black-Eyed Pea Sauté with Garlic and Olives

Prep time: 5 minutes | Cook time: 5 minutes | Serves 2

- 2 teaspoons extra-virgin olive oil
- 1 garlic clove, minced
- ½ red onion, chopped
- 1 cup cooked black-eyed peas; if canned, drain and rinse
- ½ teaspoon dried thyme
- ¼ cup water
- ¼ teaspoon salt
- ¼ teaspoon freshly ground black pepper
- 6 Kalamata olives, pitted and halved

1. Heat olive oil in a medium saucepan over medium heat. Add garlic and red onion, stirring constantly, and cook for 2 minutes until fragrant and softened. 2. Add black-eyed peas and thyme to the saucepan. Cook for 1 minute, stirring to combine flavors. 3. Stir in water, salt, pepper, and olives. Continue cooking for an additional 2 minutes, or until the mixture is heated through and flavors are well blended. Serve hot.

Per Serving:
calories: 140 | fat: 6g | protein: 5g | carbs: 18g | sugars: 8g | fiber: 5g | sodium: 426mg

Sautéed Spinach and Lima Beans

Prep time: 5 minutes | Cook time: 40 minutes | Serves 2

- Extra-virgin olive oil cooking spray
- ¼ cup chopped onion
- ½ cup low-sodium vegetable broth
- 1 cup frozen lima beans, thawed
- 2 teaspoons extra-virgin olive oil
- 2 garlic cloves, chopped
- 4 cups chopped fresh spinach
- Pinch cayenne pepper
- 2 teaspoons balsamic vinegar
- Salt, to season
- Freshly ground black pepper, to season

1. Heat a large saucepan over medium heat. Spray with cooking spray. 2. Add the onion. Sauté for about 4 minutes, or until soft and translucent. 3. Add the vegetable broth. Bring to a boil. 4. Add the lima beans and just enough water to cover. Bring to a boil. Reduce the heat to low. Cover and simmer for 30 minutes, or until the beans are tender. Set aside. 5. Heat a large skillet over medium-high heat for 30 seconds. 6. Add the olive oil and garlic. Sauté for 1 to 2 minutes, or until golden. Remove the garlic and reserve. 7. To the skillet, add the spinach and cayenne. Cover and cook for about 1 minute, or until the leaves wilt. Drain to remove any excess water. 8. Stir in the balsamic vinegar. Season with salt and pepper. 9. To serve, mound half of the spinach on a plate, top with half of the lima beans, and sprinkle with the reserved garlic.

Per Serving:
calories: 201 | fat: 7g | protein: 9g | carbs: 29g | sugars: 3g | fiber: 7g | sodium: 418mg

Vegetable Burgers

Prep time: 10 minutes | Cook time: 12 minutes | Serves 4

- 8 ounces (227 g) cremini mushrooms
- 2 large egg yolks
- ½ medium zucchini, trimmed and chopped
- ¼ cup peeled and chopped yellow onion
- 1 clove garlic, peeled and finely minced
- ½ teaspoon salt
- ¼ teaspoon ground black pepper

1. Start by placing all ingredients into a food processor. Pulse the ingredients about twenty times until they are finely chopped and well combined. 2. Divide the mixture into four equal sections and shape each portion into a burger patty. Place the patties into the ungreased air fryer basket. Adjust the air fryer temperature to 375ºF (191ºC) and air fry the burgers for 12 minutes, flipping them halfway through cooking. The burgers should be browned and firm when done. 3. Transfer the cooked burgers to a large plate and allow them to cool for 5 minutes before serving.

Per Serving:
calories: 77 | fat: 5g | protein: 3g | carbs: 6g | sugars: 2g | fiber: 1g | sodium: 309mg

Chickpea Coconut Curry

Prep time: 5 minutes | Cook time: 15 minutes | Serves 4

- 3 cups fresh or frozen cauliflower florets
- 2 cups unsweetened almond milk
- 1 (15 ounces) can coconut milk
- 1 (15 ounces) can low-sodium chickpeas, drained and rinsed
- 1 tablespoon curry powder
- ¼ teaspoon ground ginger
- ¼ teaspoon garlic powder
- ⅛ teaspoon onion powder
- ¼ teaspoon salt

1. In a large stockpot, combine cauliflower, almond milk, coconut milk, chickpeas, curry powder, ginger, garlic powder, and onion powder. Stir to combine, then cover the pot. 2. Cook the mixture over medium-high heat for 10 minutes. 3. Reduce the heat to low, uncover the pot, and stir. Continue cooking for an additional 5 minutes. 4. Season with up to ¼ teaspoon of salt, adjusting to taste.

Per Serving:
calories: 225 | fat: 7g | protein: 12g | carbs: 31g | sugars: 14g | fiber: 9g | sodium: 489mg

Greek Stuffed Eggplant

Prep time: 15 minutes | Cook time: 20 minutes | Serves 2

- 1 large eggplant
- 2 tablespoons unsalted butter
- ¼ medium yellow onion, diced
- ¼ cup chopped artichoke hearts
- 1 cup fresh spinach
- 2 tablespoons diced red bell pepper
- ½ cup crumbled feta

1. Slice eggplant in half lengthwise and scoop out flesh, leaving enough inside for shell to remain intact. Take eggplant that was scooped out, chop it, and set aside. 2. In a medium skillet over medium heat, add butter and onion. Sauté until onions begin to soften, about 3 to 5 minutes. Add chopped eggplant, artichokes, spinach, and bell pepper. Continue cooking 5 minutes until peppers soften and spinach wilts. Remove from the heat and gently fold in the feta. 3. Place filling into each eggplant shell and place into the air fryer basket. 4. Adjust the temperature to 320°F (160°C) and air fry for 20 minutes. 5. Eggplant will be tender when done. Serve warm.

Per Serving:
calories: 259 | fat: 16g | protein: 10g | carbs: 22g | sugars: 12g | fiber: 10g | sodium: 386mg

Asparagus, Sun-Dried Tomato, and Green Pea Sauté

Prep time: 10 minutes | Cook time: 10 minutes | Serves 2

- 6 packaged sun-dried tomatoes (not packed in oil)
- ½ cup boiling water
- 1 tablespoon extra-virgin olive oil
- 2 garlic cloves, minced
- ¾ pound fresh asparagus, trimmed and cut into 2-inch pieces
- ¼ cup chopped red bell pepper
- ½ cup sliced fresh button mushrooms
- ¼ cup reduced-sodium vegetable broth
- 2 tablespoons sliced almonds
- 1 large tomato, diced (about 1 cup)
- 1½ teaspoons dried tarragon
- ½ cup frozen peas
- Freshly ground black pepper, to season

1. In a small heatproof bowl, place the sun-dried tomatoes. Cover with the boiling water. Set aside. 2. In a large skillet or wok set over high heat, heat the olive oil. 3. Add the garlic. Swirl in the oil for a few seconds. 4. Toss in the asparagus, red bell pepper, and mushrooms. Stir-fry for 30 seconds. 5. Add the vegetable broth and almonds. Cover and steam for about 2 minutes. Uncover the skillet. 6. Add the tomato and tarragon. Cook for 2 to 3 minutes to reduce the liquid. 7. Drain and chop the sun-dried tomatoes. Add them and the peas to the skillet. Stir-fry for 3 to 4 minutes, or until the vegetables are crisp-tender and the liquid is reduced to a sauce. 8. Season with pepper and serve immediately.

Per Serving:
calories: 165 | fat: 8g | protein: 8g | carbs: 20g | sugars: 9g | fiber: 7g | sodium: 46mg

Cheesy Zucchini Patties

Prep time: 10 minutes | Cook time: 20 minutes | Serves 2

- 1 cup grated zucchini
- 1 cup chopped fresh mushrooms
- ½ cup grated carrot
- ½ cup nonfat shredded mozzarella cheese
- ¼ cup finely ground flaxseed
- 1 large egg, beaten
- 1 garlic clove, minced
- Salt, to season
- Freshly ground black pepper, to season
- 1 tablespoon extra-virgin olive oil
- 4 cup mixed baby greens, divided

1. In a medium bowl, stir together the zucchini, mushrooms, carrot, mozzarella cheese, flaxseed, egg, and garlic. Season with salt and pepper. Stir again to combine. 2. In a large skillet set over medium-high heat, heat the olive oil. 3. Drop 1 tablespoon of the zucchini mixture into the skillet. Continue dropping tablespoon-size portions in the pan until it is full, but not crowded. Cook for 2 to 3 minutes on each side, or until golden. Transfer to a serving plate. Repeat with the remaining mixture. 4. Place 2 cups of greens on each serving plate. Top each with zucchini patties. 5. Enjoy!

Per Serving:
calories: 252 | fat: 15g | protein: 19g | carbs: 14g | sugars: 4g | fiber: 9g | sodium: 644mg

Veggie Fajitas

Prep time: 10 minutes | Cook time: 15 minutes | Serves 4

For The Guacamole
- 2 small avocados pitted and peeled
- 1 teaspoon freshly squeezed lime juice
- ¼ teaspoon salt
- 9 cherry tomatoes, halved

For The Fajitas
- 1 red bell pepper
- 1 green bell pepper
- 1 small white onion
- Avocado oil cooking spray
- 1 cup canned low-sodium black beans, drained and rinsed
- ½ teaspoon ground cumin
- ¼ teaspoon chili powder
- ¼ teaspoon garlic powder
- 4 (6-inch) yellow corn tortillas

To Make The Guacamole 1. In a medium bowl, use a fork to mash the avocados with the lime juice and salt. 2. Gently stir in the cherry tomatoes. To Make The Fajitas 1. Cut the red bell pepper, green bell pepper, and onion into ½-inch slices. 2. Heat a large skillet over medium heat. When hot, coat the cooking surface with cooking spray. Put the peppers, onion, and beans into the skillet. 3. Add the cumin, chili powder, and garlic powder, and stir. 4. Cover and cook for 15 minutes, stirring halfway through. 5. Divide the fajita mixture equally between the tortillas, and top with guacamole and any preferred garnishes.

Per Serving:
calories: 269 | fat: 15g | protein: 8g | carbs: 30g | sugars: 5g | fiber: 11g | sodium: 175mg

Chapter 9 Vegetarian Mains

The Ultimate Veggie Burger

Prep time: 5 minutes | Cook time: 10 minutes | Serves 2

- ¾ cup shelled edamame
- ¾ cup frozen mixed vegetables, thawed
- 3 tablespoons hemp hearts
- 2 tablespoons quick-cook oatmeal
- ¼ teaspoon salt
- ¼ teaspoon onion powder
- ¼ teaspoon ground cumin
- 1 scallion, sliced
- 2 teaspoons chopped fresh cilantro
- 2 tablespoons coconut flour
- 2 large egg whites
- Extra-virgin olive oil cooking spray

1. In a food processor, combine the edamame, mixed vegetables, hemp hearts, oatmeal, salt, onion powder, cumin, scallion, cilantro, coconut flour, and egg whites. Pulse until blended, but not completely puréed. You want some texture. 2. Spray a nonstick skillet with cooking spray. Place it over medium-high heat. 3. Spoon half of the mixture into the pan. Using the back of a spoon, spread it out to form a patty. Repeat with the remaining half of the mixture. 4. Cook for 3 to 5 minutes, or until golden, and flip. Cook for about 3 minutes more, or until golden. Turn off the heat. 5. Transfer to serving plates and enjoy!

Per Serving:
calories: 154 | fat: 4g | protein: 13g | carbs: 19g | sugars: 4g | fiber: 7g | sodium: 467mg

No-Bake Spaghetti Squash Casserole

Prep time: 10 minutes | Cook time: 45 minutes | Serves 6

- Marinara
- 3 tablespoons extra-virgin olive oil
- 3 garlic cloves, minced
- One 28-ounce can whole San Marzano tomatoes and their liquid
- 2 teaspoons Italian seasoning
- 1 teaspoon fine sea salt
- ½ teaspoon red pepper flakes (optional)
- Vegan Parmesan
- ½ cup raw whole cashews
- 2 tablespoons nutritional yeast
- ½ teaspoon garlic powder
- ½ teaspoon fine sea salt
- Vegan Ricotta
- One 14-ounce package firm tofu, drained
- ½ cup raw whole cashews, soaked in water to cover for 1 to 2 hours and then drained
- 3 tablespoons nutritional yeast
- 2 tablespoons extra-virgin olive oil
- 1 teaspoon finely grated lemon zest, plus 2 tablespoons fresh lemon juice
- ½ cup firmly packed fresh flat-leaf parsley leaves
- 1½ teaspoons Italian seasoning
- 1 teaspoon garlic powder
- 1 teaspoon fine sea salt
- ½ teaspoon freshly ground black pepper
- One 3½-pound steamed spaghetti squash
- 2 tablespoons chopped fresh flat-leaf parsley

1. To make the marinara: Select the Sauté setting on the Instant Pot and heat the oil and garlic for about 2 minutes, until the garlic is bubbling but not browned. Add the tomatoes and their liquid and use a wooden spoon or spatula to crush the tomatoes against the side of the pot. Stir in the Italian seasoning, salt, and pepper flakes (if using) and cook, stirring occasionally, for about 10 minutes, until the sauce has thickened a bit. Press the Cancel button to turn off the pot and let the sauce cook from the residual heat for about 5 minutes more, until it is no longer simmering. Wearing heat-resistant mitts, lift the pot out of the housing, pour the sauce into a medium heatproof bowl, and set aside. (You can make the sauce up to 4 days in advance, then let it cool, transfer it to an airtight container, and refrigerate.) 2. To make the vegan Parmesan: In a food processor, combine the cashews, nutritional yeast, garlic powder, and salt. Using 1-second pulses, pulse about ten times, until the mixture resembles grated Parmesan cheese. Transfer to a small bowl and set aside. Do not wash the food processor bowl and blade. 3. To make the vegan ricotta: Cut the tofu crosswise into eight ½-inch-thick slices. Sandwich the slices between double layers of paper towels or a folded kitchen towel and press gently to remove excess moisture. Add the tofu to the food processor along with the cashews, nutritional yeast, oil, lemon zest, lemon juice, parsley, Italian seasoning, garlic powder, salt, and pepper. Process for about 1 minute, until the mixture is mostly smooth with flecks of parsley throughout. Set aside. 4. Return the marinara to the pot. Select the Sauté setting and heat the marinara sauce for about 3 minutes, until it starts to simmer. Add the spaghetti squash and vegan ricotta to the pot and stir to combine. Continue to heat, stirring often, for 8 to 10 minutes, until piping hot. Press the Cancel button to turn off the pot. 5. Spoon the spaghetti squash into bowls, top with the vegan Parmesan and parsley, and serve right away.

Per Serving:
calorie: 307 | fat: 17g | protein: 16g | carbs: 25g | sugars: 2g | fiber: 5g | sodium: 985mg

Orange Tofu

Prep time: 10 minutes | Cook time: 20 minutes | Serves 4

- ⅓ cup freshly squeezed orange juice (zest orange first; see orange zest ingredient below)
- 1 tablespoon tamari
- 1 tablespoon tahini
- ½ tablespoon coconut nectar or pure maple syrup
- 2 tablespoons apple cider vinegar
- ½ tablespoon freshly grated ginger
- 1 large clove garlic, grated
- ½–1 teaspoon orange zest
- ¼ teaspoon sea salt
- Few pinches of crushed red-pepper flakes (optional)
- 1 package (12 ounces) extra-firm tofu, sliced into ¼"–½" thick squares and patted to remove excess moisture

1. Preheat the oven to 400°F. 2. In a small bowl, combine the orange juice, tamari, tahini, nectar or syrup, vinegar, ginger, garlic, orange zest, salt, and red pepper flakes (if using). Whisk until well combined. 3. Pour the sauce into an 8" x 12" baking dish. 4. Add the tofu and turn to coat both sides. 5. Bake for 20 minutes. 6. Add salt to taste.

Per Serving:
calorie: 122 | fat: 7g | protein: 10g | carbs: 7g | sugars: 4g | fiber: 1g | sodium: 410mg

Grilled Vegetables on White Bean Mash

Prep time: 15 minutes | Cook time: 30 minutes | Serves 2

- 2 medium zucchini, sliced
- 1 red bell pepper, seeded and quartered
- 2 portobello mushroom caps, quartered
- 3 teaspoons extra-virgin olive oil, divided
- 1 (8-ounce) can cannellini beans, drained and rinsed
- 1 garlic clove, minced
- ½ cup low-sodium vegetable broth
- 4 cups baby spinach, divided
- Salt, to season
- Freshly ground black pepper, to season
- 1 tablespoon chopped fresh parsley
- 2 lemon wedges, divided, for garnish

1. Preheat the grill. Use a stove-top grill pan or broiler if a grill is not available. 2. Lightly brush the zucchini, red bell pepper, and mushrooms with 1½ teaspoons of olive oil. Arrange them in a barbecue grill pan. Place the pan on the preheated grill. Cook the vegetables for 5 to 8 minutes, or until lightly browned. Turn the vegetables. Brush with the remaining 1½ teaspoons of olive oil. Cook for 5 to 8 minutes more, or until tender. 3. To a small pan set over high heat, add the cannellini beans, garlic, and vegetable broth. Bring to a boil. Reduce the heat to low. Simmer for 10 minutes, uncovered. Using a potato masher, roughly mash the beans, adding a little more broth if they seem too dry. 4. Place 2 cups of spinach on each serving plate. 5. Top each with half of the bean mash and half of the grilled vegetables. Season with salt and pepper. Garnish with parsley. 6. Place 1 lemon wedge on each plate and serve.

Per Serving:
calories: 290 | fat: 9g | protein: 11g | carbs:29 g | sugars: 8g | fiber: 4g | sodium: 398mg

Stuffed Peppers

Prep time: 20 minutes | Cook time: 50 minutes | Serves 2

- ½ cup water
- ¼ cup uncooked quinoa, thoroughly rinsed
- 1 tablespoon extra-virgin olive oil
- 1 garlic clove, minced
- 6 ounces extra-firm tofu, drained and sliced
- ½ cup marinara sauce, divided
- ¼ cup finely chopped walnuts
- 1 teaspoon dried basil
- Salt, to season
- Freshly ground black pepper, to season
- 1 red bell pepper, halved and seeded
- 1 orange bell pepper, halved and seeded
- ½ cup nonfat shredded mozzarella cheese, divided
- 4 tomato slices, divided

1. Preheat the oven to 350°F. 2. In a small pot set over high heat, bring the water to a boil. 3. Add the quinoa. Reduce the heat to low. Cover and simmer for about 15 minutes, or until tender and all the water is absorbed. Let cool. Fluff with a fork. Set aside. 4. In a skillet set over medium heat, stir together the olive oil, garlic, and tofu. Cook for about 5 minutes, or until the tofu is evenly brown. 5. Mix in ¼ cup of marinara, the walnuts, and basil. Season with salt and pepper. Cook for 5 minutes more, stirring. 6. Using a wooden spoon or spatula, press one-quarter of the cooked quinoa into each pepper half. 7. Top each with about 1 tablespoon of the remaining ¼ cup of marinara. 8. Sprinkle each with about 1 tablespoon of mozzarella cheese. 9. Place 1 tomato slice on each filled pepper. 10. Finish with about 1 tablespoon of the remaining ¼ cup of mozzarella cheese. 11. Transfer the stuffed peppers to a baking dish. Place the dish in the preheated oven. Bake for 25 minutes, or until the cheese melts. 12. Serve 1 stuffed red bell pepper half and 1 stuffed orange bell pepper half to each person and enjoy!

Per Serving:
calories: 399 | fat: 21g | protein: 25g | carbs: 33g | sugars: 7g | fiber: 6g | sodium: 535mg

Crispy Cabbage Steaks

Prep time: 5 minutes | Cook time: 10 minutes | Serves 4

- 1 small head green cabbage, cored and cut into ½-inch-thick slices
- ¼ teaspoon salt
- ¼ teaspoon ground black pepper
- 2 tablespoons olive oil
- 1 clove garlic, peeled and finely minced
- ½ teaspoon dried thyme
- ½ teaspoon dried parsley

1. Sprinkle each side of the cabbage with salt and pepper. Place the cabbage into the ungreased air fryer basket, working in batches if necessary. 2. Drizzle each side of the cabbage with olive oil. Sprinkle the remaining ingredients evenly over both sides. 3. Adjust the air fryer temperature to 350°F (177°C) and air fry for 10 minutes, flipping the cabbage "steaks" halfway through the cooking time. 4. The cabbage should be browned at the edges and tender when done. 5. Serve the cabbage steaks warm.

Per Serving:
calorie: 90 | fat: 7g | protein: 2g | carbs: 7g | sugars: 3g | fiber: 3g | sodium: 170mg

Stuffed Portobello Mushrooms

Prep time: 5 minutes | Cook time: 20 minutes | Serves 4

- 8 large portobello mushrooms
- 3 teaspoons extra-virgin olive oil, divided
- 4 cups fresh spinach
- 1 medium red bell pepper, diced
- ¼ cup crumbled feta

1. Preheat the oven to 450°F. 2. Remove the stems from the mushrooms, and gently scoop out the gills and discard. Coat the mushrooms with 2 teaspoons of olive oil. 3. On a baking sheet, place the mushrooms cap-side down, and roast for 20 minutes. 4. Meanwhile, heat the remaining 1 teaspoon of olive oil in a medium skillet over medium heat. When hot, sauté the spinach and red bell pepper for 8 to 10 minutes, stirring occasionally. 5. Remove the mushrooms from the oven. Drain, if necessary. Spoon the spinach and pepper mix into the mushrooms, and top with feta.

Per Serving:
calories: 91 | fat: 4g | protein: 6g | carbs: 10g | sugars: 3g | fiber: 4g | sodium: 155mg

Roasted Veggie Bowl

Prep time: 10 minutes | Cook time: 15 minutes | Serves 2

- 1 cup broccoli florets
- 1 cup quartered Brussels sprouts
- ½ cup cauliflower florets
- ¼ medium white onion, peeled and sliced ¼ inch thick
- ½ medium green bell pepper, seeded and sliced ¼ inch thick
- 1 tablespoon coconut oil
- 2 teaspoons chili powder
- ½ teaspoon garlic powder
- ½ teaspoon cumin

1. In a large bowl, toss all ingredients together until the vegetables are thoroughly coated with oil and seasoning. 2. Transfer the vegetables into the air fryer basket. 3. Adjust the temperature to 360°F (182°C) and roast for 15 minutes. 4. Shake the basket two or three times during cooking to ensure even roasting. 5. Serve the roasted vegetables warm.

Per Serving:
calories: 112 | fat: 8g | protein: 4g | carbs: 11g | sugars: 3g | fiber: 5g | sodium: 106mg

Italian Tofu with Mushrooms and Peppers

Prep time: 5 minutes | Cook time: 10 minutes | Serves 2

- 1 teaspoon extra-virgin olive oil
- ¼ cup chopped bell pepper, any color
- ¼ cup chopped onions
- 1 garlic clove, minced
- 8 ounces firm tofu, drained and rinsed
- ½ cup sliced fresh button mushrooms
- 1 portobello mushroom cap, chopped
- 1 tablespoon balsamic vinegar
- 1 teaspoon dried basil
- Salt, to season
- Freshly ground black pepper, to season

1. Heat olive oil in a medium skillet over medium heat until it shimmers. Add bell pepper, onions, and garlic. Sauté for about 5 minutes, stirring occasionally, until the vegetables are soft. 2. Add tofu, button mushrooms, and portobello mushrooms to the skillet. Toss and stir everything together thoroughly. Reduce the heat to low to maintain a gentle simmer. 3. Stir in balsamic vinegar and sprinkle fresh basil over the mixture. Season with salt and pepper to taste. Stir well to blend all the flavors. 4. Let the dish simmer gently for 2 minutes, allowing the ingredients to meld together.

Per Serving:
calories: 142 | fat: 8g | protein: 13g | carbs: 9g | sugars: 4g | fiber: 2g | sodium: 326mg

Tofu and Bean Chili

Prep time: 10 minutes | Cook time 30 minutes | Serves 4

- 1 (15 ounces) can low-sodium dark red kidney beans, drained and rinsed, divided
- 2 (15 ounces) cans no-salt-added diced tomatoes
- 1½ cups low-sodium vegetable broth
- ½ teaspoon chili powder
- ½ teaspoon ground cumin
- ½ teaspoon garlic powder
- ½ teaspoon dried oregano
- ¼ teaspoon onion powder
- ¼ teaspoon salt
- 8 ounces extra-firm tofu

1. In a small bowl, mash ⅓ of the beans using a fork. 2. Transfer the mashed beans, along with the remaining whole beans and diced tomatoes (including their juices), into a large stockpot. 3. Stir in the broth, chili powder, cumin, garlic powder, dried oregano, onion powder, and salt. Bring the mixture to a simmer over medium-high heat and cook for 15 minutes. 4. Meanwhile, press the tofu between 3 or 4 layers of paper towels to remove excess moisture. 5. Crumble the tofu into the stockpot and stir well to combine. Simmer for an additional 10 to 15 minutes to allow flavors to meld together.

Per Serving:
calories: 207 | fat: 5g | protein: 15g | carbs: 31g | sugars: 11g | fiber: 12g | sodium: 376mg

Edamame Falafel with Roasted Vegetables

Prep time: 10 minutes | Cook time: 55 minutes | Serves 2

For the roasted vegetables
- 1 cup broccoli florets
- 1 medium zucchini, sliced
- ½ cup cherry tomatoes, halved
- 1½ teaspoons extra-virgin olive oil

For the falafel
- 1 cup frozen shelled edamame, thawed
- 1 small onion, chopped
- 1 garlic clove, chopped
- 1 tablespoon freshly squeezed lemon juice
- 2 tablespoons hemp hearts
- 1 teaspoon ground cumin
- Salt, to season
- Freshly ground black pepper, to season
- Extra-virgin olive oil cooking spray

- 2 tablespoons oat flour
- ¼ teaspoon salt
- Pinch freshly ground black pepper
- 2 tablespoons extra-virgin olive oil, divided
- Prepared hummus, for serving (optional)

To make the roasted vegetables 1. Preheat the oven to 425°F. 2. In a large bowl, toss together the broccoli, zucchini, tomatoes, and olive oil to coat. Season with salt and pepper. 3. Spray a baking sheet with cooking spray. 4. Spread the vegetables evenly atop the sheet. Place the sheet in the preheated oven. Roast for 35 to 40 minutes, stirring every 15 minutes, or until the vegetables are soft and cooked through. 5. Remove from the oven. Set aside. To make the falafel 1. In a food processor, pulse the edamame until coarsely ground. 2. Add the onion, garlic, lemon juice, and hemp hearts. Process until finely ground. Transfer the mixture to a medium bowl. 3. By hand, mix in the cumin, oat flour, salt, and pepper. 4. Roll the dough into 1-inch balls. Flatten slightly. You should have about 12 silver dollar–size patties. 5. In a large skillet set over medium heat, heat 1 tablespoon of olive oil. 6. Add 4 falafel patties to the pan at a time (or as many as will fit without crowding), and cook for about 3 minutes on each side, or until lightly browned. Remove from the pan. Repeat with the remaining 1 tablespoon of olive oil and falafel patties. 7. Serve immediately with the roasted vegetables and hummus (if using) and enjoy!

Per Serving:
calories: 316 | fat: 22g | protein: 12g | carbs: 21g | sugars: 4g | fiber: 6g | sodium: 649mg

Gingered Tofu and Greens

Prep time: 15 minutes | Cook time: 20 minutes | Serves 2

For the marinade
- 2 tablespoons low-sodium soy sauce
- ¼ cup rice vinegar
- ⅓ cup water
- 1 tablespoon grated fresh ginger

For the tofu and greens
- 8 ounces extra-firm tofu, drained, cut into 1-inch cubes
- 3 teaspoons extra-virgin olive oil, divided
- 1 tablespoon grated fresh ginger
- 2 cups coarsely shredded bok choy
- 2 cups coarsely shredded kale, thoroughly washed
- 1 tablespoon coconut flour
- 1 teaspoon granulated stevia
- 1 garlic clove, minced

- ½ cup fresh, or frozen, chopped green beans
- 1 tablespoon freshly squeezed lime juice
- 1 tablespoon chopped fresh cilantro
- 2 tablespoons hemp hearts

To make the marinade 1. In a small bowl, whisk together the soy sauce, rice vinegar, water, ginger, coconut flour, stevia, and garlic until well combined. 2. Place a small saucepan set over high heat. Add the marinade. Bring to a boil. Cook for 1 minute. Remove from the heat. To make the tofu and greens 1. In a medium ovenproof pan, place the tofu in a single layer. Pour the marinade over. Drizzle with 1½ teaspoons of olive oil. Let sit for 5 minutes. 2. Preheat the broiler to high. 3. Place the pan under the broiler. Broil the tofu for 7 to 8 minutes, or until lightly browned. Using a spatula, turn the tofu over. Continue to broil for 7 to 8 minutes more, or until browned on this side. 4. In a large wok or skillet set over high heat, heat the remaining 1½ teaspoons of olive oil. 5. Stir in the ginger. 6. Add the bok choy, kale, and green beans. Cook for 2 to 3 minutes, stirring constantly, until the greens wilt. 7. Add the lime juice and cilantro. Remove from the heat. 8. Add the browned tofu with any remaining marinade in the pan to the bok choy, kale, and green beans. Toss gently to combine. 9. Top with the hemp hearts and serve immediately.

Per Serving:
calories: 252 | fat: 14g | protein: 15g | carbs: 20g | sugars: 4g | fiber: 3g | sodium: 679mg

Chapter 10 Salads

Chapter 10 Salads

Chicken, Spinach, and Berry Salad

Prep time: 5 minutes | Cook time: 0 minutes | Serves 4

For The Salad
- 8 cups baby spinach
- 2 cups shredded rotisserie chicken
- ½ cup sliced strawberries or other berries

For The Dressing
- 2 tablespoons extra-virgin olive oil
- 2 teaspoons honey
- ½ cup sliced almonds
- 1 avocado, sliced
- ¼ cup crumbled feta (optional)
- 2 teaspoons balsamic vinegar

To Make The Salad: 1. In a large bowl, combine spinach, chicken, strawberries, and almonds. 2. Pour the dressing over the salad and toss gently to coat. 3. Divide the salad into four equal portions. Top each portion with sliced avocado and 1 tablespoon of crumbled feta cheese, if desired. To Make The Dressing: 4. In a small bowl, whisk together olive oil, honey, and balsamic vinegar until well combined.

Per Serving:
calorie: 341 | fat: 22g | protein: 26g | carbs: 14g | sugars: 5g | fiber: 7g | sodium: 99mg

Garden-Fresh Greek Salad

Prep time: 20 minutes | Cook time: 0 minutes | Serves 6

Dressing
- 3 tablespoons fresh lemon juice
- 1 tablespoon chopped fresh or 1 teaspoon dried oregano leaves
- ½ teaspoon salt

Salad
- 1 bag (10 ounces) ready-to-eat romaine lettuce
- ¾ cup chopped seeded peeled cucumber
- ½ cup sliced red onion
- ¼ cup sliced kalamata olives
- ½ teaspoon sugar
- ½ teaspoon Dijon mustard
- ¼ teaspoon pepper
- 1 clove garlic, finely chopped
- 2 medium tomatoes, seeded, chopped (1½ cups)
- ¼ cup reduced-fat feta cheese

1. In a small bowl, beat all dressing ingredients together with a whisk until smooth and well combined. 2. In a large bowl, toss all salad ingredients except for the cheese. Pour the prepared dressing over the salad and toss until everything is evenly coated. 3. Sprinkle the salad with cheese before serving.

Per Serving:
calorie: 45 | fat: 2g | protein: 3g | carbs: 6g | sugars: 3g | fiber: 2g | sodium: 340mg

Italian Potato Salad

Prep time: 10 minutes | Cook time: 25 minutes | Serves 8

- 12 new red potatoes, 3–4 ounces each, washed and skins left on
- 3 celery stalks, chopped
- 1 red bell pepper, minced
- ¼ cup chopped scallions
- 2 tablespoons olive oil
- 1 tablespoon balsamic vinegar
- ½ tablespoon red vinegar
- 1 teaspoon chopped fresh parsley
- ⅛ teaspoon freshly ground black pepper

1. Boil the potatoes in a large pot of boiling water for 20 minutes. Drain them and allow them to cool for 30 minutes. 2. Cut the potatoes into large chunks and toss them with celery, bell pepper, and scallions. 3. In a medium bowl, combine olive oil, balsamic vinegar, red wine vinegar, parsley, and pepper to make the dressing. 4. Pour the dressing over the potato salad and toss gently to coat. 5. Serve the potato salad at room temperature.

Per Serving:
calorie: 128 | fat: 4g | protein: 3g | carbs: 22g | sugars: 3g | fiber: 3g | sodium: 30mg

Strawberry-Spinach Salad

Prep time: 15 minutes | Cook time: 0 minutes | Serves 4

- ½ cup extra-virgin olive oil
- ¼ cup balsamic vinegar
- 1 tablespoon Worcestershire sauce
- 1 (10-ounce) package baby spinach
- 1 medium red onion, quartered and sliced
- 1 cup strawberries, sliced
- 1 (6-ounce) container feta cheese, crumbled
- 4 tablespoons bacon bits, divided
- 1 cup slivered almonds, divided

1. In a large bowl, whisk together olive oil, balsamic vinegar, and Worcestershire sauce until well combined. 2. Add spinach, onion, strawberries, and feta cheese to the bowl. Mix gently until all ingredients are evenly coated with the dressing. 3. Divide the salad into 4 portions. Top each portion with 1 tablespoon of bacon bits and ¼ cup of slivered almonds before serving.

Per Serving:
calorie: 417 | fat: 29g | protein: 24g | carbs: 19g | sugars: 7g | fiber: 7g | sodium: 542mg

Sunflower-Tuna-Cauliflower Salad

Prep time: 30 minutes | Cook time: 0 minutes | Serves 2

- 1 (5-ounce) can tuna packed in water, drained
- ½ cup plain nonfat Greek yogurt
- 1 teaspoon freshly squeezed lemon juice
- 1 teaspoon dried dill
- 1 scallion, chopped
- ¼ cup sunflower seeds
- 2 cups fresh chopped cauliflower florets
- 4 cups mixed salad greens, divided

1. In a medium bowl, combine tuna, yogurt, lemon juice, dill, scallion, and sunflower seeds. 2. Add cauliflower to the bowl and gently toss to coat everything evenly. 3. Cover the bowl and refrigerate the mixture for at least 2 hours, stirring occasionally. 4. To serve, place half of the tuna mixture on top of 2 cups of salad greens.

Per Serving:
calorie: 251 | fat: 11g | protein: 24g | carbs: 18g | sugars: 8g | fiber: 7g | sodium: 288mg

Herbed Tomato Salad

Prep time: 7 minutes | Cook time: 0 minutes | Serves 2 to 4

- 1 pint cherry tomatoes, halved
- 1 bunch fresh parsley, leaves only (stems discarded)
- 1 cup cilantro, leaves only (stems discarded)
- ¼ cup fresh dill
- 1 teaspoon sumac (optional)
- 2 tablespoons extra-virgin olive oil
- Kosher salt
- Freshly ground black pepper

1. In a medium bowl, gently toss together tomatoes, parsley, cilantro, dill, sumac (if using), extra-virgin olive oil, and season with salt and pepper to taste. 2. Store any leftovers in an airtight container in the refrigerator for up to 3 days, although the salad is best enjoyed on the day it's dressed.

Per Serving:
calorie: 113 | fat: 10g | protein: 2g | carbs: 7g | sugars: 3g | fiber: 3g | sodium: 30mg

Fiery Black Bean Salad

Prep time: 10 minutes | Cook time: 0 minutes | Serves 8

- 3 cups cooked black beans
- 2 tomatoes, chopped
- 2 red bell peppers, finely chopped
- 1 cup yellow corn
- 3 garlic cloves, minced
- 1 jalapeño pepper, minced
- ¼ cup fresh lime juice
- 2 tablespoons red wine vinegar
- 1 tablespoon cumin
- 1 tablespoon extra-virgin olive oil
- 2 tablespoons freshly chopped cilantro (optional)

1. Combine all ingredients in a bowl. Chill the mixture in the refrigerator for several hours to allow the flavors to blend. Serve cold.

Per Serving:
calorie: 138 | fat: 3g | protein: 7g | carbs: 23g | sugars: 3g | fiber: 7g | sodium: 8mg

Tu-No Salad

Prep time: 10 minutes | Cook time: 0 minutes | Serves 2

- 1 can (15 ounces) chickpeas, rinsed and drained
- 1 tablespoon tahini
- 2 tablespoons water
- 1 tablespoon red wine vinegar (can substitute apple cider vinegar)
- 1 tablespoon chickpea miso (or other mild-flavored miso)
- 1 teaspoon vegan Worcestershire sauce (optional)
- ½ teaspoon Dijon mustard
- ½ teaspoon coconut nectar
- 2 tablespoons minced celery
- 2 tablespoons minced cucumber
- 2 tablespoons minced apple
- ⅛ teaspoon sea salt
- Freshly ground black pepper to taste

1. In a small food processor, pulse the chickpeas until they are crumbly but not finely ground. Alternatively, you can mash them by hand. 2. In a large bowl, combine the pulsed chickpeas with tahini, water, vinegar, miso, Worcestershire sauce, mustard, agave nectar, celery, cucumber, apple, and salt. Mix everything together thoroughly. 3. Season the mixture with additional salt and pepper to taste. 4. Serve and enjoy!

Per Serving:
calorie: 264 | fat: 8g | protein: 12g | carbs: 37g | sugars: 8g | fiber: 10g | sodium: 800mg

Edamame and Walnut Salad

Prep time: 10 minutes | Cook time: 0 minutes | Serves 2

For the vinaigrette
- 2 tablespoons balsamic vinegar
- 1 tablespoon extra-virgin olive oil
- 1 teaspoon grated fresh ginger
- ½ teaspoon Dijon mustard
- Pinch salt
- Freshly ground black pepper, to season

For the salad
- 1 cup shelled edamame
- ½ cup shredded carrots
- ½ cup shredded red cabbage
- ½ cup walnut halves
- 6 cups prewashed baby spinach, divided

To make the vinaigrette: 1. In a small bowl, whisk together balsamic vinegar, olive oil, ginger, Dijon mustard, salt, and pepper. Set aside. To make the salad: 2. In a medium bowl, combine edamame, carrots, red cabbage, and walnuts. 3. Add the prepared vinaigrette to the bowl of vegetables. Toss everything together to coat evenly. 4. Divide 3 cups of spinach between 2 serving plates. 5. Top each serving of spinach with half of the dressed vegetables. 6. Serve and enjoy immediately!

Per Serving:
calorie: 341 | fat: 26g | protein: 13g | carbs: 19g | sugars: 7g | fiber: 8g | sodium: 117mg

Grilled Hearts of Romaine with Buttermilk Dressing

Prep time: 5 minutes | Cook time: 5 minutes | Serves 4

For The Romaine
- 2 heads romaine lettuce, halved lengthwise

For The Dressing
- ½ cup low-fat buttermilk
- 1 tablespoon extra-virgin olive oil
- 1 garlic clove, pressed
- 2 tablespoons extra-virgin olive oil
- ¼ bunch fresh chives, thinly chopped
- 1 pinch red pepper flakes

To Make The Romaine: 1. Heat a grill pan over medium heat until hot. 2. Brush each half of romaine lettuce with olive oil, ensuring the cut side is well coated. 3. Place the lettuce halves flat-side down on the grill pan. 4. Grill for 3 to 5 minutes, or until the lettuce slightly wilts and develops light grill marks, flipping once if desired for even grilling. To Make The Dressing: 1. In a small bowl, whisk together buttermilk, olive oil, minced garlic, finely chopped chives, and red pepper flakes until well combined. 2. Drizzle 2 tablespoons of the prepared dressing over each grilled romaine half. 3. Serve immediately while the romaine is still warm, allowing the flavors to meld.

Per Serving:
calorie: 157 | fat: 11g | protein: 5g | carbs: 12g | sugars: 5g | fiber: 7g | sodium: 84mg

Warm Barley and Squash Salad with Balsamic Vinaigrette

Prep time: 20 minutes | Cook time: 40 minutes | Serves 8

- 1 small butternut squash
- 3 teaspoons plus 2 tablespoons extra-virgin olive oil, divided
- 2 cups broccoli florets
- 1 cup pearl barley
- 1 cup toasted chopped walnuts
- 2 cups baby kale
- ½ red onion, sliced
- 2 tablespoons balsamic vinegar
- 2 garlic cloves, minced
- ½ teaspoon salt
- ¼ teaspoon freshly ground black pepper

1. Preheat the oven to 400°F. Line a baking sheet with parchment paper. 2. Peel and seed the squash, and cut it into dice. In a large bowl, toss the squash with 2 teaspoons of olive oil. Transfer to the prepared baking sheet and roast for 20 minutes. 3. While the squash is roasting, toss the broccoli in the same bowl with 1 teaspoon of olive oil. After 20 minutes, flip the squash and push it to one side of the baking sheet. Add the broccoli to the other side and continue to roast for 20 more minutes until tender. 4. While the veggies are roasting, in a medium pot, cover the barley with several inches of water. Bring to a boil, then reduce the heat, cover, and simmer for 30 minutes until tender. Drain and rinse. 5. Transfer the barley to a large bowl, and toss with the cooked squash and broccoli, walnuts, kale, and onion. 6. In a small bowl, mix the remaining 2 tablespoons of olive oil, balsamic vinegar, garlic, salt, and pepper.

Toss the salad with the dressing and serve.

Per Serving:
calories: 274 | fat: 15g | protein: 6g | carbs: 32g | sugars: 3g | fiber: 7g | sodium: 144mg

Curried Chicken Salad

Prep time: 15 minutes | Cook time: 40 minutes | Serves 2

- 4 ounces chicken breast, rinsed and drained
- 1 small apple, peeled, cored, and finely chopped
- 2 tablespoons slivered almonds
- 1 tablespoon dried cranberries
- 2 tablespoons chia seeds
- ¼ cup plain nonfat Greek yogurt
- 1 tablespoon curry powder
- 1½ teaspoons Dijon mustard
- ⅛ teaspoon salt
- ¼ teaspoon freshly ground black pepper
- 4 cups chopped romaine lettuce, divided

1. Preheat the oven to 400°F. 2. To a small baking dish, add the chicken. Place the dish in the preheated oven. Bake for 30 to 40 minutes, or until the chicken is completely opaque and registers 165°F on an instant-read thermometer. Remove from the oven. Chop into cubes. Set aside. 3. In a medium bowl, mix together the chicken, apple, almonds, cranberries, and chia seeds. 4. Add the yogurt, curry powder, mustard, salt, and pepper. Toss to coat. 5. On 2 plates, arrange 2 cups of lettuce on each. 6. Top each with one-half of the curried chicken salad. 7. Serve immediately.

Per Serving:
calorie: 240 | fat: 9g | protein: 19g | carbs: 25g | sugars: 14g | fiber: 8g | sodium: 258mg

Warm Sweet Potato and Black Bean Salad

Prep time: 5 minutes | Cook time: 35 minutes | Serves 2

- Extra-virgin olive oil cooking spray
- 1 large sweet potato, peeled and cubed
- 1 tablespoon extra-virgin olive oil
- 1 tablespoon balsamic vinegar
- 1 teaspoon dried rosemary
- ¼ teaspoon garlic powder
- ⅛ teaspoon salt
- ⅛ teaspoon freshly ground black pepper
- 1 cup canned black beans, drained and rinsed
- 2 tablespoons chopped chives

1. Preheat the oven to 450°F. 2. Place sweet potato cubes in a small baking dish coated with cooking spray. Bake uncovered for 20 to 35 minutes, or until tender. 3. In a medium serving bowl, whisk together olive oil, balsamic vinegar, rosemary, garlic powder, salt, and pepper. 4. Add black beans and cooked sweet potato to the oil and herb mixture. Toss well to coat. 5. Sprinkle with chives. 6. Serve immediately and enjoy!

Per Serving:
calorie: 235 | fat: 7g | protein: 8g | carbs: 35g | sugars: 4g | fiber: 10g | sodium: 359mg

Chapter 10 Salads

Chinese Chicken Salad

Prep time: 10 minutes | Cook time: 0 minutes | Serves 4

- 2 cups cooked chicken, diced
- 1 cup finely chopped celery
- 1 cup shredded carrots
- ¼ cup crushed unsweetened pineapple, drained
- 2 tablespoons finely diced pimiento
- Two 8-ounce cans water chestnuts, drained and chopped
- 2 scallions, chopped
- ⅓ cup low-fat mayonnaise
- 1 tablespoon light soy sauce
- 1 teaspoon lemon juice
- 8 large tomatoes, hollowed

1. In a large bowl, combine the chicken, celery, carrots, pineapple, pimiento, water chestnuts, and scallions. 2. In a separate bowl, combine the mayonnaise, soy sauce, and lemon juice. Mix well. Add the dressing to the salad, and toss. Cover, and chill in the refrigerator for 2–3 hours. 3. For each serving, place a small scoop of chicken salad into a hollowed-out tomato.

Per Serving:
calorie: 365 | fat: 16g | protein: 27g | carbs: 32g | sugars: 17g | fiber: 9g | sodium: 476mg

Wild Rice Salad

Prep time: 5 minutes | Cook time: 45 minutes | Serves 6

- 1 cup raw wild rice (rinsed)
- 4 cups cold water
- 1 cup mandarin oranges, packed in their own juice (drain and reserve 2 tablespoons of liquid)
- ½ cup chopped celery
- ¼ cup minced red bell pepper
- 1 shallot, minced
- 1 teaspoon minced thyme
- 2 tablespoons raspberry vinegar
- 1 tablespoon extra-virgin olive oil

1. Place the rinsed, raw rice and the water in a saucepan. Bring to a boil, lower the heat, cover the pan, and cook for 45–50 minutes until the rice has absorbed the water. Set the rice aside to cool. 2. In a large bowl, combine the mandarin oranges, celery, red pepper, and shallot. 3. In a small bowl, combine the reserved juice, thyme, vinegar, and oil. 4. Add the rice to the mandarin oranges and vegetables. Pour the dressing over the salad, toss, and serve.

Per Serving:
calorie: 134 | fat: 3g | protein: 4g | carbs: 24g | sugars: 4g | fiber: 3g | sodium: 12mg

Broccoli Slaw Crab Salad

Prep time: 15 minutes | Cook time: 0 minutes | Serves 4

- ⅔ cup mayonnaise
- 1 tablespoon freshly squeezed lime juice
- 1 teaspoon minced garlic
- ½ teaspoon freshly ground black pepper
- 1 (16-ounce) package broccoli slaw
- 2 (6-ounce) cans crabmeat, drained and flaked
- 1 small onion, diced
- 2 large celery stalks, chopped
- 1 large red bell pepper, seeded and chopped
- Chopped fresh parsley, for garnish

1. In a large bowl, whisk together mayonnaise, lime juice, garlic, and pepper until the mixture is smooth. 2. Add broccoli slaw, crab meat, onion, celery, and bell pepper to the bowl. Mix everything together until all ingredients are well coated with the dressing. 3. Garnish the salad with parsley before serving.

Per Serving:
calorie: 279 | fat: 14g | protein: 26g | carbs: 13g | sugars: 3g | fiber: 2g | sodium: 572mg

Haricot Verts, Walnut, and Feta Salad

Prep time: 10 minutes | Cook time: 15 minutes | Serves 12

- ½ cup walnuts, toasted
- 1½ pounds fresh haricot verts, trimmed and halved
- ½ cup cooked green lentils
- 1 medium red onion, sliced into rings
- ½ cup peeled, seeded, and diced cucumber
- ⅓ cup crumbled fat-free feta cheese
- ¼ cup extra-virgin olive oil
- ¼ cup white wine vinegar
- ¼ cup chopped fresh mint leaves
- 1 garlic clove, minced

1. Place the walnuts in a small baking dish in a 350°F oven for 5–10 minutes until lightly browned. Remove from the oven, and set aside. 2. Steam the haricot verts about 4–5 minutes, or until desired degree of crispness. 3. In a salad bowl, combine the haricot verts with the walnuts, lentils, red onion rings, cucumber, and feta cheese. 4. Combine all the dressing ingredients together, and toss with the vegetables. Chill in the refrigerator for 2–3 hours before serving.

Per Serving:
calorie: 119 | fat: 7g | protein: 5g | carbs: 11g | sugars: 3g | fiber: 4g | sodium: 61mg

Grilled Romaine with White Beans

Prep time: 5 minutes | Cook time: 8 minutes | Serves 4 to 6

- 3 tablespoons extra-virgin olive oil, divided
- 2 large heads romaine lettuce, halved lengthwise
- 2 tablespoons white miso
- 1 tablespoon water, plus more as needed
- 1 (15-ounce) can white beans, rinsed and drained
- ½ cup chopped fresh parsley

1. Preheat the grill or a grill pan. 2. Drizzle 2 tablespoons of extra-virgin olive oil over the cut sides of the romaine lettuce. 3. In a medium bowl, whisk the remaining 1 tablespoon of extra-virgin olive oil with the white miso and about 1 tablespoon of water. Add more water, if necessary, to reach a thin consistency. Add the white beans and parsley to the bowl, stir, adjust the seasonings as desired, and set aside. 4. When the grill is hot, put the romaine on the grill and cook for 1 to 2 minutes on each side or until lightly charred with grill marks. Remove the lettuce from the grill and repeat with remaining lettuce halves. Set the lettuce aside on a platter or individual plates and top with the beans.

Per Serving:
calorie: 242 | fat: 10g | protein: 11g | carbs: 31g | sugars: 4g | fiber: 11g | sodium: 282mg

Pomegranate "Tabbouleh" with Cauliflower

Prep time: 20 minutes | Cook time: 5 minutes | Serves 4 to 6

- ⅓ cup extra-virgin olive oil, divided
- 4 cups grated cauliflower (about 1 medium head)
- Juice of 1 lemon
- ¼ red onion, minced
- 4 large tomatoes, diced
- 3 large bunches flat-leaf parsley, chopped
- 1 large bunch mint, chopped
- ½ cup pomegranate arils
- Kosher salt
- Freshly ground black pepper

1. In a large skillet, heat 2 tablespoons of extra-virgin olive oil. When it's hot, add the cauliflower and sauté for 3 to 5 minutes or until it starts to crisp. Remove the skillet from the heat and allow the cauliflower to cool while you prep the remaining ingredients. 2. In a large bowl, combine the remaining extra-virgin olive oil with the lemon juice and red onion. Mix well, then mix in the tomatoes, parsley, mint, and pomegranate arils. 3. After the cauliflower cools, 5 to 7 minutes, add it to the bowl with the other ingredients. Season with salt and pepper to taste and serve. 4. Store any leftovers in an airtight container in the refrigerator for 3 to 5 days.

Per Serving:
calorie: 205 | fat: 15g | protein: 4g | carbs: 17g | sugars: 9g | fiber: 5g | sodium: 50mg

Crunchy Pecan Tuna Salad

Prep time: 20 minutes | Cook time: 0 minutes | Serves 1

- ½ medium apple, finely chopped
- 2 medium ribs celery, finely chopped
- ¼ large red onion, finely chopped
- 2 tablespoons (16 g) coarsely chopped pecans
- ¼ cup (46 g) canned navy beans, drained, rinsed, and mashed
- 2 ounces (57 g) canned tuna packed in water, drained and rinsed
- 1 tablespoon (14 g) mayonnaise (see Tip)
- ½ tablespoon (8 g) Dijon mustard
- 1 tablespoon (15 ml) fresh lemon juice
- Black pepper, as needed

1. In a large bowl, combine apple, celery, onion, pecans, beans, and tuna. 2. In a small bowl, mix together mayonnaise, mustard, lemon juice, and black pepper. 3. Add the mayonnaise mixture to the tuna mixture and stir until everything is evenly combined. 4. Serve the tuna salad immediately, or refrigerate it for 2 to 3 hours, or overnight, to chill and allow the flavors to meld before serving.

Per Serving:
calorie: 197 | fat: 11g | protein: 11g | carbs: 16g | sugars: 7g | fiber: 5g | sodium: 179mg

Pasta Salad–Stuffed Tomatoes

Prep time: 10 minutes | Cook time: 0 minutes | Serves 4

- 1 cup uncooked whole-wheat fusilli
- 2 small carrots, sliced
- 2 scallions, chopped
- ¼ cup chopped pimiento
- 1 cup cooked kidney beans
- ½ cup sliced celery
- ¼ cup cooked peas
- 2 tablespoons chopped fresh parsley
- ¼ cup calorie-free, fat-free Italian salad dressing
- 2 tablespoons low-fat mayonnaise
- ¼ teaspoon dried marjoram
- ¼ teaspoon freshly ground black pepper
- 4 medium tomatoes

1. Cook the fusilli in boiling water until cooked, about 7 to 8 minutes; drain. 2. In a large bowl, combine the macaroni with the remaining salad ingredients (except the tomatoes), and toss well. Cover, and chill in the refrigerator 1 hour or more. 3. With the stem end down, cut each tomato into 6 wedges, cutting to, but not through, the base of the tomato. Spread the wedges slightly apart, and spoon the pasta mixture into the tomatoes. Chill until ready to serve.

Per Serving:
calorie: 214 | fat: 3g | protein: 10g | carbs: 40g | sugars: 6g | fiber: 8g | sodium: 164mg

Chapter 11
Stews and Soups

Chapter 11 Stews and Soups

Beef and Mushroom Barley Soup

Prep time: 10 minutes | Cook time: 1 hour 20 minutes | Serves 6

- 1 pound beef stew meat, cubed
- ¼ teaspoon salt
- ¼ teaspoon freshly ground black pepper
- 1 tablespoon extra-virgin olive oil
- 8 ounces sliced mushrooms
- 1 onion, chopped
- 2 carrots, chopped
- 3 celery stalks, chopped
- 6 garlic cloves, minced
- ½ teaspoon dried thyme
- 4 cups low-sodium beef broth
- 1 cup water
- ½ cup pearl barley

1. Season the meat with the salt and pepper. 2. In an Instant Pot, heat the oil over high heat. Add the meat and brown on all sides. Remove the meat from the pot and set aside. 3. Add the mushrooms to the pot and cook for 1 to 2 minutes, until they begin to soften. Remove the mushrooms and set aside with the meat. 4. Add the onion, carrots, and celery to the pot. Sauté for 3 to 4 minutes until the vegetables begin to soften. Add the garlic and continue to cook until fragrant, about 30 seconds longer. 5. Return the meat and mushrooms to the pot, then add the thyme, beef broth, and water. Set the pressure to high and cook for 15 minutes. Let the pressure release naturally. 6. Open the Instant Pot and add the barley. Use the slow cooker function on the Instant Pot, affix the lid (vent open), and continue to cook for 1 hour until the barley is cooked through and tender. Serve.

Per Serving:
calories: 245 | fat: 9g | protein: 21g | carbs: 19g | sugars: 3g | fiber: 4g | sodium: 516mg

Italian Vegetable Soup

Prep time: 20 minutes | Cook time: 5 to 9 hours | Serves 6

- 3 small carrots, sliced
- 1 small onion, chopped
- 2 small potatoes, diced
- 2 tablespoons chopped parsley
- 1 garlic clove, minced
- 3 teaspoons sodium-free beef bouillon powder
- 1¼ teaspoons dried basil
- ¼ teaspoon pepper
- 16-ounce can red kidney beans, undrained
- 3 cups water
- 14½-ounce can stewed tomatoes, with juice
- 1 cup diced, extra-lean, lower-sodium cooked ham

1. In the inner pot of your Instant Pot, start by layering the carrots, onion, potatoes, parsley, garlic, beef bouillon, basil, pepper, and kidney beans. It's important not to stir them at this stage. 2. Pour water over the layered ingredients until they are just covered. 3. Secure the lid of the Instant Pot, ensuring the valve is set to sealing. Depending on your preferred cooking time: For Low Slow Cook mode, set the Instant Pot to cook for 8–9 hours. For High Slow Cook mode, set it to cook for 4½–5½ hours. During this time, the vegetables will cook and absorb the flavors of the broth and seasonings. 4. Once the cooking time is complete, carefully release the pressure manually or allow it to release naturally, depending on your preference and the Instant Pot model. 5. Remove the lid and gently stir in the diced tomatoes and ham to incorporate them into the soup. 6. Secure the lid again and switch the Instant Pot to High Slow Cook mode. Cook for an additional 10–15 minutes to ensure the tomatoes and ham are heated through and flavors meld together.

Per Serving:
calories: 156 | fat: 1g | protein: 9g | carbs: 29g | sugars: 8g | fiber: 5g | sodium: 614mg

Thai Corn and Sweet Potato Stew

Prep time: 10 minutes | Cook time: 20 minutes | Serves 4

- 1 small can (5.5 ounces) light coconut milk
- 1 cup chopped onion
- ½ cup chopped celery
- 2 cups cubed sweet potato (can use frozen)
- ¾ to 1 teaspoon sea salt
- 2 cups water
- 1½ tablespoons Thai yellow or red curry paste
- 1½ cups frozen corn kernels
- 1½ cups chopped red bell pepper
- 1 package (12 to 14 ounces) tofu, cut into cubes, or 1 can (14 ounces) black beans, rinsed and drained
- 2½ tablespoons freshly squeezed lime juice
- 4 to 5 cups baby spinach leaves
- ⅓ to ½ cup fresh cilantro or Thai basil, chopped
- Lime wedges (optional)

1. In a soup pot over high heat, warm 2 tablespoons of the coconut milk. Add the onion, celery, sweet potato, and ¾ teaspoon of the salt, and sauté for 4 to 5 minutes. Add the water, Thai paste, and remaining coconut milk. Increase the heat to high to bring to a boil. Cover and reduce the heat to medium-low, and let the mixture simmer for 8 to 10 minutes, or until the sweet potato has softened. Turn off the heat, and use an immersion blender to puree the soup base. Add the corn, bell pepper, and tofu or beans, and turn the heat to medium-low. Cover and cook for 3 to 4 minutes to heat through. Add the lime juice, spinach, and cilantro or basil, and stir until the spinach has just wilted. Taste, and season with the remaining ¼ teaspoon salt, if desired. Serve with the lime wedges (if using).

Per Serving:
calorie: 223 | fat: 7g | protein: 10g | carbs: 36g | sugars: 11g | fiber: 6g | sodium: 723mg

Buttercup Squash Soup

Prep time: 15 minutes | Cook time: 10 minutes | Serves 6

- 2 tablespoons extra-virgin olive oil
- 1 medium onion, chopped
- 4 to 5 cups Vegetable Broth or Chicken Bone Broth
- 1½ pounds buttercup squash, peeled, seeded, and cut into 1-inch chunks
- ½ teaspoon kosher salt
- ¼ teaspoon ground white pepper
- Whole nutmeg, for grating

1. Set the electric pressure cooker to the Sauté setting. When the pot is hot, pour in the olive oil. 2. Add the onion and sauté for 3 to 5 minutes, until it begins to soften. Hit Cancel. 3. Add the broth, squash, salt, and pepper to the pot and stir. (If you want a thicker soup, use 4 cups of broth. If you want a thinner, drinkable soup, use 5 cups.) 4. Close and lock the lid of the pressure cooker. Set the valve to sealing. 5. Cook on high pressure for 10 minutes. 6. When the cooking is complete, hit Cancel and allow the pressure to release naturally. 7. Once the pin drops, unlock and remove the lid. 8. Use an immersion blender to purée the soup right in the pot. If you don't have an immersion blender, transfer the soup to a blender or food processor and purée. (Follow the instructions that came with your machine for blending hot foods.) 9. Pour the soup into serving bowls and grate nutmeg on top.

Per Serving:
calories: 320 | fat: 16g | protein: 36g | carbs: 7g | sugars: 3g | fiber: 2g | sodium: 856mg

Favorite Chili

Prep time: 10 minutes | Cook time: 35 minutes | Serves 5

- 1 pound extra-lean ground beef
- 1 teaspoon salt
- ½ teaspoons black pepper
- 1 tablespoon olive oil
- 1 small onion, chopped
- 2 cloves garlic, minced
- 1 green pepper, chopped
- 2 tablespoons chili powder
- ½ teaspoons cumin
- 1 cup water
- 16-ounce can chili beans
- 15-ounce can low-sodium crushed tomatoes

1. Press Sauté button and adjust once to Sauté More function. Wait until indicator says "hot." 2. Season the ground beef with salt and black pepper. 3. Add the olive oil into the inner pot. Coat the whole bottom of the pot with the oil. 4. Add ground beef into the inner pot. The ground beef will start to release moisture. Allow the ground beef to brown and crisp slightly, stirring occasionally to break it up. Taste and adjust the seasoning with more salt and ground black pepper. 5. Add diced onion, minced garlic, chopped pepper, chili powder, and cumin. Sauté for about 5 minutes, until the spices start to release their fragrance. Stir frequently. 6. Add water and 1 can of chili beans, not drained. Mix well. Pour in 1 can of crushed tomatoes. 7. Close and secure lid, making sure vent is set to sealing, and pressure cook on Manual at high pressure for 10 minutes. 8. Let the pressure release naturally when cooking time is up. Open the lid carefully.

Per Serving:
calories: 213 | fat: 10g | protein: 18g | carbs: 11g | sugars: 4g | fiber: 4g | sodium: 385mg

Creamy Sweet Potato Soup

Prep time: 15 minutes | Cook time: 10 minutes | Serves 6

- 2 tablespoons avocado oil
- 1 small onion, chopped
- 2 celery stalks, chopped
- 2 teaspoons minced garlic
- 1 teaspoon kosher salt
- ½ teaspoon freshly ground black pepper
- 1 teaspoon ground turmeric
- ½ teaspoon ground cinnamon
- 2 pounds sweet potatoes, peeled and cut into 1-inch cubes
- 3 cups Vegetable Broth or Chicken Bone Broth
- Plain Greek yogurt, to garnish (optional)
- Chopped fresh parsley, to garnish (optional)
- Pumpkin seeds (pepitas), to garnish (optional)

1. Set the electric pressure cooker to the Sauté setting. When the pot is hot, pour in the avocado oil. 2. Sauté the onion and celery for 3 to 5 minutes or until the vegetables begin to soften. 3. Stir in the garlic, salt, pepper, turmeric, and cinnamon. Hit Cancel. 4. Stir in the sweet potatoes and broth. 5. Close and lock the lid of the pressure cooker. Set the valve to sealing. 6. Cook on high pressure for 10 minutes. 7. When the cooking is complete, hit Cancel and allow the pressure to release naturally. 8. Once the pin drops, unlock and remove the lid. 9. Use an immersion blender to purée the soup right in the pot. If you don't have an immersion blender, transfer the soup to a blender or food processor and purée. (Follow the instructions that came with your machine for blending hot foods.) 10. Spoon into bowls and serve topped with Greek yogurt, parsley, and/or pumpkin seeds (if using).

Per Serving:
calories: 175 | fat: 5g | protein: 5g | carbs: 29g | sugars: 4g | fiber: 4g | sodium: 706mg

Asparagus Soup

Prep time: 5 minutes | Cook time: 10 minutes | Serves 2

- 1 pound asparagus, woody ends removed, sliced into 1-inch pieces
- 1 (8 ounces) can cannellini beans, drained and rinsed
- 2 cups reduced-sodium vegetable broth
- 1 medium shallot, thinly sliced
- 1 garlic clove, thinly sliced
- ½ teaspoon dried thyme
- ½ teaspoon dried marjoram leaves
- ⅛ teaspoon salt
- Freshly ground black pepper, to season

1. In a large saucepan set over high heat, stir together the asparagus, cannellini beans, vegetable broth, shallot, garlic, thyme, marjoram, and salt. Bring to a boil. Reduce the heat to medium-low. Cover and simmer for about 5 minutes, or until the asparagus is tender. 2. In a large blender or food processor, purée the soup until smooth, scraping down the sides, if necessary. Season with pepper. 3. Serve immediately and enjoy!

Per Serving:
calories: 83 | fat: 1g | protein: 6g | carbs: 17g | sugars: 7g | fiber: 7g | sodium: 712mg

Creamy Chicken Wild Rice Soup

Prep time: 15 minutes | Cook time: 15 minutes | Serves 5

- 2 tablespoons margarine
- ½ cup yellow onion, diced
- ¾ cup carrots, diced
- ¾ cup sliced mushrooms (about 3–4 mushrooms)
- ½ pound chicken breast, diced into 1-inch cubes
- 6.2-ounce box Uncle Ben's Long Grain & Wild Rice

Fast Cook
- 2 14-ounce cans low-sodium chicken broth
- 1 cup skim milk
- 1 cup evaporated skim milk
- 2 ounces fat-free cream cheese
- 2 tablespoons cornstarch

1. Select the Sauté feature and add the margarine, onion, carrots, and mushrooms to the inner pot. Sauté for about 5 minutes until onions are translucent and soft. 2. Add the cubed chicken and seasoning packet from the Uncle Ben's box and stir to combine. 3. Add the rice and chicken broth. Select Manual, high pressure, then lock the lid and make sure the vent is set to sealing. Set the time for 5 minutes. 4. After the cooking time ends, allow it to stay on Keep Warm for 5 minutes and then quick release the pressure. 5. Remove the lid; change the setting to the Sauté function again. 6. Add the skim milk, evaporated milk, and cream cheese. Stir to melt. 7. In a small bowl, mix the cornstarch with a little bit of water to dissolve, then add to the soup to thicken.

Per Serving:
calories: 316 | fat: 7g | protein: 27g | carbs: 35g | sugars: 10g | fiber: 1g | sodium: 638mg

Minted Sweet Pea Soup

Prep time: 10 minutes | Cook time: 10 minutes | Serves 2 to 4

- 2 tablespoons extra-virgin olive oil
- 1 small yellow onion, minced
- Pinch kosher salt
- Pinch freshly ground black pepper
- 2 garlic cloves, minced
- 1 zucchini, diced
- 4 cups low-sodium vegetable broth
- 3 cups frozen peas
- Juice of 1 lemon
- ½ cup plain Greek yogurt (optional)
- ½ cup thinly sliced fresh mint
- 2 tablespoons chopped pistachios (optional)

1. Heat the extra-virgin olive oil in a medium stockpot over medium heat. Add the onion, salt, and pepper and sauté until translucent. 2. Add the garlic and zucchini and sauté until tender, about 3 minutes. 3. Transfer the vegetables to a blender and puree them with the vegetable broth, peas, and lemon juice. 4. Adjust the seasonings as desired and serve the soup warmed in a saucepan over medium heat or cooled in the refrigerator. To cool it in an ice bath, transfer the soup to a medium bowl and nestle that in a large bowl filled with ice water. 5. Serve with a dollop of optional Greek yogurt (if using) and topped with mint and pistachios (if using). 6. Store the cooled soup in an airtight container in the refrigerator for up to 5 days, with garnishes kept separately.

Per Serving:
calories: 181 | fat: 6g | protein: 8g | carbs: 27g | sugars: 13g | fiber: 6g | sodium: 442mg

Carrot Soup

Prep time: 15 minutes | Cook time: 25 minutes | Serves 6

- 4 cups store-bought low-sodium vegetable broth, divided
- 2 celery stalks, halved
- 1 small yellow onion, roughly chopped
- ½ fennel bulb, cored and roughly chopped
- 1 (1-inch) piece fresh ginger, peeled and chopped
- 1 pound carrots, peeled and halved
- 2 teaspoons ground cumin
- 1 garlic clove, peeled
- 1 tablespoon almond butter

1. Select the Sauté setting on an electric pressure cooker, and combine ½ cup of broth, the celery, onion, fennel, and ginger. Cook for 5 minutes, or until the vegetables are tender. 2. Add the carrots, cumin, garlic, remaining 3½ cups of broth, and the almond butter. 3. Close and lock the lid, and set the pressure valve to sealing. 4. Change to the Manual/Pressure Cook setting, and cook for 15 minutes. 5. Once cooking is complete, quick-release the pressure. Carefully remove the lid, and let cool for 5 minutes. 6. Using a stand mixer or an immersion blender, carefully purée the soup. Serve with a heaping plate of greens.

Per Serving:
calories: 97 | fat: 3g | protein: 3g | carbs: 17g | sugars: 10g | fiber: 4g | sodium: 177mg

Hearty Italian Minestrone

Prep time: 10 minutes | Cook time: 50 minutes | Serves 8

- ½ cup sliced onion
- 1 tablespoon extra-virgin olive oil
- 4 cups low-sodium chicken broth
- ¾ cup diced carrot
- ½ cup diced potato (with skin)
- 2 cups sliced cabbage or coarsely chopped spinach
- 1 cup diced zucchini
- ½ cup cooked garbanzo beans (drained and rinsed, if canned)
- ½ cup cooked navy beans (drained and rinsed, if canned)
- One 14.5-ounce can low-sodium tomatoes, with liquid
- ½ cup diced celery
- 2 tablespoons fresh basil, finely chopped
- ½ cup uncooked whole-wheat rotini or other shaped pasta
- 2 tablespoons fresh parsley, finely chopped, for garnish

1. In a large stockpot over medium heat, sauté the onion in oil until it becomes slightly browned. Add the chicken broth, carrot, and potato. Cover the pot and cook over medium heat for 30 minutes. 2. Add the remaining ingredients to the pot and continue cooking for an additional 15 to 20 minutes, or until the pasta is fully cooked through. 3. Garnish the soup with parsley and serve hot.

Per Serving:
calories: 101 | fat: 2g | protein: 6g | carbs: 17g | sugars: 4g | fiber: 4g | sodium: 108mg

Chock-Full-of-Vegetables Chicken Soup

Prep time: 5 minutes | Cook time: 15 minutes | Serves 2

- 1 tablespoon extra-virgin olive oil
- 8 ounces chicken tenders, cut into bite-size chunks
- 1 small zucchini, finely diced
- 1 cup sliced fresh button mushrooms
- 2 medium carrots, thinly sliced
- 2 celery stalks, thinly sliced
- 1 large shallot, finely chopped
- 1 garlic clove, minced
- 1 tablespoon dried parsley
- 1 teaspoon dried marjoram
- ⅛ teaspoon salt
- 2 plum tomatoes, chopped
- 2 cups reduced-sodium chicken broth
- 1½ cups packed baby spinach

1. In a large saucepan set over medium-high heat, heat olive oil. 2. Add the chicken. Cook for 3 to 4 minutes, stirring occasionally, or until browned. Transfer to a plate. Set aside. 3. To the saucepan, add the zucchini, mushrooms, carrots, celery, shallot, garlic, parsley, marjoram, and salt. Cook for 2 to 3 minutes, stirring frequently, until the vegetables are slightly softened. 4. Add the tomatoes and chicken broth. Increase the heat to high. Bring to a boil, stirring occasionally. Reduce the heat to low. Simmer for 5 minutes, or until the vegetables are tender. 5. Stir in the spinach, cooked chicken, and any accumulated juices on the plate. Cook for about 2 minutes, stirring, until the chicken is heated through. 6. Serve hot and enjoy!

Per Serving:
calories: 262 | fat: 10g | protein: 32g | carbs: 16g | sugars: 3g | fiber: 6g | sodium: 890mg

Taco Soup

Prep time: 5 minutes | Cook time: 20 minutes | Serves 4

- Avocado oil cooking spray
- 1 medium red bell pepper, chopped
- ½ cup chopped yellow onion
- 1 pound 93% lean ground beef
- 1 teaspoon ground cumin
- ½ teaspoon salt
- ½ teaspoon chili powder
- ½ teaspoon garlic powder
- 2 cups low-sodium beef broth
- 1 (15-ounce) can no-salt-added diced tomatoes
- 1½ cups frozen corn
- ⅓ cup half-and-half

1. Start by heating a large stockpot over medium-low heat. Once the pot is hot, spray the cooking surface with cooking spray to prevent sticking. Add diced bell pepper and onion to the pot. Sauté the vegetables for about 5 minutes, stirring occasionally, until they begin to soften and become fragrant. 2. Next, add ground beef to the pot along with ground cumin, salt, chili powder, and garlic powder. Break apart the ground beef with a spoon or spatula as it cooks. Continue cooking for 5 to 7 minutes, or until the beef is browned and cooked through, ensuring to stir occasionally to evenly cook the meat and incorporate the spices. 3. Once the beef is cooked, pour in the beef broth, diced tomatoes along with their juices, and corn kernels (fresh or canned). Increase the heat to medium-high and bring the mixture to a simmer. Allow it to simmer for about 10 minutes to blend the flavors together and to ensure the corn is heated through. 4. After simmering, remove the pot from the heat. Stir in the half-and-half to add a creamy richness to the soup. Mix well until the half-and-half is fully incorporated into the soup mixture.

Per Serving:
calories: 487 | fat: 21g | protein: 39g | carbs: 35g | sugars: 8g | fiber: 5g | sodium: 437mg

Turkey Carcass Broth

Prep time: 15 minutes | Cook time: 4 to 10 hours | Makes about 8 cups

- 1 turkey carcass, broken up into pieces
- 2 medium onions, coarsely chopped
- 3 medium carrots, coarsely chopped
- 3 medium stalks celery with leaves, coarsely chopped
- 8 cups chicken stock
- 2 teaspoons dried thyme
- 1 teaspoon dried sage leaves
- 1 bay leaf
- 4 whole black peppercorns
- Salt

1. Put all the ingredients except the salt in the insert of a 5- to 7-quart slow cooker. Cover and cook on high for 4 to 5 hours or on low for 8 to 10 hours. 2. Season with salt. Strain the broth through a colander to remove the large solids, then strain again through a fine mesh sieve. 3. Cool the stock to room temperature, then store in airtight containers in the refrigerator for up to 5 days or in the freezer for up to 6 months.

Per Serving:
1 cup: calories: 92 | fat: 2g | protein: 12g | carbs: 8g | sugars: 3g | fiber: 1g | sodium: 127mg

Potlikker Soup

Prep time: 15 minutes | Cook time: 20 minutes | Serves 6

- 3 cups store-bought low-sodium chicken broth, divided
- 1 medium onion, chopped
- 3 garlic cloves, minced
- 1 bunch collard greens or mustard greens including stems, roughly chopped
- 1 fresh ham bone
- 5 carrots, peeled and cut into 1-inch rounds
- 2 fresh thyme sprigs
- 3 bay leaves
- Freshly ground black pepper

1. Select the Sauté setting on an electric pressure cooker, and combine ½ cup of chicken broth, the onion, and garlic and cook for 3 to 5 minutes, or until the onion and garlic are translucent. 2. Add the collard greens, ham bone, carrots, remaining 2½ cups of broth, the thyme, and bay leaves. 3. Close and lock the lid and set the pressure valve to sealing. 4. Change to the Manual/Pressure Cook setting, and cook for 15 minutes. 5. Once cooking is complete, quick-release the pressure. Carefully remove the lid. Discard the bay leaves. 6. Serve.

Per Serving:
calories: 107 | fat: 3g | protein: 12g | carbs: 12g | sugars: 3g | fiber: 5g | sodium: 556mg

Gazpacho

Prep time: 15 minutes | Cook time: 0 minutes | Serves 4

- 3 pounds ripe tomatoes, chopped
- 1 cup low-sodium tomato juice
- ½ red onion, chopped
- 1 cucumber, peeled, seeded, and chopped
- 1 red bell pepper, seeded and chopped
- 2 celery stalks, chopped
- 2 tablespoons chopped fresh parsley
- 2 garlic cloves, chopped
- 2 tablespoons extra-virgin olive oil
- 2 tablespoons red wine vinegar
- 1 teaspoon honey
- ½ teaspoon salt
- ¼ teaspoon freshly ground black pepper

1. Prepare all the ingredients for gazpacho. In a blender jar, add ripe tomatoes (cored and roughly chopped), tomato juice, finely diced onion, peeled and diced cucumber, diced bell pepper (any color you prefer), chopped celery, fresh parsley leaves, minced garlic cloves, a drizzle of olive oil, a splash of vinegar (like red wine vinegar), a touch of honey for sweetness, and a pinch each of salt and pepper. 2. Pulse the blender until the ingredients are well combined but still slightly chunky. This should create a textured soup with visible pieces of vegetables for added freshness and crunch. 3. Taste the gazpacho and adjust the seasonings according to your preference. You might want to add more salt, pepper, or vinegar for acidity. 4. Once satisfied with the taste, transfer the gazpacho to a nonreactive, airtight container. This could be a glass or plastic container with a tight-fitting lid. 5. Refrigerate the gazpacho for up to 3 days to allow the flavors to meld together. This chilling time also enhances the refreshing quality of the soup. 6. When ready to serve, stir the gazpacho well and ladle it into bowls. Garnish with additional chopped vegetables, a drizzle of olive oil, or fresh herbs if desired. Enjoy your homemade gazpacho chilled and bursting with summer flavors!

Per Serving:
calories: 170 | fat: 8g | protein: 5g | carbs: 24g | sugars: 16g | fiber: 6g | sodium: 332mg

Golden Chicken Soup

Prep time: 10 minutes | Cook time: 20 minutes | Serves 4 to 6

- 1 tablespoon extra-virgin olive oil
- 1 yellow onion, chopped
- 2 teaspoons garlic powder
- 1 tablespoon ginger powder
- 2 teaspoons turmeric
- ½ teaspoon freshly ground black pepper
- 6 cups low-sodium chicken broth
- 3 (5 to 6 ounces) boneless, skinless chicken breasts
- 4 celery stalks, cut into ¼-inch-thick slices
- 1 fennel bulb, thinly sliced

1. Heat the extra-virgin olive oil in a large stockpot over medium heat. Sauté the onion until translucent, about 3 minutes. Add the garlic powder, ginger powder, turmeric, black pepper, and chicken broth. 2. Bring to a boil, then carefully add the chicken, celery, and fennel. Reduce the heat to medium-low, cover, and simmer until the internal temperature of the chicken is 160°F, 5 to 10 minutes. 3. Remove the chicken breasts and allow them to cool for 5 minutes while the soup keeps simmering. 4. Shred the chicken using two forks and return it to the stockpot. Heat the soup for about 1 minute and adjust the seasonings as desired. 5. Store the cooled soup in an airtight container in the refrigerator for 3 to 5 days.

Per Serving:
calories: 107 | fat: 4g | protein: 10g | carbs: 10g | sugars: 3g | fiber: 2g | sodium: 370mg

Tomato-Basil Soup with Grilled Cheese Croutons

Prep time: 10 minutes | Cook time: 20 minutes | Serves 4 to 6

For the tomato soup
- 2 tablespoons extra-virgin olive oil
- 1 onion, chopped
- 1 tablespoon minced garlic
- 3 pounds fresh tomatoes, cored and chopped, or canned diced tomatoes
- 8 cups low-sodium vegetable broth
- 4 tablespoons tomato paste
- ½ cup coconut milk
- ½ teaspoon garlic powder
- Pinch kosher salt
- Pinch freshly ground black pepper
- ⅓ cup fresh basil, chopped

For the grilled cheese croutons
- 1 tablespoon butter or cooking spray
- 4 slices whole-wheat bread
- 4 ounces cheese (cheddar or Gruyère), shredded
- Freshly ground black pepper (optional)

To make the tomato soup 1. Heat the extra-virgin olive oil in a medium stockpot over medium heat. Sauté the onion and minced garlic until translucent, about 3 minutes. 2. Add the tomatoes and vegetable broth, increase the heat to medium-high, cover, and simmer until the tomato skin wrinkles and pulls back from the tomato flesh, 8 to 10 minutes. 3. Add the tomato paste, coconut milk, garlic powder, salt, and pepper and simmer for 3 to 5 minutes. 4. Transfer the soup to a blender and blend until smooth, in batches if necessary. Leave the center piece out of the lid and cover the lid with a clean kitchen towel while blending to allow the steam to escape. 5. Pour the soup back into the stockpot. 6. Serve the soup topped with basil and the grilled cheese croutons (if using). 7. Store the cooled soup in an airtight container in the refrigerator for 3 to 5 days. Keep the garnishes separate. To make the grilled cheese croutons 8. Meanwhile, apply the butter on one side of each slice of bread. 9. Put a small nonstick skillet over medium heat, and place 1 slice of bread in the skillet, buttered-side down. Top with half of the cheese and season with pepper (if using). Then top with the second slice of bread, buttered-side up. When the underside is golden brown, 3 to 4 minutes, turn the sandwich. Cook until the second side of the bread is golden and crispy. 10. Repeat with the remaining ingredients. 11. Cut each sandwich into 1-inch squares and use them to garnish the soup.

Per Serving:
calories: 307 | fat: 15g | protein: 12g | carbs: 38g | sugars: 14g | fiber: 7g | sodium: 931mg

Chapter 12

Desserts

Chapter 12 Desserts

Tapioca Berry Parfaits

Prep time: 10 minutes | Cook time: 6 minutes | Serves 4

- 2 cups unsweetened almond milk
- ½ cup small pearl tapioca, rinsed and still wet
- 1 teaspoon almond extract
- 1 tablespoon pure maple syrup
- 2 cups berries
- ¼ cup slivered almonds

1. Pour the almond milk into the electric pressure cooker. Stir in the tapioca and almond extract. 2. Close and lock the lid of the pressure cooker. Set the valve to sealing. 3. Cook on High pressure for 6 minutes. 4. When the cooking is complete, hit Cancel. Allow the pressure to release naturally for 10 minutes, then quick release any remaining pressure. 5. Once the pin drops, unlock and remove the lid. Remove the pot to a cooling rack. 6. Stir in the maple syrup and let the mixture cool for about an hour. 7. In small glasses, create several layers of tapioca, berries, and almonds. Refrigerate for 1 hour. 8. Serve chilled.

Per Serving:
½ cup: calories: 174 | fat: 5g | protein: 3g | carbs: 32g | sugars: 11g | fiber: 3g | sodium: 77mg

Crumb Pie Shell

Prep time: 10 minutes | Cook time: 10 minutes | Serves 10

- 1¼ cups finely crumbled high-fiber bran crisp breads (such as Fiber Rich+ Bran Crisp Breads)
- 2 tablespoons canola oil
- 1 tablespoon water
- ⅛ teaspoon cinnamon

1. Preheat your oven to 325 °F (165°C). In a medium mixing bowl, thoroughly combine all the ingredients until evenly mixed. Make sure everything is well incorporated. 2. Take a 10-inch pie pan and spread the mixture evenly across the bottom and up the sides of the pan. Use your fingers or the back of a spoon to press the mixture firmly into place, ensuring it forms a solid crust. 3. Place the pie shell in the preheated oven and bake for 8 to 10 minutes. This brief baking time helps to set and firm up the crust. 4. Once baked, you can optionally refrigerate the pie shell until you're ready to use it. This step helps the crust to cool and set completely, making it easier to fill with your desired filling later on. Now, your pie shell is ready to be filled with sweet or savory fillings as per your recipe's requirements. Enjoy your homemade pie crust!

Per Serving:
calories: 78 | fat: 4g | protein: 2g | carbs: 10g | sugars: 1g | fiber: 1g | sodium: 99mg

Berry Smoothie Pops

Prep time: 5 minutes | Cook time: 0 minutes | Serves 6

- 2 cups frozen mixed berries
- ½ cup unsweetened plain almond milk
- 1 cup plain nonfat Greek yogurt
- 2 tablespoons hemp seeds

1. Place all the ingredients into the blender jar. Ensure the blender is tightly sealed. 2. Process the ingredients until they are finely blended. This step might take a few minutes to achieve a smooth consistency, depending on the power of your blender. 3. Prepare 6 clean ice pop molds. Pour the blended mixture evenly into each mold, leaving a little space at the top to allow for expansion during freezing. 4. Insert ice pop sticks into each mold. Make sure the sticks are centered and fully submerged into the mixture. 5. Place the filled molds into the freezer. Allow them to freeze for 3 to 4 hours, or until the ice pops are completely firm. 6. Once frozen, remove the molds from the freezer. To release the ice pops, briefly run warm water over the outside of the molds to loosen them. Gently pull on the sticks to remove the ice pops from the molds. 7. Serve and enjoy your refreshing homemade ice pops! These steps ensure your ice pops turn out perfectly frozen and easy to enjoy.

Per Serving:
calorie: 70 | fat: 2g | protein: 5g | carbs: 9g | sugars: 2g | fiber: 3g | sodium: 28mg

Cherry Delight

Prep time: 20 minutes | Cook time: 50 minutes | Serves 12

- 20-ounce can cherry pie filling, light
- ½ package yellow cake mix
- ¼ cup light, soft tub margarine, melted
- ⅓ cup walnuts, optional
- 1 cup water

1. Grease a 7" springform pan then pour the pie filing inside. 2. Combine dry cake mix and margarine (mixture will be crumbly) in a bowl. Sprinkle over filling. Sprinkle with walnuts. 3. Cover the pan with foil. 4. Place the trivet into your Instant Pot and pour in 1 cup of water. Place a foil sling on top of the trivet, then place the springform pan on top. 5. Secure the lid and make sure lid is set to sealing. Press Steam and set for 50 minutes. 6. When cook time is up, release the pressure manually, then carefully remove the springform pan by using hot pads to lift the pan up by the foil sling. Place on a cooling rack for 1–2 hours.

Per Serving:
calories: 137| fat: 4g | protein: 1g | carbs: 26g | sugars: 19g | fiber: 1g | sodium: 174mg

Chocolate Cupcakes

Prep time: 10 minutes | Cook time: 20 minutes | Serves 12

- 3 tablespoons canola oil
- ¼ cup agave nectar
- ¼ cup egg whites
- 1 teaspoon vanilla
- 1 teaspoon cold espresso or strong coffee
- ½ cup fat-free milk
- 1¼ cups quinoa flour
- ¼ cup ground walnuts
- 6 tablespoons cocoa powder
- 2 teaspoons baking powder
- ¼ teaspoon baking soda

1. Preheat your oven to 375 °F (190°C) to ensure it's fully heated by the time you finish preparing the batter. 2. In a medium-sized bowl, combine the following ingredients: oil (such as olive oil or vegetable oil), agave nectar (a natural sweetener), egg whites (ensure they're at room temperature), vanilla extract (for flavor), espresso (brewed and cooled), and milk (dairy or non-dairy of your choice). Use a whisk or electric mixer to beat these ingredients together until well combined and smooth. 3. In a separate bowl, combine the dry ingredients: quinoa flour (a gluten-free alternative rich in protein), chopped walnuts (for texture and flavor), cocoa powder (unsweetened), baking powder (to help the muffins rise), and baking soda (to aid in the muffins' texture). Stir or whisk these dry ingredients together until evenly mixed. 4. Gradually add the combined dry ingredients (from step 3) into the bowl with the wet ingredients (from step 2). Mix everything together until a smooth batter forms. Be careful not to overmix, as this can make the muffins dense. 5. Prepare a muffin tin by lining it with paper liners. Spoon the batter evenly into the lined muffin cups, filling each cup about two-thirds full. 6. Place the filled muffin tin in the preheated oven. Bake at 375 °F (190 °C) for approximately 20 minutes. Check the muffins around the 18-minute mark by inserting a toothpick into the center of a muffin; if it comes out clean or with just a few crumbs attached, the muffins are done. 7. Once baked, remove the muffin tin from the oven and place it on a wire rack to cool for about 5-10 minutes. Then, carefully remove the muffins from the tin and allow them to cool completely on the wire rack. 8. Once cooled, your quinoa flour espresso walnut muffins are ready to be enjoyed as a delicious and nutritious treat!

Per Serving:
calories: 113 | fat: 5g | protein: 3g | carbs: 15g | sugars: 4g | fiber: 2g | sodium: 43mg

Watermelon-Lime Granita

Prep time: 15 minutes | Cook time: 0 minutes | Serves 10

- 1 pound seedless watermelon flesh, cut into 1-inch chunks
- 2 tablespoons agave syrup
- 2 tablespoons freshly squeezed lime juice

1. Begin by lining a baking sheet with parchment paper. Ensure the baking sheet fits comfortably in your freezer. Spread the watermelon chunks in a single layer on the parchment paper-lined sheet. Make sure the chunks are evenly spaced apart. Place the baking sheet in the freezer and allow the watermelon to freeze for at least 20 minutes, or until the chunks are firm. 2. Once the watermelon chunks are frozen solid, carefully transfer them to a blender. Add agave syrup (a natural sweetener) and freshly squeezed lime juice to the blender with the frozen watermelon chunks. Blend the mixture on high speed until it becomes smooth and liquefied. 3. Prepare a 9-by-13-inch shallow baking dish. Pour the blended watermelon mixture into the dish, spreading it out evenly. 4. Return the baking dish to the freezer. Allow the watermelon mixture to freeze for approximately 2 hours, or until it becomes firm around the edges and slushy in the center. 5. Every 30 minutes during the freezing process, take a fork and gently scrape the surface of the mixture. This helps to break up any large ice crystals and creates a light, fluffy texture similar to shaved ice. 6. Continue scraping and fluffing the granita every half hour until the entire mixture has been transformed into slushy crystals. 7. Once the watermelon granita reaches your desired consistency, it's ready to serve. Spoon the granita into serving dishes or glasses, and enjoy immediately as a refreshing summer treat. 8. Store any leftover granita in an airtight container in the freezer. It can be kept for up to 1 month, though it's best enjoyed freshly made.

Per Serving:
calories: 23 | fat: 0g | protein: 0g | carbs: 6g | sugars: 5g | fiber: 0g | sodium: 1mg

Mixed-Berry Snack Cake

Prep time: 15 minutes | Cook time: 28 to 33 minutes | Serves 8

- ¼ cup low-fat granola
- ½ cup buttermilk
- ⅓ cup packed brown sugar
- 2 tablespoons canola oil
- 1 teaspoon vanilla
- 1 egg
- 1 cup whole wheat flour
- ½ teaspoon baking soda
- ½ teaspoon ground cinnamon
- ⅛ teaspoon salt
- 1 cup mixed fresh berries (such as blueberries, raspberries and blackberries)

1. Preheat your oven to 350°F (175°C). Spray an 8- or 9-inch round pan with cooking spray to prevent sticking. 2. Place the granola in a resealable food-storage plastic bag. Seal the bag and slightly crush the granola using a rolling pin or meat mallet. Set the crushed granola aside. 3. In a large bowl, combine buttermilk, brown sugar, oil, vanilla extract, and egg. Stir these wet ingredients together until smooth and well combined. 4. Add flour, baking soda, ground cinnamon, and salt to the bowl with the wet ingredients. Stir gently until the dry ingredients are just moistened and incorporated into the batter. Be careful not to overmix. 5. Gently fold in half of the berries into the batter. This ensures even distribution of the berries throughout the coffee cake. 6. Spoon the batter into the prepared round pan, spreading it out evenly with a spatula. 7. Sprinkle the remaining half of the berries evenly over the top of the batter in the pan. Then, sprinkle the crushed granola over the berries. 8. Place the pan in the preheated oven and bake for 28 to 33 minutes, or until the top of the coffee cake is golden brown and springs back when lightly touched in the center. 9. Once baked, remove the pan from the oven and place it on a cooling rack. Allow the coffee cake to cool in the pan for about 10 minutes. 10. Serve the coffee cake warm directly from the pan. It's delicious as is or you can optionally serve it with a dollop of whipped cream or a scoop of vanilla ice cream.

Per Serving:
calorie: 160 | fat: 5g | protein: 3g | carbs: 26g | sugars: 12g | fiber: 1g | sodium: 140mg

Crispy Pistachio Chocolate Bark

Prep time: 5 minutes | Cook time: 0 minutes | Serves 16

- 1 cup (180 g) dairy-free 70% dark chocolate chips, melted
- ¼ cup (6 g) crisped rice cereal
- ½ cup (50 g) crushed pistachios

1. Prepare by lining a large baking sheet with parchment paper. This will prevent the chocolate from sticking and make cleanup easier. 2. In a medium bowl, combine the chopped chocolate (or chocolate chips) and rice cereal. Stir well to evenly distribute the cereal throughout the chocolate. 3. Spread the chocolate and rice cereal mixture evenly onto the prepared baking sheet. Use a spatula or the back of a spoon to smooth and spread the mixture to your desired thickness. Aim for about ¼ inch (6 mm) thickness for the bark. 4. Sprinkle the shelled and chopped pistachios evenly over the surface of the chocolate mixture. Press the pistachios lightly into the chocolate using your hands or the back of a spoon. This ensures that the pistachios adhere to the chocolate. 5. Place the baking sheet with the prepared bark into the freezer. Allow it to freeze for approximately 1 hour, or until the chocolate is completely set and firm. 6. Once the bark is firm, remove it from the freezer. Using your hands or a knife, break the chocolate bark into approximately 16 pieces. The pieces can be irregular in shape for a rustic look. 7. Serve and enjoy your homemade chocolate pistachio bark! Store any leftover bark in an airtight container in the refrigerator to maintain freshness.

Per Serving:
calorie: 101 | fat: 7g | protein: 2g | carbs: 11g | sugars: 8g | fiber: 2g | sodium: 8mg

Lemon Dessert Shots

Prep time: 30 minutes | Cook time: 0 minutes | Serves 12

- 10 gingersnap cookies
- 2 ounces ⅓-less-fat cream cheese (Neufchâtel), softened
- ½ cup marshmallow crème (from 7 ounces jar)
- 1 container (6 ounces) fat-free Greek honey vanilla yogurt
- ½ cup lemon curd (from 10 ounces jar)
- 36 fresh raspberries
- ½ cup frozen (thawed) lite whipped topping

1. In 1-quart resealable food-storage plastic bag, place cookies; seal bag. Crush with rolling pin or meat mallet; place in small bowl. 2. In medium bowl, beat cream cheese and marshmallow crème with electric mixer on low speed until smooth. Beat in yogurt until blended. Place mixture in 1-quart resealable food-storage plastic bag; seal bag. In 1-pint resealable food-storage plastic bag, place lemon curd; seal bag. Cut ⅛-inch opening diagonally across bottom corner of each bag. 3. In bottom of each of 12 (2-oz) shot glasses, place 1 raspberry. For each glass, pipe about 2 teaspoons yogurt mixture over raspberry. Pipe ¼-inch ring of lemon curd around edge of glass; sprinkle with about 1 teaspoon cookies. Repeat. 4 Garnish each dessert shot with dollop of about 2 teaspoons whipped topping and 1 raspberry. Place in 9-inch square pan. Refrigerate 30 minutes or until chilled but no longer than 3 hours.

Per Serving:
calorie: 110 | fat: 3g | protein: 2g | carbs: 18g | sugars: 14g | fiber: 0g | sodium: 70mg

Crustless Peanut Butter Cheesecake

Prep time: 10 minutes | Cook time: 10 minutes | Serves 2

- 4 ounces (113 g) cream cheese, softened
- 2 tablespoons confectioners' erythritol
- 1 tablespoon all-natural, no-sugar-added peanut butter
- ½ teaspoon vanilla extract
- 1 large egg, whisked

1. In a medium bowl, mix cream cheese and erythritol until smooth. Add peanut butter and vanilla, mixing until smooth. Add egg and stir just until combined. 2. Spoon mixture into an ungreased springform pan and place into air fryer basket. Adjust the temperature to 300ºF (149ºC) and bake for 10 minutes. Edges will be firm, but center will be mostly set with only a small amount of jiggle when done. 3. Let pan cool at room temperature 30 minutes, cover with plastic wrap, then place into refrigerator at least 2 hours. Serve chilled.

Per Serving:
calorie: 363 | fat: 32g | protein: 12g | carbs: 5g | sugars: 2g | fiber: 0g | sodium: 317mg

Double-Ginger Cookies

Prep time: 45 minutes | Cook time: 8 to 10 minutes | Makes 5 dozen cookies

- ¾ cup sugar
- ¼ cup butter or margarine, softened
- 1 egg or ¼ cup fat-free egg product
- ¼ cup molasses
- 1¾ cups all-purpose flour
- 1 teaspoon baking soda
- ½ teaspoon ground cinnamon
- ½ teaspoon ground ginger
- ¼ teaspoon ground cloves
- ¼ teaspoon salt
- ¼ cup sugar
- ¼ cup orange marmalade
- 2 tablespoons finely chopped crystallized ginger

1. In medium bowl, beat ¾ cup sugar, the butter, egg and molasses with electric mixer on medium speed, or mix with spoon. Stir in flour, baking soda, cinnamon, ground ginger, cloves and salt. Cover and refrigerate at least 2 hours, until firm. 2. Heat oven to 350°F. Lightly spray cookie sheets with cooking spray. Place ¼ cup sugar in small bowl. Shape dough into ¾-inch balls; roll in sugar. Place balls about 2 inches apart on cookie sheet. Make indentation in center of each ball, using finger. Fill each indentation with slightly less than ¼ teaspoon of the marmalade. Sprinkle with crystallized ginger. 3. Bake 8 to 10 minutes or until set. Immediately transfer from cookie sheets to cooling racks. Cool completely, about 30 minutes.

Per Serving:
1 Cookie: calorie: 45 | fat: 1g | protein: 0g | carbs: 9g | sugars: 5g | fiber: 0g | sodium: 40mg

Strawberry Cream Cheese Crepes

Prep time: 10 minutes | Cook time: 10 minutes | Serves 4

- ½ cup old-fashioned oats
- 1 cup unsweetened plain almond milk
- 1 egg
- 3 teaspoons honey, divided
- Nonstick cooking spray
- 2 ounces low-fat cream cheese
- ¼ cup low-fat cottage cheese
- 2 cups sliced strawberries

1. In a blender jar, process the oats until they resemble flour. Add the almond milk, egg, and 1½ teaspoons honey, and process until smooth. 2. Heat a large skillet over medium heat. Spray with nonstick cooking spray to coat. 3. Add ¼ cup of oat batter to the pan and quickly swirl around to coat the bottom of the pan and let cook for 2 to 3 minutes. When the edges begin to turn brown, flip the crepe with a spatula and cook until lightly browned and firm, about 1 minute. Transfer to a plate. Continue with the remaining batter, spraying the skillet with nonstick cooking spray before adding more batter. Set the cooked crepes aside, loosely covered with aluminum foil, while you make the filling. 4. Clean the blender jar, then combine the cream cheese, cottage cheese, and remaining 1½ teaspoons honey, and process until smooth. 5. Fill each crepe with 2 tablespoons of the cream cheese mixture, topped with ¼ cup of strawberries. Serve.

Per Serving:
calories: 149 | fat: 6g | protein: 6g | carbs: 20g | sugars: 10g | fiber: 3g | sodium: 177mg

Blender Banana Snack Cake

Prep time: 5 minutes | Cook time: 30 to 32 minutes | Serves 9

- ¼ cup coconut nectar or pure maple syrup
- ¼ cup water
- 2 teaspoons vanilla
- 1 teaspoon cinnamon
- ½ teaspoon nutmeg
- ¼ teaspoon sea salt
- 3½ cups sliced, well-ripened bananas
- 1 cup whole grain spelt flour
- ½ cup rolled oats
- 2 teaspoons baking powder

1. Preheat the oven to 350°F. Lightly coat an 8" x 8" pan with cooking spray and line the bottom of the pan with parchment paper. 2. In a blender, combine the nectar or syrup, water, vanilla, cinnamon, nutmeg, salt, and 3 cups of the sliced bananas. Puree until smooth. Add the flour, oats, baking powder, and the remaining ½ cup of bananas. Pulse a couple of times, until just combined. (Don't puree; you don't want to overwork the flour.) Transfer the mixture into the baking dish, using a spatula to scrape down the sides of the bowl. Bake for 30 to 32 minutes, until fully set. (Insert a toothpick in the center and see if it comes out clean.) Transfer the cake pan to a cooling rack. Let cool completely before cutting.

Per Serving:
calorie: 141 | fat: 1g | protein: 3g | carbs: 32g | sugars: 14g | fiber: 4g | sodium: 177mg

Pumpkin Cheesecake Smoothie

Prep time: 10 minutes | Cook time: 0 minutes | Serves 1

- 2 tablespoons cream cheese, at room temperature
- ½ cup canned pumpkin purée (not pumpkin pie mix)
- 1 cup almond milk
- 1 teaspoon pumpkin pie spice
- ½ cup crushed ice

1. Prepare your blender. Ensure it is clean and ready for use. 2. Gather all the ingredients as listed in your recipe. This typically includes liquids like juices or milk, fruits, vegetables, and any additional flavorings or sweeteners. 3. Place all of the ingredients into the blender jar. Make sure the lid is securely fastened to avoid any spills during blending. 4. Start blending the ingredients on a low speed to begin breaking them down. 5. Gradually increase the blender speed to high to fully blend all the ingredients until smooth. Blend for about 1-2 minutes, or until there are no visible chunks and the mixture has a smooth consistency. 6. Stop the blender and carefully remove the lid. Use a spatula to scrape down the sides of the blender jar if necessary, ensuring all ingredients are well incorporated. 7. Pour the blended mixture into glasses or a serving container.

Per Serving:
calories: 230 | fat: 11g | protein: 11g | carbs: 25g | sugars: 16g | fiber: 4g | sodium: 216mg

Superfood Brownie Bites

Prep time: 15 minutes | Cook time: 0 minutes | Makes 30

- 1 cup raw nuts (walnuts, pecans, or cashews)
- ½ cup hulled hemp seeds
- ⅓ cup raw pepitas
- ½ cup raw cacao powder
- 1 cup pitted dates
- 2 tablespoons coconut oil
- 1 teaspoon vanilla extract

1. Line a baking sheet with parchment paper. 2. Place the nuts, hemp seeds, and pepitas in a food processor and pulse until the ingredients are a meal consistency. Add the cacao powder, dates, coconut oil, and vanilla extract and pulse until the mixture holds together if you pinch it with your fingers. The dough should ball up and appear glossy, and not be too sticky and wet. If it doesn't stick together enough to form a dough consistency, add water in drops until the correct consistency is reached. Be careful not to add too much liquid. If you do, add more cacao to balance the texture. 3. Scoop out the brownie bite mixture in 1-tablespoon amounts and roll the mixture into balls. Set the balls on the baking sheet and then chill them in the refrigerator for at least 10 minutes to hold their shape. 4. Transfer the balls to a container with a lid and store in the refrigerator until ready to eat. You could eat these immediately, but they are more likely to crumble. 5. Store brownies in an airtight container in the refrigerator for 5 to 7 days.

Per Serving:
calories: 145 | fat: 11g | protein: 4g | carbs: 11g | sugars: 7g | fiber: 3g | sodium: 2mg

Chocolate Almond Butter Fudge

Prep time: 10 minutes | Cook time: 0 minutes | Makes 9 Pieces

- 2 ounces unsweetened baking chocolate
- ½ cup almond butter
- 1 can full-fat coconut milk, refrigerated overnight, thickened cream only
- 1 teaspoon vanilla extract
- 4 (1-gram) packets stevia (or to taste)

1. Line a 9-inch square baking pan with parchment paper. Ensure the parchment paper overhangs the edges of the pan for easy removal of the fudge later. 2. In a small saucepan, place the chocolate and almond butter. Heat the saucepan over medium-low heat, stirring constantly to prevent burning or sticking, until both the chocolate and almond butter are completely melted and smooth. Remove the saucepan from the heat and allow the mixture to cool slightly. 3. In a medium bowl, combine the melted chocolate and almond butter mixture with the cream from the coconut milk (just the solid part that has separated), vanilla extract, and stevia (a natural sweetener). Use a whisk or spatula to blend everything together until smooth and well combined. Taste the mixture and adjust the sweetness to your liking by adding more stevia if desired. 4. Pour the smooth mixture into the prepared baking pan lined with parchment paper. Use a spatula to spread the mixture evenly across the pan, smoothing the top. 5. Place the baking pan in the refrigerator and chill the fudge for at least 3 hours, or until it is completely firm and set. 6. Once chilled and firm, remove the fudge from the refrigerator. Lift the fudge out of the pan using the parchment paper overhang. Place it on a cutting board and cut into squares or desired shapes using a sharp knife. 7. Serve and enjoy your homemade chocolate almond butter fudge! Store any leftover fudge in an airtight container in the refrigerator for up to a week.

Per Serving:
1 piece: calories: 169 | fat: 11g | protein: 8g | carbs: 11g | sugars: 7g | fiber: 3g | sodium: 64mg

Appendix 1: Measurement Conversion Chart

VOLUME EQUIVALENTS (DRY)

US STANDARD	METRIC (APPROXIMATE)
1/8 teaspoon	0.5 mL
1/4 teaspoon	1 mL
1/2 teaspoon	2 mL
3/4 teaspoon	4 mL
1 teaspoon	5 mL
1 tablespoon	15 mL
1/4 cup	59 mL
1/2 cup	118 mL
3/4 cup	177 mL
1 cup	235 mL
2 cups	475 mL
3 cups	700 mL
4 cups	1 L

WEIGHT EQUIVALENTS

US STANDARD	METRIC (APPROXIMATE)
1 ounce	28 g
2 ounces	57 g
5 ounces	142 g
10 ounces	284 g
15 ounces	425 g
16 ounces (1 pound)	455 g
1.5 pounds	680 g
2 pounds	907 g

VOLUME EQUIVALENTS (LIQUID)

US STANDARD	US STANDARD (OUNCES)	METRIC (APPROXIMATE)
2 tablespoons	1 fl.oz.	30 mL
1/4 cup	2 fl.oz.	60 mL
1/2 cup	4 fl.oz.	120 mL
1 cup	8 fl.oz.	240 mL
1 1/2 cup	12 fl.oz.	355 mL
2 cups or 1 pint	16 fl.oz.	475 mL
4 cups or 1 quart	32 fl.oz.	1 L
1 gallon	128 fl.oz.	4 L

TEMPERATURES EQUIVALENTS

FAHRENHEIT (F)	CELSIUS (C) (APPROXIMATE)
225 °F	107 °C
250 °F	120 °C
275 °F	135 °C
300 °F	150 °C
325 °F	160 °C
350 °F	180 °C
375 °F	190 °C
400 °F	205 °C
425 °F	220 °C
450 °F	235 °C
475 °F	245 °C
500 °F	260 °C

Appendix 2: The Dirty Dozen and Clean Fifteen

The Environmental Working Group (EWG) is a nonprofit, nonpartisan organization dedicated to protecting human health and the environment Its mission is to empower people to live healthier lives in a healthier environment. This organization publishes an annual list of the twelve kinds of produce, in sequence, that have the highest amount of pesticide residue-the Dirty Dozen-as well as a list of the fifteen kinds of produce that have the least amount of pesticide residue-the Clean Fifteen.

THE DIRTY DOZEN

- The 2016 Dirty Dozen includes the following produce. These are considered among the year's most important produce to buy organic:

Strawberries	Spinach
Apples	Tomatoes
Nectarines	Bell peppers
Peaches	Cherry tomatoes
Celery	Cucumbers
Grapes	Kale/collard greens
Cherries	Hot peppers

- The Dirty Dozen list contains two additional items kale/collard greens and hot peppers-because they tend to contain trace levels of highly hazardous pesticides.

THE CLEAN FIFTEEN

- The least critical to buy organically are the Clean Fifteen list. The following are on the 2016 list:

Avocados	Papayas
Corn	Kiw
Pineapples	Eggplant
Cabbage	Honeydew
Sweet peas	Grapefruit
Onions	Cantaloupe
Asparagus	Cauliflower
Mangos	

- Some of the sweet corn sold in the United States are made from genetically engineered (GE) seedstock. Buy organic varieties of these crops to avoid GE produce.

Appendix 3: Recipes Index

A

Air Fryer Chicken-Fried Steak	29
Artichokes Parmesan	69
Asian Fried Rice	22
Asian Salmon in a Packet	47
Asparagus Soup	87
Asparagus, Sun-Dried Tomato, and Green Pea Sauté	74
Asparagus-Pepper Stir-Fry	71
Autumn Pork Chops with Red Cabbage and Apples	29
Avo-Tuna with Croutons	52

B

Bacon and Tomato Frittata	15
Bacon-Wrapped Asparagus	66
Bacon-Wrapped Scallops	46
Baked Avocado and Egg	11
Baked Chicken Dijon	44
Baked Garlic Scampi	52
Balsamic Brussels Sprouts	68
Balsamic Green Beans and Fennel	71
Banana Protein Pancakes	12
Barley Squash Risotto	23
Bavarian Beef	31
BBQ Bean Burgers	23
BBQ Ribs and Broccoli Slaw	31
Beef and Mushroom Barley Soup	86
Beef and Vegetable Shish Kabobs	30
Beet Greens and Black Beans	24
Berry Smoothie Pops	92
Black-Eyed Pea Sauté with Garlic and Olives	73
Blender Banana Snack Cake	95
Blood Sugar–Friendly Nutty Trail Mix	55
Blooming Onion	64
Blueberry Cornmeal Muffins	17
Bran Apple Muffins	14
Breakfast Egg Bites	17
Breakfast Millet with Nuts and Strawberries	14
Breakfast Sausage	13
Broccoli Cheese Chicken	37
Broccoli Salad	66
Broccoli Slaw Crab Salad	83
Broiled Dijon Burgers	33
Brussels Sprout Hash and Eggs	15
Brussels Sprouts with Pecans and Gorgonzola	70
Buttercup Squash Soup	87
Butterflied Beef Eye Roast	26
Buttermilk-Ginger Smothered Chicken	39

C

Callaloo Redux	70
Candied Pecans	56
Carrot Soup	88
Cast Iron Hot Chicken	39
Cauliflower Hush Puppies	70
Cauliflower with Lime Juice	69
Charcuterie Dinner For One	50
Cheesy Zucchini Patties	74
Cherry Delight	92
Chicken Kabobs	58
Chicken Nuggets	37
Chicken Paprika	39
Chicken Patties	38
Chicken Provençal	40
Chicken with Spiced Sesame Sauce	38
Chicken, Spinach, and Berry Salad	80
Chickpea Coconut Curry	73
Chinese Asparagus	68
Chinese Chicken Salad	83
Chinese Spareribs	34
Chipotle Twice-Baked Sweet Potatoes	71
Chock-Full-of-Vegetables Chicken Soup	89
Chocolate Almond Butter Fudge	96
Chocolate Cupcakes	93
Chocolate-Zucchini Muffins	12
Chorizo Mexican Breakfast Pizzas	13
Chunky Red Pepper and Tomato Sauce	64
Cilantro Lime Chicken Thighs	40
Cinnamon Toasted Pumpkin Seeds	56
Classic Oven-Roasted Carrots	64
Coconut-Ginger Rice	19
Coddled Eggs and Smoked Salmon Toasts	10

Coffee-and-Herb-Marinated Steak	26
Crab Cakes with Honeydew Melon Salsa	49
Crab-Filled Mushrooms	57
Crab-Stuffed Avocado Boats	52
Creamy Apple-Cinnamon Quesadilla	60
Creamy Cheese Dip	60
Creamy Chicken Wild Rice Soup	88
Creamy Nutmeg Chicken	43
Creamy Spinach Dip	60
Creamy Sweet Potato Soup	87
Creole Steak	30
Crispy Cabbage Steaks	76
Crispy Pistachio Chocolate Bark	94
Crumb Pie Shell	92
Crunchy Pecan Tuna Salad	84
Crustless Peanut Butter Cheesecake	94
Cucumber Pâté	55
Curried Chicken Salad	82
Curried Rice with Pineapple	20

D

Dandelion Greens with Sweet Onion	65
Double-Berry Muffins	10
Double-Ginger Cookies	94

E

Easy Beef Curry	34
Easy Breakfast Chia Pudding	17
Easy Lentil Burgers	19
Easy Tuna Patties	51
Edamame and Walnut Salad	81
Edamame Falafel with Roasted Vegetables	78
Edamame-Tabbouleh Salad	21

F

Favorite Chili	87
Fennel and Chickpeas	67
Fiery Black Bean Salad	81
Fresh Pot Pork Butt	33
Fried Zucchini Salad	65

G

Garden-Fresh Greek Salad	80

Garlic Dill Wings	39
Garlic Galore Rotisserie Chicken	37
Garlic Herb Radishes	68
Garlic Roasted Radishes	64
Gazpacho	90
Ginger and Mint Dip with Fruit	61
Gingered Tofu and Greens	78
Gingered-Pork Stir-Fry	29
Ginger-Garlic Cod Cooked in Paper	51
Ginger-Glazed Salmon and Broccoli	46
Gluten-Free Carrot and Oat Pancakes	10
Golden Chicken Soup	90
Gouda Egg Casserole with Canadian Bacon	15
Grain-Free Apple Cinnamon Cake	14
Greek Chicken	40
Greek Chicken Stuffed Peppers	42
Greek Stuffed Eggplant	74
Greek Stuffed Tenderloin	31
Greek Yogurt Sundae	16
Green Beans with Garlic and Onion	65
Green Goddess White Bean Dip	55
Grilled Fish with Jicama Salsa	53
Grilled Hearts of Romaine with Buttermilk Dressing	82
Grilled Herb Chicken with Wine and Roasted Garlic	36
Grilled Lemon Mustard Chicken	38
Grilled Romaine with White Beans	84
Grilled Rosemary Swordfish	52
Grilled Vegetables on White Bean Mash	76
Ground Turkey Lettuce Cups	61
Ground Turkey Tetrazzini	43
Guacamole	57
Guacamole with Jicama	56

H

Haricot Verts, Walnut, and Feta Salad	83
Hearty Italian Minestrone	88
Herbed Beans and Brown Rice	23
Herbed Buttermilk Chicken	40
Herbed Cornish Hens	37
Herbed Tomato Salad	81
"Honey" Mustard Sauce	67
Herbed Whole Turkey Breast	42
Herb-Roasted Turkey and Vegetables	43
Homemade Sun-Dried Tomato Salsa	58
Horseradish Mashed Cauliflower	68

I

Italian Bean Burgers	20
Italian Potato Salad	80
Italian Sausages with Peppers and Onions	32
Italian Tofu with Mushrooms and Peppers	77
Italian Vegetable Soup	86

J

Jalapeño Popper Pork Chops	33
Jerk Chicken Kebabs	42

L

Lemon Butter Cod with Asparagus	53
Lemon Dessert Shots	94
Lemon Pepper Salmon	48
Lemony White Bean Puree	56
Lobster Fricassee	48
Low-Carb Peanut Butter Pancakes	11
Low-Sugar Blueberry Muffins	57

M

Marjoram-Pepper Steaks	27
Minted Sweet Pea Soup	88
Mixed-Berry Snack Cake	93
Monterey Jack Cheese Quiche Squares	60

N

No-Bake Spaghetti Squash Casserole	75
Not Slow-Cooked Collards	65

O

Orange Tofu	75
Orange-Marinated Pork Tenderloin	29
Oregano Tilapia Fingers	51

P

Parmesan Mackerel with Coriander	50
Pasta Salad–Stuffed Tomatoes	84
Peppercorn-Crusted Baked Salmon	52
Pizza Eggs	12
Plum Smoothie	16
Poached Eggs	11
Pomegranate "Tabbouleh" with Cauliflower	84
Pork Butt Roast	28
Pork Chop Diane	27
Pork Milanese	30
Pork Tacos	32
Potato-Bacon Gratin	11
Potlikker Soup	89
Pumpkin Cheesecake Smoothie	95

Q

Quinoa Pilaf with Salmon and Asparagus	50
Quinoa Vegetable Skillet	22

R

Ratatouille Baked Eggs	17
Red Beans	20
Rice with Spinach and Feta	22
Roasted Carrot and Herb Spread	61
Roasted Delicata Squash	66
Roasted Eggplant	69
Roasted Garlic	70
Roasted Lemon and Garlic Broccoli	68
Roasted Peppers and Eggplant	67
Roasted Pork Loin	27
Roasted Salmon with Honey-Mustard Sauce	53
Roasted Salmon with Salsa Verde	50
Roasted Veggie Bowl	77

S

Saffron-Spiced Chicken Breasts	36
Sage and Garlic Vegetable Bake	20
Salmon Florentine	48
Salmon with Brussels Sprouts	49
Salmon with Provolone Cheese	47
Sautéed Garlicky Mushrooms	65
Sautéed Mixed Vegetables	66
Sautéed Spinach and Lima Beans	73
Sautéed Spinach and Tomatoes	69
Scallion Grits with Shrimp	12
"Smothered" Steak	28
Scallops and Asparagus Skillet	51
Sea Bass with Ginger Sauce	53
Sherried Peppers with Bean Sprouts	67

Shrimp Étouffée	47
Slow Cooker Chipotle Beef Stew	27
Slow-Cooked Simple Lamb and Vegetable Stew	32
Smoky Spinach Hummus with Popcorn Chips	58
Smoky Whole Chicken	41
Smothered Sirloin	26
Snow Peas with Sesame Seeds	67
Southern Boiled Peanuts	59
Southwestern Quinoa Salad	19
Spaghetti Squash	69
Spanakopita Egg White Frittata	16
Spice-Rubbed Chicken Thighs	38
Spice-Rubbed Turkey Breast	42
Spicy Chicken Cacciatore	44
Spicy Corn and Shrimp Salad in Avocado	47
Spinach and Artichoke Dip	62
Spinach and Feta Egg Bake	13
Steak with Bell Pepper	28
Stewed Green Beans	24
Strawberry Cream Cheese Crepes	95
Strawberry-Spinach Salad	80
Stuffed Peppers	76
Stuffed Portobello Mushrooms	76
Summer Veggie Scramble	13
Sunflower-Tuna-Cauliflower Salad	81
Sunshine Burgers	21
Superfood Brownie Bites	96
Sweet Potato Fennel Bake	24

T

Taco Soup	89
Tapioca Berry Parfaits	92
Tarragon Cod in a Packet	46
Teriyaki Chicken and Broccoli	44
Teriyaki Salmon	49
Texas Caviar	21
Thai Corn and Sweet Potato Stew	86

Thanksgiving Turkey Breast	36
The Ultimate Veggie Burger	75
Tilapia with Pecans	49
Tofu and Bean Chili	77
Tofu, Kale, and Mushroom Breakfast Scramble	15
Tomato-Basil Soup with Grilled Cheese Croutons	90
Tu-No Salad	81
Turkey and Quinoa Caprese Casserole	41
Turkey Carcass Broth	89
Turkey Rollups with Veggie Cream Cheese	57

V

Vegetable Beef Soup	28
Vegetable Burgers	73
Vegetable Kabobs with Mustard Dip	59
Veggie Fajitas	74
Veggie Unfried Rice	22
Veggies and Kasha with Balsamic Vinaigrette	21
Vietnamese Meatball Lollipops with Dipping Sauce	59

W

Warm Barley and Squash Salad with Balsamic Vinaigrette	82
Warm Sweet Potato and Black Bean Salad	82
Watermelon-Lime Granita	93
White Bean–Oat Waffles	16
Whole Veggie-Stuffed Trout	48
Wild Rice Salad	83
Wine-Poached Chicken with Herbs and Vegetables	41

Z

Zoodles Carbonara	33
Zucchini Fritters	66
Zucchini Hummus Dip with Red Bell Peppers	58